# A Squatter's Republic

Western Histories
William Deverell, series editor
Published for the Huntington-USC Institute on California and the West
by University of California Press and the Huntington Library

1 *The Father of All: The de la Guerra Family, Power, and Patriarchy in Mexican California,* by Louise Pubols

2 *Alta California: Peoples in Motion, Identities in Formation, 1769–1850,* edited by Steven W. Hackel

3 *American Heathens: Religion, Race, and Reconstruction in California,* by Joshua Paddison

4 *Blue Sky Metropolis: The Aerospace Century in Southern California,* edited by Peter J. Westwick

5 *Post-Ghetto: Reimagining South Los Angeles,* edited by Josh Sides

6 *Where Minds and Matters Meet: Technology in California and the West,* edited by Volker Janssen

7 *A Squatter's Republic: Land and the Politics of Monopoly in California, 1850–1900,* by Tamara Venit Shelton

# A Squatter's Republic

Land and the Politics of Monopoly
in California, 1850–1900

by Tamara Venit Shelton

Published for the Huntington-USC Institute on California and the West
by University of California Press, Berkeley, California, and
the Huntington Library, San Marino, California

Series jacket design by Lia Tjandra
Interior design by Doug Davis
Copyediting by Nola Butler
Indexing by Daniela Blei
Printed by Sheridan Books in the United States of America

*Library of Congress Cataloging-in-Publication Data*

Shelton, Tamara Venit.
  A squatter's republic : land and the politics of monopoly in California, 1850-1900 /
Tamara Venit Shelton.
      pages cm. -- (Western histories ; 7)
  Includes bibliographical references and index.
  ISBN 978-0-87328-255-0 (alk. paper)
1. Land tenure--California--History--19th century 2. Land use--California--
History--19th century. 3. Monopolies--California--History--19th century.
4. Squatters--California--History--19th century. 5. California--History--
19th century. 6. United States--History--19th century. I. Title.
  HD211.C2S54 2013
  333.3'179409034--dc23
                              2013008466

# Contents

# Acknowledgments

First and foremost, my thanks go to William Deverell, professor of history at the University of Southern California, who invited me to submit a book proposal to the Western Histories series and then shepherded the manuscript through the publication process with efficiency and encouragement. I am honored to contribute to this fine collection of scholarship on California and the West.

Research for this project would not have been possible without the assistance of many librarians and archivists across California, Kansas, and New York. Special thanks go to Peter Blodgett at the Huntington Library, David Kessler at the Bancroft Library, Patricia Johnson and Carson Hendricks at the Center for Sacramento History, and Jim Reed at History San Jose. Funding from Stanford Humanities and Social Sciences, Amherst College, the Andrew W. Mellon Foundation, the Huntington Library, the David Potter Memorial Scholarship Fund, the Reed College Office of the Dean of the Faculty, and Claremont McKenna College supported research and revisions. To these institutions and foundations, I am immensely grateful.

This project began as a dissertation, and over the years it has existed in many other incarnations—as an idea, a conference paper, an article, a book proposal, and now, a book. From there to here, my most heartfelt thanks go to Richard White, Margaret Byrne Professor of American History at Stanford University, whose generosity with his time, intellect, and humor knows no equal. It was my unbelievable good fortune to have had him as my dissertation advisor. He inspired me to make bigger arguments and to strive for loftier goals than I would have dared on my own. Even now as an assistant professor, I find that I rely on Richard's advice as much as I did as a graduate student. The words *thank you* seem insufficient. I am indebted to him for his continued guidance and support.

As a graduate student and beyond, I have benefited from the mentorship of Albert Camarillo and Gordon Chang, whose cheerful encouragement was as valuable to me as their assiduous feedback. My thanks also go to those who read sections of the manuscript or commented on conference papers and other presentations. I am grateful to the following teachers, colleagues, and friends: Andrew Berger, Andrea Davies, Nate Gillespie, Tamar Herzog, David Igler, Linda Ivey, Michael Magliari, Dan McGarry, Jeff Morgan, Richard Orsi, Natalia Mehlman Petrzela, Don Pisani, Anat Plocker, Claire Potter, Rachel St. John, Marni Sandweiss, Julia Sarreal, Jeffrey Sklansky, Cecilia Tsu, David Vaught, Lissa Wadewitz, Phoebe Kropp Young, Michael Zakim, and Kari Zimmerman. My first academic home after graduate school was the history department at Reed College. My colleagues at Reed, Michael Breen, Jacqueline Dirks, Douglas Fix, David Garrett, Benjamin Lazier, Mary Ashburn Miller, Margot Minardi, and David Sacks, all contributed to the evolution of this project from dissertation to finished book through their helpful comments and conversations. Many thanks also go to Daniela Blei, a colleague and friend, who helped edit and otherwise prepare this manuscript for publication.

Cameron Shelton's boundless encouragement, enthusiasm, and love have kept me going even when I felt most out of steam. I am a better scholar and person because he has shared his intellect and energy with me. Our daughter, Evelyn Anne Shelton, makes everything more meaningful and more worthwhile.

Finally, it is difficult to express the depth of my gratitude for my mother and father, Corinne Fong Venit and Stewart Venit. They taught me to value learning and to embrace new challenges. Their support allowed me to dream big dreams for myself. I can never repay them, so I can only hope to make them proud. This book is dedicated to them.

## THE LAND QUESTION

W hat nineteenth-century Americans called "the land question" was in fact two questions: First, who had the right to own land? And second, how much land should they be allowed to own? These were the fundamental questions, and they created others about the nature of property rights, freedom, and the dangerous power of monopoly. The political ideology of agrarian republicanism taught nineteenth-century Americans to associate landownership with economic independence and the virtue necessary for self-governance. The seeming abundance of "free" land in the western United States promised to increase opportunities for landownership and, by extension, class mobility and democracy. Thus, the alienable rights of property became a means of thinking about the inalienable rights of humankind.

*A Squatter's Republic: Land and the Politics of Monopoly in California* follows the rise and fall of the land question from 1850 to 1900; through this investigation, it also traces the rise and fall of a particularly nineteenth-century vision of landed independence. The land question was at the heart of political and economic reform in the Gilded Age, and its history is the history of America's transformation from agrarian republic to industrial empire. As the borders of the United States stretched west, the land question became part of a dialogue about wealth and opportunity in the nation. Wherever Indian, Mexican, Asian, and white Westerners encountered one another, the land question ostensibly explained differences of class, race, and gender and determined whose rights deserved protection. In the 1850s, as sectional strife gripped the country and civil war loomed, the land question entered debates over the expansion of slavery into the western territories and became shorthand for expressing the politics of free soil and free labor. And as the American economy corporatized, consolidated, and grew, the land question surfaced again as part of debates over industrialization and new immigration from Asia and Europe and as a way

1

of thinking through the rights of wageworkers to organize and to reform capitalism. By the end of the nineteenth century, however, the land question had receded from the center of the American political economy and culture; *A Squatter's Republic* endeavors to explain why that happened.

This book considers the land question through the antimonopolist reform movements it inspired in late nineteenth-century California. To a modern audience, the word *antimonopoly* may conjure images of the Rough Rider president, Theodore Roosevelt, valiantly trust-busting robber baron John D. Rockefeller's Standard Oil, but the history of American antimonopolism stretches back a century before the Progressive Era and encompasses far more than the opposition to large, industrial corporations. For most of the nineteenth century, Americans were far more afraid of "land monopoly" than industrial monopoly. Between 1850 and 1900, California became the locus of one of the most influential antimonopolist land-reform movements in the United States.[1] In California, where a land rush closely followed the Gold Rush, the land question took on particular urgency and importance. The Gold Rush was supposed to have been a leveling influence, making rich men out of anyone who could shoulder a pickaxe or shake a pan. Their California was the squatter's republic, a society for the white man who claimed no more land than he could use, who promised to uphold agrarian republican ideals and put down monopoly, the nemesis of democracy.

After the initial euphoria of the Gold Rush, California settled into the boom-and-bust cycles that epitomized the Gilded Age economy. The most accessible gold deposits were quickly exhausted, and by the early 1850s, more capital-intensive forms of mining had largely replaced placer mining. Meanwhile, unresolved Mexican land grants, land speculation, and the proliferation of commercial farms complicated public-land distribution and disappointed would-be settlers.[2] Within a decade, the state's economic growth had become stagnant and new migration dwindled. Although the completion of the United States's first transcontinental railroad in 1869 brought hope for restored prosperity, it failed to meet expectations. The railroad did help shorten the effective distance between California and eastern markets, but it also opened the gates to the Panic of 1873, a banking crisis that set off a national depression. Underemployed white laborers began to congregate in the public squares of such cities as San Francisco, and they roamed the countryside in search of wage work. At the same time, once-elite Mexican families began to crack under the stress of ongoing land litigation and taxes. Drought ravaged their ranches and pushed the beleaguered families further toward the brink of bankruptcy. Many were driven to mortgage or sell their property.[3] California Indian populations were also gripped by poverty. Newspapers and federal Indian agents reported that Indians were destitute and even starving on land reserved for them.[4] Against these signs of despair, the immense fortunes of industrial barons and railroad tycoons provided a cruel counterpoint and evidence that California's golden promise had favored the few and not the many.[5]

Land monopolies became symbolic of that broken promise. Drawing from common law definitions of *monopoly* as unreasonable restraint on competition, anti–land monopolists reasoned that large, concentrated landholding and land withheld from production constituted monopolies because they created artificial scarcity, drove up the price of land, and diminished the ability of small proprietors to compete for freehold tenure.[6] Land monopoly implied a failure to work the land and make it productive, and so a land monopolist was anyone who owned land that he did not personally cultivate. He either hired laborers and tenants to do the work or withheld it for speculation, undermining the formation of an independent citizenry and a moral society. Land monopolies, the emblems of concentrated wealth and its pernicious, antidemocratic consequences, became the scapegoat for Gilded Age California's economic woes.

Californians used anti–land monopolism as a platform from which to launch a broad spectrum of political economic reforms in their state and beyond. The opposition to land monopoly became entwined with the public discourse on Mexican land rights, industrial labor relations, immigration from China, and the rise of railroad and other corporate monopolies. As a reform ideology, anti–land monopolism assumed that monopolies were unnatural, inefficient, and immoral. Monopolies were signs of a corrupt political economy, often the product of government negligence or unfair privileges bestowed on a few undeserving individuals at the expense of the masses. Anti–land monopolists argued that a democratic government had the moral and economic imperative to eradicate monopolies and to prioritize the rights of small proprietors above all others. The assumption that the small proprietors' republic would be a white republic was a fundamental part of anti–land monopolism, and the opposition to land monopoly became inextricable from the racial politics of its time. As conquest and new immigration diversified the population of California and the nation, the many contested meanings of whiteness and non-whiteness became refracted through the land question.

Land reform, as a number of scholars have emphasized, had been central to antebellum working-class cultures and politics, and it maintained that significance well into the Gilded Age.[7] As *A Squatter's Republic* details, antimonopolist reformers extended the logic of landownership to all forms of private property and gave land rights for small producers a foundational role in the opposition to other Gilded Age monopolies in banking, energy, transportation, and communication. The opposition to land monopoly provided a familiar set of images and a common vocabulary to articulate the fears and hopes with which late nineteenth-century Americans encountered new capital-intensive technologies, large-scale corporations, and expansive federal powers. The fight against consolidated power and the support for agrarian ideals of independence gave common cause to farmers and industrial workers alike. By the late nineteenth century, all major political parties included antimonopolist resolutions in their platforms, and antimonopolism defined the reform efforts of such industrial unions as the Knights of Labor, and such agrarian groups as the Greenbackers, the Farmers' Alliance, and the Populists.

Antimonopolism became the driving reform ideology of America's Gilded Age. Nonetheless, it remains a concept that historians have frequently mischaracterized. Historians tend to portray antimonopolism in one of three ways: as a backward-looking agrarianism, as an incipient form of socialism, or as a thinly veiled expression of liberal capitalism.[8] For Gilded Age reformers, however, antimonopolism represented a distinctly alternative way in which to organize the political economy. Nineteenth-century Americans did not see their economic alternatives as a choice between traditional socialism and laissez-faire capitalism, or as a choice between reverting to an agrarian economy and embracing modern industrialism.[9] With the land question as their guide, antimonopolists called for government to break up monopolies through laws and taxes designed to eradicate speculation and landlordism. They envisioned a political economy that would give land to independent producers, protect their freedom to compete, and facilitate their social mobility.

The opposition to land monopoly provided a useful framework for thinking about industrial monopolies, but only to a point. In the last two decades of the nineteenth century, new ideas about monopoly, inspired by observations of railroad operations, began to spread. Land monopoly, with its insistence on the moral and economic superiority of diffuse ownership and competition, was ill suited to describe the proper organization of capital-intensive industries like the railroads, whose high fixed costs made them work most efficiently under consolidated ownership and in the absence of competition. Reformers confronting a modernizing America thus had to modernize antimonopolism. During the 1880s and 1890s, antimonopolism reformulated its role for the state while continuing to avoid the extremes of socialism and laissez-faire capitalism as well as the extremes of anti–land monopolism. The late nineteenth-century anti-monopolist political economy established terms for government involvement in those industries deemed most essential to mass production: transportation, communication, energy, and banking. Doing so, reformers hoped, would permit small, independent capitalists to benefit from industrial efficiencies and to continue to support the republican ideals on which the nation was founded. Government regulation or public ownership of monopolies promised to prevent the worst abuses of laborers and consumers while keeping the engine of progress motoring down the track. By the end of the century, antimonopolists no longer wished to kill monopolistic capitalism; they wanted to control it.

California taught the nation how to cope with monopoly. The state was at the center of the railroad controversies that transformed the anti-monopolist political economy at the end of the nineteenth century. The Southern Pacific Railroad Company became a lightning rod for complaints about special government privileges and, rightly or wrongly, the prime example of all that was wrong with the Gilded Age.[10] California politicians and antimonopolists of both parties attacked the Southern Pacific for its immense land holdings, control of routes and rates, manipulation of labor and capital markets, and abuse of political privilege. But they also understood the significance of the railroad to the economic development of California and the nation. California antimonopolists both feared and desired the transformations wrought by large-scale, capital-intensive industrialization like the railroad, which promised progress and prosperity but not necessarily to all in equal measure. The opposition to land monopoly could not encompass that ambivalence. It gradually receded from the center of antimonopolist industrial reform and was relegated to rural and agricultural matters.

Divorced from the land question, antimonopolism became far less radical as a reform ideology and far less clear about the terms of its moral economy. By the end of the century, many reformers had come to accept monopolies as natural, even inevitable, forms of industrial organization. They sought to make consolidated ownership more benevolent, to maximize its benefits to society, and to minimize its costs. This brand of anti-monopolism defined the institutions that guided federal policies toward trusts and monopolies and set the tone for the interactions among government, citizens, and the economy in the Progressive Era.

## *Land and Freedom in the Early Republic*

Although anti–land monopolism has deep and diffuse historical roots, American ideas about land and landownership stemmed most directly from traditions of liberalism, agrarianism, and republicanism, which were inherited from the European Enlightenment.[11] Agrarianism, as it originated in late seventeenth- and eighteenth-century British and French political philosophy, held that working with the land endowed cultivators with special capacities for virtue and independence. Liberalism added the notion that occupancy and use extended natural rights of ownership. Republicanism deemed that small, independent landowners (or freeholders), unaffected by external control or persuasion, were ideally and uniquely qualified for self-governance. American land reformers frequently cited as their intellectual forebears such seventeenth- and eighteenth-century British and French political theorists as John Locke, James Harrington, François Quesnay, and Victor Riqueti, the marquis de Mirabeau. What these philosophers shared was a belief that private property was sacrosanct, that it was the bedrock of a stable society, and that its protection was the raison d'être of the state. Their ideas inspired a range of British and American land-reform theories that were influential in the United States in the late eighteenth century, from the proto-socialism of Thomas Spence and the communitarianism of Charles Fourier and Robert Dale Owen to the individualism of Thomas Paine and Thomas Jefferson.[12]

In the early American republic, it was Jefferson who most famously articulated the connection between cultivating a freehold and cultivating a virtuous citizenry. In his *Notes on the State of Virginia*, written and published in the 1780s, Jefferson claimed, "Those who labour in the earth are the chosen people of God, if ever he had a chosen people, whose breasts he has made his peculiar deposit for substantial and genuine virtue."[13] America, where land was relatively plentiful, offered its people a unique opportunity to construct a society composed of freeholders. Not surprisingly, the political implications for the social organization and wealth distribution inspired by these principles became known as *Jeffersonian agrarianism*. In the decades after the American Revolution, Jefferson and others aspired to make the United States a nation of small, independent freeholders. Jefferson claimed that "corruption of morals in the mass of cultivators is a phenomenon of which no age nor nation has furnished an example."[14] Jefferson's political influence on the young republic promulgated the concept that small freeholders were arbiters of democratic values, which made the freehold essential to the continued freedom and independence of American citizens.[15] Although Jefferson eventually loosened the ties between personal independence and independent land tenure, nineteenth-century Americans continued to believe that the freehold was vital to the success of the American republic, and that it required governmental protection from privileged, arbitrary, and concentrated power, or, in short, monopolies.[16]

In the antebellum period, American policy reflected the principles of antimonopolism by prioritizing the distribution of public lands to small freeholders. In the 1830s, Jacksonian Democrats in Congress called for a liberal distribution of public lands in the same spirit with which they had called for the death of the Second Bank of the United States.[17] Both measures aimed to eliminate the special privileges of monopoly and to promote economic independence and equal opportunity among white men.[18] Inexpensive public land would make landownership possible for more Americans, who would otherwise be dependent on wages and landlords. The Democratic Missouri senator Thomas Hart Benton wrote:

> Tenantry is unfavorable to freedom. It lays the foundation for separate orders in society, annihilates the love of country, and weakens the spirit of independence. The tenant has, in fact, no country, no hearth, no domestic altar, no household god. The freeholder, on the contrary, is the national supporter of a free government, and it should be the policy of republics to multiply their freeholders as it is the policy of monarchies to multiply tenants.[19]

A large base of independent proprietors would protect the United States from the dependency and degeneracy that many associated with the old-world tenants and peasants of Europe. In this sense, there was more at stake in the disposal of western land than access to the natural resources and enormous economic potential of the American West. The fate of the West was the fate of the republic.

Congressional debates over public-land policy culminated in the Preemption Act of 1841, which allowed each American citizen to purchase 160 acres of public land for the bargain price of $1.25 per acre after it had been surveyed. The price per acre was crucial because it had the potential to determine which class of settlers could afford to buy public land. A high price would have excluded laborers and small farmers of limited means and favored large landholders and speculators. The $1.25-per-acre price was a triumph for Jacksonian Democrats like Benton. It signaled to ordinary American settlers that their government would prioritize their land rights over those of wealthier landowners and speculators.[20] Yet the key aspect of the Preemption Act of 1841 was that it legalized squatting—settling on land that the occupant neither owned nor rented—by permitting individuals to occupy the land before it was surveyed. Squatters had always moved out ahead of the survey line. Squatting was one among many methods of land acquisition in the West where, under the broad category of "settler," an individual might squat, rent, buy, speculate, or engage in a little of each at different times and on different parcels of land.[21] The Preemption Act gave squatters a new advantage in purchasing. A squatter needed only to locate an unoccupied section of public land, erect a shelter, fence, or other improvement, and file a preemption claim with the local land office. At the end of fourteen months, he had the right of first purchase before a public auction in which he might be outbid. For the aspiring settler, then, squatting had the lowest barriers to entry and the highest potential for return on investment. Preemption required only small initial costs for a filing fee and improvements, and a squatter could earn an income from working the land without paying property taxes until he had fulfilled the occupancy requirement.

The Preemption Act did not quiet the public outcry for free land. If anything, it turned up the volume for would-be preemptors who did not feel the law went far enough. In the 1840s, farmers and laborers organized to demand that all public land be reserved for "actual settlers"—that is, individuals who planned to occupy and cultivate the land themselves and not for those who wanted to hold it for speculation or rent it to tenants. In 1844, newspaper printer George Henry Evans organized the National Reform Association, a group of New York City artisans promoting preemption rights and federal assistance to settlers leaving eastern cities. The National Reformers blamed the emergent industrial economy for an 1837 economic depression, increased immigration to cities in the 1840s, and the surfeit of workers that diminished labor's bargaining power with employers.[22] They believed that inexpensive western farmland could function as a "safety-valve" for an oversaturated urban labor market by alleviating population pressures in the city, thus reducing labor competition and maintaining high wages. The anti–land monopolist reform agenda of the National Reformers included acreage limits on public-land claims to discourage speculation and support for the anti-rent movement of tenant farmers in upstate New York. The "anti-renters" believed laboring on the land gave tenant farmers natural rights of ownership, and through legal and extralegal channels, anti-renters aimed to take titles from "idle" landlords and transfer them to tenants.[23] Ultimately, the anti-rent movement failed to effect any change in New York land laws, and the National Reform Association disintegrated in the 1850s. Many of its leaders grew old and died, and some of its younger members traveled to the West to seek new opportunities in farming, commerce, or, in the case of twenty-five-year-old James McClatchy, gold hunting in California.[24]

*A Squatter's Republic* begins with the California Gold Rush, a moment when McClatchy and other unsuccessful forty-niners looked to landownership after their dreams of golden riches did not pan out. They hoped to squat on inexpensive public land, file preemption claims, and purchase it once the land had been surveyed, but their goals were obstructed by private claims to Mexican land grants. The U.S. government had treaty obligations to uphold these grants, which squatters identified as monopolies because of their immense size. When bitter, occasionally violent, disputes erupted between squatters and other landholders over property rights, squatters became California's first antimonopolists.[25] In asserting that the land rights of small freeholders should supersede all others, the California squatters established a vocabulary of reform that would be revisited by later generations of antimonopolists.

*A Squatter's Republic* is a history of seemingly simple questions: Who should have the right to own land, and how much? The land question was about land, to be sure, but it was also about laborers and capitalists, race and freedom, government and citizens. Its rise and fall in Gilded Age California underscores the symbolic and material significance of the American West to the nation's political economy and culture.

And like all good stories about the American West, this one begins with violence.

## CHAPTER ONE

SQUATTERS AND SPECULATORS: THE FOUNDATIONS OF
ANTI–LAND MONOPOLISM IN CALIFORNIA

The sound of gunfire interrupted Samuel W. Brown's lunch on August 14, 1850. An employee of the Fremont Mining and Trading Company, Brown had sailed from New York to Sacramento, California, and was docked in the Sacramento River near the city's levee. From his ship's deck, he observed a clash on shore between squatters and the sheriff's posse. In a letter to his wife, he described the scene:

> We saw a large party of armed men on foot and on horseback passing up the levee confusedly and hastily and shouting as they went.... Soon we heard the report of firearms—looked out and found the whole city in commotion. Crowds of men were rushing into I Street. The crowds [were] soon out of our sight and we returned to the cabin. In a few minutes a neighbor ran into the cabin and told us that the sheriff's posse and the squatters' party had had a fight and that fifteen men were killed. That the leader of the squatters was dead and that the mayor was wounded and the fight was going on.[1]

The street fight was the result of tensions between squatters and speculators over the right to own city lots in Sacramento. The squatters believed that the township was public land, which, according to federal laws, they had the right to occupy and purchase from the government. They claimed that speculators illegally monopolized city lots, which made it more expensive and difficult for squatters to become landowners. For their part, speculators believed that the township was not public land, but that it was, in fact, encompassed by two private land grants that had been made to the Swiss pioneer John A. Sutter: the first grant was made by the Mexican governor of Alta California, Juan Bautista Alvarado, in 1841, and the second was made by his successor, Manuel Micheltorena, in 1845. Sutter had subdivided his grants and sold off city lots to other settlers, as was commonly done at the time, but these settlers were dubbed "speculators" by pistol-brandishing squatters.[2]

On that hot August day in Sacramento, local authorities sided with the so-called speculators, and the squatters retaliated by invoking a higher, "natural" law derived from traditions of liberal agrarianism. They insisted that their occupancy and use of the land endowed them with rights of ownership that should supersede all counterclaims and justified their defiance of the local legal system. Good governance, squatters asserted, diffused opportunities for landownership and prevented land monopoly. In the Gold Rush era, squatters became California's first anti–land monopolists, and their opposition to land monopoly defined the terms and stakes of land disputes across the new state. Their land-reform agenda reflected a larger vision for how a government should protect its citizens, how a democratic society should apportion property rights, and how California might realize the promise of the American republic.

## Land Rights in a Conquered California

When the Treaty of Guadalupe Hidalgo ended the Mexican–American War in 1848, Mexico formally ceded to the United States a vast territory, covering present-day California as well as Arizona, New Mexico, and parts of Colorado, Nevada, and Utah. Because California was sparsely populated at the time of acquisition, new American migrants expected there would be an abundance of unclaimed public land open to settlement. In other territories annexed in the nineteenth century, the federal government had enacted liberal public-land policies that were designed to accelerate and facilitate permanent migration. In Missouri and Louisiana, Congress broke up some of the large Spanish estates to free up land for American settlers, and in Oregon Territory, pioneering families received federal grants of up to 640 acres while single men received half of that.[3] Migrants to California hoped the government would treat settlers in the newly acquired Mexican territories with the same generosity.

What American migrants to California did not know was exactly where the available land would be. Two obstacles stood between squatters and the land they aimed to occupy and use: Indian land rights and the Mexican private land grants. Between the two, squatters associated Mexican private land grants more closely with monopoly. When compared with the enormous land grants extended to Mexican citizens, Indian landholdings seemed rather insignificant. Under Mexican rule, Indians had held modest land rights—independently and collectively, informally and formally. Indians who occupied the remote interior of California, distant from settlements, evaded and resisted colonial interference so as to continue to occupy their land as they always had. They moved seasonally through hunting, fishing, and gathering grounds, occasionally supplementing their income with trade and raiding.[4] Indians living along the coasts and rivers near non-Indians became more enmeshed in colonial communities and exercised limited land rights where they lived and worked.[5] In 1834, the Mexican provincial government "secularized" the California missions and seized most of the church's landholdings. While the majority of the appropriated land became the property of Mexican ranchers, powerful political figures, military officials, and some Indian individuals and groups also benefited. Indians, who had been more or (usually) less willing occupants and servants at the missions, received private grants and communal property rights to grazing lands, orchards, vineyards, and fields. The Mexican provincial governor José Figueroa issued a proclamation distributing mission lands to individual Indian heads of household or single males over twenty-one years of age in lots from one hundred to four hundred square varas. (One vara was roughly the equivalent of a yard.) Yet, these grants were not the equivalent of titles; Indians could not subdivide, sell, or mortgage their land. Moreover, accepting the allotment obligated Indians to labor on communal lands administered by the governor's commissioner.[6] In a few instances, individual Indians, both men and women, successfully petitioned for private land grants through special service to the mission or the province.[7] The median size of grants to Indian individuals was about 2,200 acres, as compared to the median size of 9,000 acres among grants to Mexican individuals. By the time the United States began to review and patent the grants, approximately half of the Indian grantees had sold part or all of their claims to non-Indians.[8]

After California became part of the United States, Indians found their land rights further curtailed. State and federal Indian policy worked in concert to dismantle Indian land rights in California and to promote white settlement. Although the 1824 Mexican constitution made Indians citizens, the U.S. government did not recognize them as such, and Indians were excluded from treaty provisions that protected Mexican private property rights. American military governors overseeing California Indian affairs between 1846 and 1849 assumed that Indian-occupied lands were part of the public domain, with some portion eventually to be set

aside for reservations, a practice consistent with American federal policy in other parts of the country. Meanwhile, the Gold Rush sent waves
of invaders into the mountainous interior, which provoked violent confrontations between the new arrivals and the old inhabitants and precipitated a marked decline in Indian populations. Between 1850 and 1855,
the number of California Indians dropped from one hundred thousand
to fifty thousand, and it continued to fall thereafter.[9] The federal government remained conspicuously hands-off in California's early territorial years. Amid the chaos of the Gold Rush and in the absence of federal
guidance, subagents for the government scrambled to maintain peaceful
white–Indian relations, to secure Indian labor for California's farms and
mines, and to suppress raiding and violence. The 1850 Act for the Government and Protection of Indians was the state's stopgap measure to
institutionalize Indian land rights and reassert white supremacy over Indians. The legislation set aside farmland for Indians where they lived and
worked but made no reference to any rights to traditional hunting, fishing, or gathering grounds or to the private land grants extended by the
Mexican government. The act also outlined terms of indenture that
bound Indian workers to their white employers.[10] The U.S. Congress did
not establish Indian reservations until 1853, and when it did, it allotted
only twenty-five thousand acres for each of five permanent reservations,
where Indians were encouraged but not forced to go.[11] Until 1865, several
additional temporary reservations functioned as detention centers for
Indians forcibly relocated by state militia and guarded by federal troops.
The majority of California Indians remained off-reservation, and they
either fled to remote, isolated areas or found themselves subject to indenture laws.[12] In a climate so altogether hostile toward Indian liberties,
Indian land tenure did not seem like much of a threat to squatters.

Mexican land grantees, on the other hand, were cause for concern.
Two factors made Mexican land grantees the obvious challenge to squatters' claims: first, the U.S. government's treaty commitment to uphold
the private property rights of Mexican citizens, and second, the immense
size of the grants.[13] The grants could cover as much as forty-eight thousand acres, an area larger than some counties in eastern states.[14] Although later estimates figured that the land grants covered only 9 percent
of California's land, squatters believed that the land grantees controlled
the most arable and well-situated territory.[15]

Settlers gathered information about land values in California through
a variety of sources. For the public domain, they relied on government
officials to disseminate the data. In public-land states like California,

Congress appointed a surveyor general, whose deputies sectioned off tracts and evaluated the quality of the soil and the presence of water, timber, and minerals. (Land with known mineral deposits would not be made open to private entry.) Survey results were freely available at local land offices where registers and other officers recorded and administered the distribution of land at the government minimum price of $1.25 per acre, or twice that for land adjacent to railroads. In theory, settlers could consult with the land office to locate and assess the value of unoccupied tracts.[16] In practice, settlers tended to move faster than the surveyors, especially in California, with its torrent of Gold Rush migration. Congress failed to appoint a surveyor general in California until 1851 and, out of negligence, ignorance, or delusion, the state appropriated a mere twenty-five thousand dollars for official surveys.[17] (Over the next ten years, surveying California became a money pit for congressional funds, with more than $1.7 million spent to map roughly 20 million acres.) Yet the lack of a general survey was not an impediment to settlement. After all, it was widely believed that surveyors were prone to corruption and incompetence, and thus their findings were often suspect. As in the case of John Sutter and the squatters of Sacramento, wealthy individuals with the means or groups of settlers pooling their resources often engaged the services of independent surveyors.[18] More often, California settlers sought out and relied on subjective and informal valuations of land. For public and private land sales, would-be California proprietors plumbed local knowledge and scoured travel accounts and newspaper articles, which opined, with more or less imaginative embellishment, on the value of California land. California newspapers published the results of public auctions, including the size and price of final sales.[19] County records of deeds, censuses, and tax-assessment rolls also pointed to the potential productivity and market value of the property under evaluation.[20] Enterprising businessmen capitalized on the public records system to develop a private industry providing and managing land-value information. Private agents scouted out available land while firms of conveyancers, abstractors, and attorneys facilitated the transfer of titles. These ancillary businesses provided independent sources of information and security for aspiring landowners assessing the value of potential acquisitions.[21] Settlers wanted to know: How many cattle might they graze? What kind of crop yield could they expect? Were there adequate sources of timber and water and access to transportation to sustain their enterprise? Improvements by prior inhabitants—including cleared fields, fences, structures, and irrigation ditches—also raised the value of a given tract, which made compensation for improvements a hot-button political issue for evicted squatters in the 1850s.[22] Location was, of course, critical to land's value, and settlers gravitated toward land with proximity to waterways, roads, and urban areas.[23] In the cities, land adjacent to the main plaza or major commercial arteries was most highly valued. The squatters' riot of 1850 that Samuel Brown witnessed from his ship in the Sacramento River illustrates just that point, as squatters and speculators squabbled over the lots along the river, the city's main point of disembarkation and transportation. By all these criteria, would-be proprietors estimated relative land values and fretted that the Mexican land grants already monopolized the best that the state had to offer.

Concerns about Mexican land monopolies went beyond simple calculations of value, profit, and opportunity. New migrants to California, steeped in the political culture of agrarian republicanism, worried about the social consequences of monopoly as well. Israel Shipman Pelton Lord, an Illinois doctor who came to California to prospect for gold, remarked in his diary in November 1849, "A most stupendous scheme of land monopoly is contemplated by the holders." He went on to articulate the themes that would become central to the squatters' antimonopolist argument. The holders of Mexican land grants were "land sharks," speculators, and landlords, not cultivators: "If they succeed and the old claims are confirmed, the whole land will continue [as] a wilderness of tangled briars and vines and shrubs and weeds and grass except where the fire and flood clean it off, or it will be held under a worse tenure than the farming land of England or Ireland."[24] Lord was certain that California land that was under the control of Mexican land grantees would remain unimproved and unproductive, and its society would resemble the polarized European societies of peasants and aristocrats. The problem of land monopoly was inextricable from the problem of race. In an 1850 letter to an Illinois newspaper, *The Free Trader*, Alonzo Delano, a gold prospector who arrived in Sacramento shortly after Lord, cautioned his readers, "Should the government recognize these Mexican grants, it places the multitude at the mercy of the few, engrafting in fact the peon system of Mexico or the feudal tenure of Europe upon our Republican institutions in California, making a few lords of the soil with a multitude of dependents upon their will, a state of things to which our Anglo-Saxon race are strangers and to which they will not submit."[25] Delano was not alone in his fear that land monopoly would diminish the squatters' opportunities for independence and, by extension, degrade the "Anglo-Saxon" race. Whiteness, landholding, and citizenship were mutually reinforcing categories

that formed the foundations of the American republic in the newly acquired territories of the Far West. Land monopoly, particularly Mexican
land monopoly, threatened to undermine those foundations.

Some migrants also began to suspect (and hope) that many of the
Mexican land grants were invalid. They gleaned what information they
could about Mexican land grants from letters sent by friends and family
or from travelers' reports published in eastern newspapers. The word
from the West was that the grants were poorly documented, unsystem-
atically archived, even outright fraudulent. In 1850, Henry Haight, a
young lawyer who would later become governor of California, described
the state of Mexican land grants in a letter to his father: "It is confusion
worse confounded."[26] It was rumored that many of the grants had not
been surveyed and were, as a result, overlapping or ill-defined. Israel Lord
wrote in his diary in November 1849: "I have no means of knowing [the
land grants'] extent, but from the number of ranches and the apparent
size of some of them, I should not wonder if they are found, like the same
kind of grants in Texas, to overlap in some portions, if not the whole
country, like the shingles on a roof."[27] New migrants to California expected to encounter uncertain and unresolved boundaries between public and private land.

They also worried that, despite all the questions and concerns, Congress would approve some or perhaps all titles under Mexican land
grants. In addition to the Treaty of Guadalupe Hidalgo's promises to
Mexican property holders, there was precedent for the authorization of
foreign titles after judicial reviews in Louisiana Territory and Florida.[28]
In 1849, the federal government had two conflicting reports on the state
of Mexican land grants in California. The first report by Captain Henry
Halleck surveyed Mexican public records in the Monterey archive and
determined that many of the grants lacked adequate maps and surveys or
had been falsified. Halleck recommended that the United States carefully
scrutinize each one.[29] The other report found and recommended the near
opposite. The author of this report, William Carey Jones, had been a land
lawyer in Louisiana Territory and had powerful political connections
through his father-in-law, Jacksonian Democrat and U.S. senator from Missouri, Thomas Hart Benton. Jones acknowledged that some grants were invalid due to "antedating"—that is, they were issued after Mexico ceded
control of California to the United States but drawn up as if they were issued before. And Jones agreed with Halleck that some of the grants
lacked clearly defined boundaries. However, Jones claimed that these im-
perfect grants were relatively few in number, and a congressional review

board would find them easy to identify and to resolve.[30] Jones's research for the report was more extensive than Halleck's—he consulted archives in Monterey, San Francisco, San Jose, Los Angeles, San Diego, and Mexico City—but he also had personal incentive to cast the grants in the most favorable light possible. Jones and his brother-in-law, John C. Frémont, were knee-deep in California land speculation and had purchased claims to Mexican land grants from the original grantees. Frémont, who was famous for shepherding the 1846 Bear Flag Revolt that declared California's independence from Mexico, held the rights to a particularly dubious grant. Jones probably realized that a close scrutiny of Mexican land grants would threaten Frémont's claim. Senator Benton supported his son-in-law's assessment and urged Congress to expedite confirmation of all Mexican land grants except for the most blatantly fraudulent.[31] Yet despite Benton's call for a summary confirmation of the Mexican land grants in California, Congress decided to follow Halleck's suggestion and, as it had in other acquired territories, pursue a policy of close scrutiny.

But it did not do so immediately. Three years elapsed between the signing of the Treaty of Guadalupe Hidalgo and the establishment of a board of commissioners to review the Mexican land grants. In that time, California's land problems became a crisis. As the historian Paul Wallace Gates has noted, "In a slowly developing frontier community such tardiness would have produced no serious consequences," but in California, there was a gold rush.[32] In 1848 and 1849, nearly one hundred thousand new migrants arrived. The surge in population drove up demand for land in the auriferous hills, the agricultural valleys, and the emerging urban centers.[33] Real estate along rivers was particularly desirable to merchants supplying gold prospectors, and new cities, including Sacramento, sprang up wherever that geography and population intersected.

## A Gold Rush Entrepôt

The city of Sacramento, perched on a muddy riverbank near the junction of the Sacramento and American Rivers, was a popular supply point for hopeful gold miners en route to the Sierra Nevada Mountains, and in 1850, it was the second largest of California's cities, with seven thousand residents (fig. 1).[34] Newspaperman Samuel Upham, who arrived in Sacramento in 1850 by way of San Francisco, observed that while "a year ago it contained scarcely half a dozen tents and shanties . . . [Sacramento's] growth during the past ten months has been almost magical."[35] Upham described the gold rush entrepôt as an egalitarian paradise:

Here labor asks its own price, and its beck commands capital. No chartered institutions have monopolized the great avenues to wealth; no aristocracy, grown proud from the long possession of exclusive privileges, can obtain a foothold or assert supremacy. Circumstances have established a level, in which it is honorable to be, from which everyone has an equal chance to rise, and where merit is the only sure guarantee of success. Neither business nor capital can oppress labor in California. Whenever its rights are invaded, the gulches and canyons that lead down the western slope of the Sierra Nevada will furnish a safe retreat, where labor will obtain a rich reward, until its end is gained and the powers that oppress it yield to necessity and consent to do justice. A general independence is observable in the people here, which is the inevitable result of their mutual relation. All classes are alike dependent upon each other, and obligations are mutually incurred. The rich men of to-day were adventurers yesterday. How natural, then, that they should respect labor, by which they have accomplished their success. Few can be found who have secured a competency by their own exertions who do not feel a conscious pride in acknowledging it. Labor will continue to hold the first position in California. Rich and exhaustless as are her natural resources, they have slumbered in the bowels of the earth since creation, and the world could never be benefited by them, without the judicious application of bone and muscle— *the real capital of the world.*[36]

Upham's description captured the classic mid-nineteenth-century ideal of the West. Sacramento was a place where laborers enjoyed the opportunity to become independent, where the increasingly calcified institutions of the East held no sway, and where a classless America would flourish. In the nineteenth-century vernacular, *independence* connoted qualities of manliness, and references to the gendered nature of independence studded Upham's descriptions of the Sacramento pioneers: "Those who have immigrated here are, in most cases, the cream of the populace. A manly, vigorous, intelligent race of freemen, capable of meeting any emergency."[37] By 1850, the "emergency" was apparent.

Unsuccessful miners retreated to Sacramento from the Sierra Nevada Mountains. Many of them had learned about land rights from their experiences in the gold fields, where miners enjoyed land-use laws designed to facilitate mineral discovery and extraction. Miners could not purchase mineral lands from the government, but they could work a claim without renting or otherwise paying for it. Their occupancy and use secured their entitlement. As aspiring landowners, the erstwhile miners hoped that the government would extend similarly liberal laws in urban and rural areas to promote commercial and agricultural development.[38] They set up tents, shanties, and other makeshift homes along the river and on the bridle path connecting the city to Sutter's fort.[39] Upon his arrival in Sacramento in December 1849, Israel Lord noted in his diary: "The first thing that strikes the attention of an observing man is the want of order—the utter confusion and total disorder which prevail on every hand ... The whole town plot, except a few crooked, winding footpaths, among tents and through alleys, and a devious wagon way through the streets, and the ground occupied by tents and buildings, is covered with boxes and barrels, empty or filled with all kinds of goods, in passable, indifferent, or bad order, or totally ruined."[40] Another recent arrival, William Prince, a tree and plant broker from Long Island, described the scene to his wife in an 1849 letter: "This is a flourishing town built up since last January and contains about 500 houses (so called), 7/8 of which are mere canvas or sheeting on slight rafters."[41]

In the earliest moments of the California Gold Rush, John Sutter claimed ownership of the slapdash township. Sutter had become a citizen of Mexico, and in 1841, he received a private grant from Governor Alvarado to eleven square leagues (approximately forty-eight thousand acres). The grant failed to specify a southern boundary, and Sutter's surveyor, Jean Jacques Vioget, misidentified the latitudes. Four years later, Sutter petitioned the Mexican government for a *sobrante* grant, entitling him to twenty-two leagues of surplus lands excluded from the 1841 grant. Sutter later insisted that Governor Micheltorena complied with the request but the original document had been lost.[42] As a result, the boundaries of Sutter's grants were, to say the least, open to some interpretation, and Sutter unsurprisingly interpreted his claim to encompass the increasingly valuable land of Sacramento.[43] He then subdivided his grant and sold the rights to portions of it to other settlers, speculators, and merchants.[44]

Sacramento speculators, in turn, offered to rent and sell city lots to squatters at exorbitant prices. Prince, who went to Sacramento when he

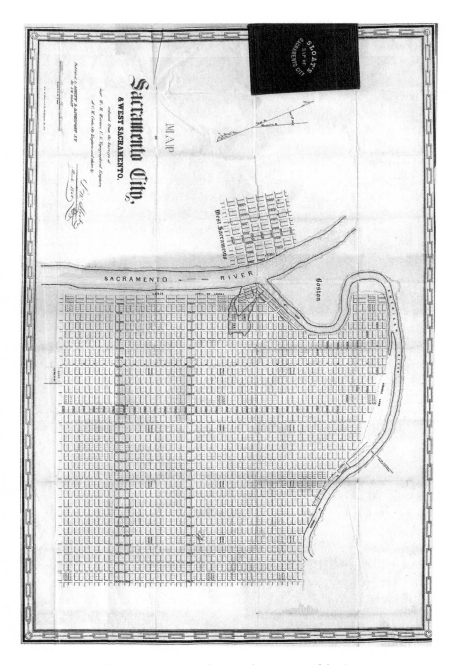

FIGURE 1.  Map of Sacramento, 1850, showing the junction of the Sacramento
and American Rivers. Eleanor McClatchy Collection, 1982-004-0068, Center for
Sacramento History.

failed at gold mining, lamented to his wife: "I shall not realize my expectations here. . . . Had I gone deep into speculation in lots on my first arrival, I should have done well, but I did not come for that and went direct to the mines."[45] But even squatters wealthy enough to buy city lots did not have the incentive. They anticipated that Sutter's grant, like all Mexican land grants, would eventually be subject to federal review, and if the grant were deemed invalid, the land would revert to public domain and be sold for the government minimum price.[46] In Sacramento, it became open season for squatting. As early as April 1849, the problem of squatting moved Sutter's son, who worked for his father as a land agent, to take out space in the *Placer Times*: "Notice to Squatters: All persons are hereby cautioned not to settle without my permission, on any land of mine in this Territory."[47] Sacramento speculators, believing Sutter's grant was protected by the Treaty of Guadalupe Hidalgo, acted aggressively to secure the titles that they had purchased from him, and since many of the biggest speculators were often city officials, they had the political connections to expedite evictions. Sacramento's mayor, Hardin Bigelow, owned real estate valued at fifty-five thousand dollars, according to the 1850 U.S. Census.[48]

To many squatters, it began to seem that the local law was corrupt and controlled by speculators. In response, they organized the Sacramento City Settlers' Association in the fall of 1849, elected officers, and declared:

> [The Association] believing the ground, generally, in and around Sacramento City, to be Public Land; and desiring to promote the prosperity and harmony of persons settling thereon, has resolved. . . . Every Member of the Association will use his best exertions for the support of his fellow-associates, against any and every innovation of their JUST RIGHTS.[49]

The association collected funds to employ an independent surveyor to map and record all its members' claims. In doing so, the association aimed to replace a corrupt system of land distribution with a more "just" bureaucracy controlled by "actual" settlers. By claiming that the township was public land, the squatters connected their cause to a larger, national defense of preemption rights and small freeholding. In the United States, these were institutions traditionally associated with republicanism and democracy, and the Sacramento squatters made themselves the defenders of those values in the newly acquired territory of California.

Charles Robinson, a doctor from Fitchburg, Massachusetts, who had the distinction of being the first Sacramento squatter forcibly removed from a claim, became the association's president. In September 1849, Henry A. Schoolcraft, a speculator, district magistrate, and recorder, had petitioned the city council for Robinson's removal from a lot near the I Street levee. Although Schoolcraft claimed the lot as his own, the doctor had built the foundations of a house on it. The city tore them down, and Robinson unsuccessfully sued the city for destruction of private property.[50] Robinson's defeat and the loss of his home inspired him to lead a movement against Sacramento's speculators and the local government that backed them. Those who knew Robinson back in Massachusetts were later surprised to hear of his involvement in the 1850 Sacramento riot. They "couldn't account for so quiet a person heading an armed mob."[51] But Robinson's followers in California regarded his taciturnity as steely determination. A lawyer for the Settlers' Association and Sacramento's city notary, John Hill McKune, recalled, "His manner was quiet and he made no effort to captain the crew by any histrionic gesture, but in a few minutes he secured the undivided attention of the whole meeting consisting of almost two thousand people and before he closed they were ready (like the Athenians on the Agora who listed to Demosthenes) 'let us march against Philip, let us fight for our country, let us conquer or die.'"[52]

Like Robinson, the other members of the Settlers' Association were of a professional class that included doctors, lawyers, farmers, and printers.[53] They were a mix of native-born Americans and emigrants from the British Isles, some of whom had come to California alone and some who arrived with their wives and children. At least two Sacramento squatters—James McClatchy and Henry Caulfield—came to the Settlers' Association with firsthand experience in eastern land-reform conflict. Both men had participated in New York's Anti-Rent Wars in the 1840s. The "Anti-Renters" had sought to overhaul New York's leasehold system and permit tenants to buy the land they worked. Their movement attempted to enact an agrarian ideal of small, freeholder farms on old New York manor grounds.[54] New York City labor leader George Henry Evans organized financial and political support for the upstate tenant farmers under his organization, the National Reform Association. Evans equated land reform with labor reform because he believed that surplus urban labor would naturally gravitate toward available rural lands, thus maintaining high wages in the cities.[55] In the 1840s, due in large part to Evans's enthusiasm and charisma, land reform became the cause célèbre among artisan laborers in New York City. McClatchy, just barely

FIGURE 2. James McClatchy stands behind George Henry Evans in an undated composite photograph with other members of the Land Reform Association, as the National Reform Association was sometimes later called. Eleanor McClatchy Collection, 1982-005-0017, Center for Sacramento History.

twenty and working as a printer, was among the youngest members of the National Reform Association (fig. 2).[56] After emigrating from Ireland in 1840, McClatchy became an employee of the *New-York Tribune* and a protégé of its editor, Horace Greeley. Already a member of the National Reform Association, Greeley introduced McClatchy to Evans.[57] Like McClatchy, Henry Caulfield was an Irish immigrant who had come to the United States in his youth, and like McClatchy, he had participated in the Anti-Rent Wars, but not as a land reformer. He was a member of Albany's Emmet Guards, a local militia that suppressed anti-rent activities in Columbia County in 1844. In 1849, both McClatchy and Caulfield caught gold fever. McClatchy traveled across Mexico and up the coast of California, while Caulfield went to California via Cape Horn. After brief, unstoried careers as miners, both men took up residence in Sacramento, where McClatchy resumed work as a printer and editor and Caulfield became a carpenter.[58] Three thousand miles from New York, Caulfield and McClatchy found themselves allies in the battle to make California squatters into landowners.

The members of the Settlers' Association were united by a common fear that land monopolies denied squatters the opportunity to own land and to profit from Sacramento's growth. While their broadsheets and oratory expressed a deep antipathy toward so-called land-sharks and speculators, Sacramento County records indicate that they, too, engaged in speculation, although usually on a smaller scale than their wealthier neighbors. Approximately one quarter of Sacramento County residents who filed preemption claims between 1852 and 1854 also held titles to land valued anywhere from two hundred dollars to thirteen thousand three hundred dollars, with a median of one thousand dollars. According to county tax assessor records, this value was typically spread over two or more lots, most without improvements, which suggests that squatter-landowners were holding land for future sale, not for current use.[59] Caulfield was one example. In the years just after the 1850 riot, he filed two preemption claims with the county recorder's office: one in 1852 and another in 1853. Just a year later, in 1854, the county tax assessor recorded twenty-three lots under title to Caulfield. These lots ranged in value from forty to two hundred and fifty dollars. Caulfield had not improved a single one of his lots, a sign that he was not using or occupying them.[60]

Other members of the Sacramento City Settlers' Association similarly moved between strategies of public land preemption and private purchase. Such diversification was prudent, given the insecurity of all California titles, and it effectively blurred the line between squatter and speculator.[61] In the 1850s, McClatchy bought a title from Peter Burnett, the first governor of California, who was on the Settlers' Association's list of most detested land speculators.[62] As a backup, McClatchy had a preemption claim on file for the same lot, just in case the Sutter grant and, thus, Burnett's title should be rejected by a federal review. By 1860, in addition to the town lot he occupied, McClatchy had acquired 320 acres outside of the city. The 1860 census listed the value of his real estate at two thousand dollars.[63] B. R. Nickerson, the vice president of the Settlers' Association, owned real estate valued at twenty thousand dollars and even identified himself as a "speculator" to the 1850 census taker.[64] Association member and lawyer McKune also speculated in city lots while simultaneously defending the rights of squatters in court. In 1853,

McKune owned two city lots, valued at a total of nine hundred dollars, and by 1860, his real estate holdings had grown to five thousand dollars in value.[65]

The difference between Sacramento squatters and the men that they dubbed speculators was one of scale of wealth, with clear differences only at the extremes. The 1850 census listed the squatter lawyer C. A. Tweed's real estate at ten thousand dollars in value and his partner Lewis Aldrich's holdings at one thousand dollars. The city assessor recorded that Tweed's wife independently owned two city lots in value of nine hundred eighty dollars. John Madden, whose eviction directly precipitated the riot in August 1850, owned two thousand dollars in real estate in Sacramento. In 1852, just two years after the riots, the county tax assessor valued the land of the three wealthiest squatters: W. Merritt at $13,300, Caulfield at $11,710, and Selah Russell at $9,555. Members of the Settlers' Association often owned real estate valued at one thousand dollars or more. In contrast, tax assessors estimated that Samuel Brannan, the largest landowner in the city of Sacramento and a notorious Mormon apostate, held land with a market value of $118,500 in 1852.[66] But Brannan was unusually wealthy; other landowners identified as speculators by the Settlers' Association held property on the same scale as the average squatter. In 1852, T. L. Chapman, who was also on the association's published list of reviled speculators, owned land in value of just $1,600, above the median value of squatters' landholdings—$1,050.[67] Although the historian Roy Robbins once summed up the history of public lands as "the struggle between these two forces of squatterism and speculation, between the poor man and the man of wealth," the Sacramento squatters were, in reality, neither strictly squatters nor poor men.[68]

## A Squatter Riot

In the winter of 1849, Sacramento grew both larger and poorer, which exacerbated tensions between squatters and speculators. Mining camps in the Sierras closed down for the winter, which left miners without income for several months. They straggled into town alongside the last of the year's overland migrants, swelling the population at a time when supplies were at their lowest. The effects of the seasonal closure of the region's largest industry rippled out to traders, draymen, and builders, who also found themselves out of work.[69] In January 1850, Israel Lord wrote in his diary, "They are squatting all along the river, at short intervals, on both sides, and building shantees, and making brush fences."[70] To make matters worse, it began to rain, and the city of Sacramento flooded. William Prince observed the residents traveling by boat through the inundated streets: "The street has had 50 boats of 15 to 25 feet long . . . going about carrying passengers, goods, etc."[71] All residents, squatter and speculator alike, took to what little high ground remained in the city.

By the end of March, the flood waters had abated. As the city dried out, hope for renewed prosperity returned. The riverfront once again filled up with tents and shanties and soon became so crowded that boats could not unload their cargo. Merchants and claimants to city lots protested that the squatters were obstructing trade.[72] City council president A. M. Winn sided with the merchants. Calling the squatters "the great evil," Winn complained to the council that "a legitimate business cannot compete with those who occupy public grounds without expense. It is unjust because the very property occupied by those who only retard the progress of improvement belongs in fact to those who have purchased and improved the lots." He urged the council to pass stricter ordinances against unlawful occupation of city lots and to support the eviction efforts of the local authorities.[73] Meanwhile, large speculators like Brannan paid vigilantes to evict squatters and to handle the heavy labor of tearing down homes, fences, and any other squatter improvements. Evictions became a local spectacle, with crowds of spectators cheering the demolition. The vigilante squads gave the conflict a new, vicious cast.[74] Among Brannan's victims was the Settlers' Association president, Charles Robinson, who had just begun work on a second house after losing the first one to Henry Schoolcraft. Robinson stood by as Brannan's hired men laid waste to his work, a foundation that projected ambitiously from the embarcadero out over the river on pilings, but this time, Robinson did not stand alone.[75] A winter spent huddled together on the only dry land in town had created a new sense of solidarity among the city squatters as well as a new energy and commitment to the defense of their land rights. The association assisted new immigrants settling on unoccupied lots and provided armed-guard protection from Brannan's men and city officials.[76] Members also pitched in to help new arrivals build shelters and other improvements.[77]

In March, the Settlers' Association attempted to bolster their claim to land rights in Sacramento by publishing a report that asserted that the township—and more specifically, the riverfront—was public land. The report contained a translation of Sutter's 1841 grant, which the squatters had located in a nearby archive. The association's official surveyor and register, Colonel John Plumbe, who had been a surveyor for the Allegheny

Mountain railway in 1829, contributed an analysis of the grant's terms. Plumbe contested the grant on three counts: first, that Governor Alvarado had deeded the land to Sutter *and* his colonists; second, that the private land grant—like all Mexican land grants—excluded the flood plains along the Sacramento River where many squatters resided; and third, that the southern boundary did not extend far enough to encompass the city itself.[78] These conclusions led Plumbe to remark that "in all cases where cities or towns have been laid out upon any of the *public lands of the United States*, Congress has secured the *right of preemption to every occupant of a lot*: and no doubt can be entertained of its extending to the enterprising citizens of distant California, the benefits of the same principles of mere justice as have heretofore been enjoyed by those of Iowa, Wisconsin, and other States."[79] Plumbe's interpretation of the Preemption Act of 1841 was wishful thinking; the act did not guarantee "every occupant a lot." But such gifts of free land constituted the dreams of antimonopolists like Plumbe, who hoped that the government would prioritize the claims of small freeholders above all others.

On May 10, the speculator–squatter conflict edged closer to its violent climax when speculators John P. Rodgers and DeWitt Burnett filed suit in the Sacramento Recorder's Court against John Madden, who was squatting on the corner of N and Second Streets. Madden contended that the property was public, and that he had occupied it since March and made improvements to ready his preemption claim. Rodgers and Burnett insisted that they bought the lot from Sutter, and it was most certainly not open to preemption. The court sided with Rodgers and Burnett and ordered Madden off the lot.[80] Galvanized by the Madden decision, Sacramento speculators increased the frequency and force of evictions. Samuel Brown sympathized with the evicted squatters in a letter to his wife: "My feelings and principles but not my interests are strongly on the side of the squatters and I have been strongly tempted to join the 'Association' and speak at its meetings." He believed the speculators to be unscrupulous, "filching honest men's gains and moneys, abusing without the shadow of right property which each citizen of the United States had an equal claim to," and the Sacramento Settlers' Association, he declared, would "put down this monopoly" of public land.[81]

In yet another broadsheet, the squatters extended a "notice to immigrants" unschooled in the cunning of Sacramento land monopolists: "There are in our City a number of men with remarkable principles, who go among those who have newly arrived and offer to sell or lease to them the *Public Land* in and about this place, thus imposing upon the unsuspecting." The "notice" urged new arrivals to thwart the speculators' schemes and occupy the land that was public: "The vacant land in Sacramento City and vicinity, is open for *ALL*, free of charge; but, they can make either of the following gentlemen a present of a few thousand dollars, if they have it to spare. Such favors are eagerly sought and exultingly received by them. In fact, some of them are so solicitous in this matter, that, if they are not given *something*, they will *almost not like it*, and even threaten to *sue* people who will not contribute to their support."[82] Undeterred by public shaming, the speculators continued the evictions throughout the summer of 1850, each time inspiring Robinson to call a frenzied meeting of squatters.[83] Newspaper accounts estimated the crowds surpassed one hundred, but these numbers included not only would-be preemptors but also curious spectators and members of the opposition. Samuel Brannan, lawyers for the speculators, and judges often appeared at the gatherings to defend the evictions.[84] The crowds inspired dramatic oratory. At a meeting on the first of July, M. A. Milligan, a member of the Settlers' Association's board of arbitrators, made "an eloquent appeal about the sacred right of the homestead—a right which every man was bound to protect in justice to himself."[85] On another occasion, James McClatchy cried, "Let us put up all the fences pulled down, *and put up the men who pulled them down!*"[86] Applause and stamping feet expressed approval for McClatchy's proposed lynching of the Sacramento speculators.

On August 8, Madden filed an appeal with the County Court, which, despite legal assistance from McKune, Aldrich, and Tweed, proved futile. Four days later, Judge E. J. Willis rejected Madden's appeal and had a writ of restitution drawn up. Anticipating the Settlers' Association's next action, Willis intimated that the law would not permit an appeal to a higher court. The squatters again circulated broadsheets and called public meetings in which they reiterated their charges of land monopoly by Sacramento speculators: "It is well known that a few individuals have seized upon nearly all the arable public lands in this country." Squatters levied a number of accusations against the speculators: "First, they have used brute force and torn down the buildings of the settlers and driven them from their homes by riotous mobs. Second, they have used threats of violence even to the taking of life, if the occupant or settler persisted in defending his property, and thus extorted from the timid their rightful possessions."[87] The squatters also decried the judicial system—Willis's decision convinced them that the courts were in the pockets of the speculators—and they called into question the authority of the newly formed California

legislature: a "pretend" legislature, they scoffed, still too new to have received official recognition from the U.S. Congress, yet already corrupt
enough to give speculators legal cover to evict squatters.[88] The squatters
accused the legislature of acting without authority and violating the Constitution's promise to protect the property rights of American citizens.[89]
On the eve of the riot, the squatters posted a notice that was in essence
a squatters' declaration of independence, warning of impending retalia-
tion: "The settlers and others on the first show of violence to their persons or property . . . have deliberately resolved to appeal to arms, and
protect their sacred rights, if need be, with their lives." By claiming that
property rights were "sacred," the squatters defended their call to arms as
service to a higher law. The sanctity and supremacy of natural rights
could not be brought low by unjust courts and a pretend legislature. The
broadsheet ended with an ominous warning: "The property and lives of
those who take the field against them will share the fate of war."[90]

When the "war" came, it was short-lived but bloody. On August 13,
Sheriff Joseph McKinney attempted to deliver a writ of restitution to Madden, but he found his path blocked by McClatchy and Michael Moran,
another member of the association. McKinney arrested McClatchy and
Moran and tossed them onto the brig docked near the levee on the Sacramento River. The sheriff vowed to return to Madden's lot before ten
o'clock the following morning to remove any personal property and de-
molish his home. In response, Robinson called a meeting near the levee
for "squatters and all other republicans," a carefully chosen label that highlighted the squatters' connection to American ideals. Denied appeal and
forced to suffer the indignity of two association members' imprisonment,
Robinson realized it was time to fight.

Getting angry squatters to meetings had been easy, but rounding up
volunteers to riot in the streets proved difficult. Even if, as McKune described him, Robinson had the oratorical skill of Demosthenes, the squatters were not the Athenians staving off the Macedonians. They were
would-be landowners, for whom squatting was often more a matter of
pragmatism than ideology. Many of them feared armed defense by local
law enforcement. The night of the arrests, Robinson confessed his troubles and anxieties in a letter to a friend: "Will you call me rash if I tell you
that I took these steps to this point when I could get but twenty-five men
to pledge themselves on paper to sustain me, and many of them, I felt,
were timid?"[91] On the morning of August 14, Robinson and the Settlers'
Association treasurer, John Malony, rode to the agreed-upon rendezvous
point and found no one waiting for them. Later, Robinson recalled with

bitterness: "Evidently the courage that manifested itself so defiantly at squatter meetings, with no enemy in sight, had all oozed out of these brave men. Some of the loudest and apparently the boldest were found in bed trembling like aspen leaves."[92] Robinson and Malony managed to rustle up fifteen men to join their ranks, including Henry Caulfield, who had a reputation as a ruffian and could always be counted on to join a fight.[93] With Malony hastily appointed as captain, the ragtag squatters' army took up guns, pistols, and swords and began to march toward Madden's house.

By the time they reached the lot on the corner of N and Second Streets, Sheriff McKinney and his men had removed Madden's furniture and demolished most of the house. The squatters had also drawn a crowd—some jeering, some applauding. Various newspaper reports estimated the size of the crowd to be from thirty to one thousand. At about noon, the burgeoning group paraded to the levee near I Street where the brig was docked.[94] On I Street, the squatters encountered Mayor Bigelow and other city officials. Malony directed his men to shoot the mayor. Bigelow received bullets to the cheek, thigh, and abdomen, but it was the fourth bullet to his thumb that nearly killed him when gangrene later set in and a doctor had to amputate his entire arm. (The unfortunate mayor finally succumbed to cholera while recovering from the surgery.) Among the other city officials, four, including the son of John P. Rodgers, whose case against Madden had sparked the riot, sustained injuries, but James Woodland, the city assessor, was the only fatality. He was felled by a single bullet and expired on the spot.[95] Earlier that morning, his wife had given birth to their third child.[96]

Robinson took a bullet to the side. The shot missed his heart by an inch and lodged near his spine. The injury was not fatal, but it made him unable to run from the scene of the fight. He took refuge on a balcony of the Bininger Hotel, where his friend McKune found him. Five minutes later, Sheriff McKinney and his officers ("pretended officers," according to McKune) discovered them, and they carried Robinson to the brig on a stretcher, over McKune's protests.[97] As the firing subsided, it became evident that the squatters had suffered more fatalities than the mayor's men. Malony and two of the other squatters died of gunshot wounds. The rest of the group fled upriver to the house of James Allen, a slave-owning squatter from Missouri who operated a tavern on the outskirts of town.[98] The sheriff's men pursued the fleeing rioters but only captured Caulfield, whom they tied belly-down onto a horse and carried back into town. After some debate over whether to hang Caulfield from a tree, the sheriff's men

decided to save themselves the trouble and threw him in the brig with
Robinson, McClatchy, and the others.[99]

The next morning, the city buried Woodland, and McKinney and his
men rode out to raid Allen's tavern. A scout for the sheriff reported that
the squatters were assembled in the front room while Allen's wife lay ill
with typhoid fever in the back.[100] Poor Mrs. Allen would not live to die of
typhoid. As the second shootout began, she became one of its first victims,
along with the Allens' adopted son and their slave. McKinney was also shot
to death, which widowed his sixteen-year-old wife of just four months.[101]
Two squatters were shot and killed, and the sheriff's men rounded up the
four surviving squatters for the brig.[102] Allen took three bullets, and
the trail of blood he left between his house and the river convinced some
authorities that he had died.[103] Gravely wounded but far from incapaci-
tated, Allen made his way upriver about forty miles to a gold mining
camp called Hangtown (Placerville). He hid out there just long enough to
generate anxious rumors of an allied uprising of miners and squatters.[104]
Many miners felt sympathy for the squatters' cause. If Congress one day
overturned the liberal mineral land–use laws, miners expected they
would have to seek preemption rights on their claims, which aligned their
interests with those of the squatters. But the miner–squatter alliance
never materialized in Sacramento. At some unknown point, Allen left
Hangtown and returned to Missouri.[105] Sutter and the so-called speculators retained control of their city lots.

## Beyond Sacramento

Any history of the Squatter Riot of 1850 in Sacramento prompts the question: What are the broader implications of a brief, ineffective insurrection?
For the most part, Sacramento was a peaceful, seasonally soggy city, where
rival land claimants lived side by side. The riot was an extreme and aber-
rant event, indeed, but it was not unique in California's history. In the two
decades after the Gold Rush, squatter conflicts erupted in rural and urban
areas—in the goldfields, on the farms, and in the cities alike. Differences in
land use, climate, and population across the state may have altered the tim-
ing. Squatters and other landholders clashed in Gold Rush regions with
the first waves of immigration, but conflict did not reach the less densely
populated agricultural and ranching areas until the end of the 1850s. Yet
such differences did not affect the fundamental nature of the disputes;
wherever property rights were in doubt, which was to say, everywhere in
California, fights ensued in the courts and, occasionally, in the streets. The
severity of these conflicts ranged from petty, day-to-day disagreements to

armed resistance and riots.[106] Newspapers and local histories gave dramatic monikers to armed standoffs and the occasional exchange of gunfire. The Bodega War (1859), the San Jose Settlers' War (1861), the Healdsburg War (1862), and the Battle of Mussel Slough (1880) earned California squatters a range of reputations, from ruffians and criminals to Jeffersonian idealists and defenders of democracy.

The ongoing uncertainty about the legitimacy of Mexican land grants in the 1850s and 1860s encouraged squatters to resist eviction, perhaps most aggressively in the cities where prime real estate was relatively scarce. In San Francisco, four separate Mexican grants made claim to the city. In 1853, local newspapers noted that "one title had just seemed as good or as bad as another; *possession* being better than any."[107] Consequently, San Francisco became a scene for turf wars and skirmishes between individuals and gangs of squatters, who were deliberately occupying "lands known to be claimed by others."[108] To squatters, the overlapping grants were a clear sign of fraud, and they felt sure the city would revert to public domain. San Francisco squatters spread out across the city, put up improvements, and filed preemption claims. An article in the *Alta California* newspaper reported squatting on Kearny, Bush, and Mission Streets, and "even on the almost impossible heights of Telegraph Hill." To secure their possession of city lots, the squatters built fences under the cloak of darkness: "The squatters are wide awake, particularly during the nighttime, and a piece of ground over which one passes in the afternoon, free of all encumbrance, he finds the following morning fenced in."[109] The *Annals of San Francisco*, a compilation of articles by local newspaper men printed in 1855, reported that, "when daylight and the proprietor came, the intruder defied ejection. To seek redress from the tribunals whose judgments had led to these encroachments was only ridiculous; so the parties generally fought it out among themselves, with the aid of friends and long purses to hire help, until both suffered considerably in the battle."[110] As in Sacramento, San Francisco squatters organized protective associations and sought extralegal resolutions where they felt the law and the authorities had failed them. In 1849, 1854, and again, in 1867, riots of a similar scale to the one in Sacramento erupted in San Francisco. Squatters resisted writs of ejectment with force of arms and were ultimately suppressed by militia, city authorities, and police.[111]

Violence made for colorful "frontier" anecdotes and, consequently, received the most attention in the press, but the relationship between squatters and other landholders was not always so antagonistic. Squatters and claimants to Mexican land grants largely found ways to accommodate one another, and these accommodations revealed the alignment of interests between squatters and their supposed rivals. In rural counties such as Sonoma, to the north of San Francisco Bay, claimants to Mexican land grants often leased land to squatters for farming or stock raising. Such an arrangement was mutually advantageous in a time of insecure land titles. While squatters protected themselves from harassment, ejectment, and the potential loss of their improvements, land grantees exacted some remuneration for the use of their land and spared themselves the costs of a legal or literal fight. After a wave of immigration swept through rural Sonoma County, one local history recalled that "bachelor ranchos," encampments of mostly male squatters, "sprang up like mushrooms."[112] The so-called bachelors rented land from the grant holders "at prices not much above what they would have had to pay had it been government land."[113] In his history of Putah Creek, a rural community in the Sacramento Valley, David Vaught has shown that claimants there often sold or rented land to squatters or employed them as laborers. Shared aspirations united them: "They all wanted Putah Creek to be a great agricultural community worthy of all the booster rhetoric."[114]

Not only did squatters and large landholders often find ways to work together, but the former also tended to become the latter with time. In Alameda County, some of the most prominent and wealthy landowners got their start as squatters. Horace W. Carpentier squatted on land when he arrived in Alameda County in 1850, but within a few years, he had become famous as Oakland's most rapacious land speculator and the notorious swindler of the Peralta family, who held some of the largest Mexican land grants.[115] A. J. Moon and Edson Adams similarly got their start in Oakland as squatters and eventually became the first members of the city's board of trustees. They then used their political clout to ensure that Carpentier's path to land monopolization in the city of Oakland remained unobstructed.[116] A county history of Oakland from 1883 also identified two of the original Oakland immigrants, "Mason and Wickware, now of San Francisco [who] were called squatters in those days, not 'capitalists.'"[117] There was no permanent social stigma from squatting, no scarlet "S" emblazoned on the lapels of the nineteenth century's wealthiest Californians.

## Conclusion

When Charles Robinson called Sacramento's "squatters and all other republicans" to arms in 1850, the squatters did not answer because of shared moral opposition to speculation or republican antipathy toward self-aggrandizement and excess. Squatters had as much in common with the speculators they claimed to oppose as they had with one another. Squatting and speculating were two strategies for land acquisition. Both aimed to secure property rights so that land values might increase and new California settlements might flourish. But "speculation" had deeply entrenched negative connotations in the American republic. The Sacramento squatters elevated the stakes of their cause by equating it with the opposite of speculation—antimonopolism, natural rights, and landed republicanism. They presented their land rights as the fulfillment of the promise of the West and of the republic itself, the promise of enduring equality and democracy. That rhetoric was persuasive and won supporters. In the coming decade, squatters' rights, undergirded by a culturally entrenched political ideology, dominated state politics.

## CHAPTER TWO

THE SQUATTER VOTE: SQUATTERS' RIGHTS AND
PARTY POLITICS FROM CALIFORNIA TO KANSAS

On the evening of August 14, 1850, Charles Robinson and James
McClatchy were fellow inmates aboard a Sacramento prison
brig. The charge was inciting a riot. Six years later, and a thousand miles to the east in Kansas Territory, Robinson found himself in another jail. This time, the charge was treason. Robinson had immigrated
to Kansas in October 1854 to help shepherd the free soil movement. The
Kansas-Nebraska Act of 1854, which allowed residents to vote on
whether to permit slavery in the territories, provoked a confrontation
between antislavery and proslavery settlers in Kansas, as each side organized and identified itself as the legitimate territorial government. The
antislavery government made Robinson its governor, and the proslavery
government made him a traitor. In 1856, proslavery authorities arrested
Robinson as he attempted to flee the territory and imprisoned him in
Leavenworth, a town in northeast Kansas. Concerned for his friend,
McClatchy wrote to Robinson, and Robinson replied:

> I am in the midst of another excitement more violent if
> possible than was that in Sacramento. It seems as though
> the Devil was to pay in this Country at the present time
> and [there is] no money in the treasury.... There is but
> a step from the sublime to the ridiculous, and but one
> from the governor's office to the gallows, so it seems.[1]

From the Sacramento prison brig to the Leavenworth jail, Robinson and
McClatchy witnessed and participated in the changing political circumstances and meanings of squatting in the 1850s. Squatterism originated
as an antimonopolist defense of small freeholders, but in the 1850s, as
squatters became more politically active and organized, other values
began to cluster around the concept: values of free labor and popular

sovereignty, slaveholding and secessionism. In the years leading up to the Civil War, squatters' rights to own the land they used and occupied served multiple and even opposite agendas.

The history of squatters' rights in "Bleeding Kansas" during its territorial era has been well studied, and California simultaneously became a testing ground for the many meanings of squatters' rights.[2] In Kansas and California, settlers rallied behind squatters' rights not only to acquire inexpensive land but also to shape their nation's political culture. Democrats and a new political party, the Republicans, vied for the "squatter vote" in California. Each party claimed to defend the rights of small, independent landowners and promoted legislation that liberalized preemption laws. In the decade before the Civil War, the party rivalry secured a central place for squatters in California politics, and their land rights inevitably became enmeshed in the state's response to slavery and, ultimately, secession. Even thousands of miles distant from the theater of war, Californians were not immune to its effects. The nation's crisis gave California squatters a new vocabulary with which to defend their land rights as essential to the survival of the American republic.

## After the Sacramento Squatter Riot

Charles Robinson may have been the first prisoner elected to office in California. After the riot, while Robinson sat on Sacramento's prison brig awaiting bail, his friends nominated him for the state assembly. They had considered putting him up for a senate seat, but as John Hill McKune later recalled, "On more mature reflection we determined that his chances for the assembly were better."[3] Robinson received 869 votes, coming in third to secure one of Sacramento's three legislative seats. Local newspapers attributed Robinson's win to the concerted effort to elect a "squatter candidate."[4] Shortly after the October election, with Robinson out on bond, he and McClatchy began to publish a weekly newspaper to promote preemption rights and denounce large *speculators*, a term they used interchangeably with *land monopolists*. They called their paper the *Settlers and Miners Tribune*, and they used its pages to extol the virtues of land limits, protections for squatters' improvements, and more lenient preemption laws.[5] The *Tribune* came in handy as a mouthpiece for their cause when the paper's editors were indicted with the other squatters who had participated in the August riot. In November 1850, less than a month after the publication of the first issue of the *Tribune*, the squatter-rioters were formally charged with conspiracy to obstruct the law and the murder of James Woodland, the city tax assessor. The indictment called the defendants "persons of evil minds and dispositions" and claimed that they "wickedly and unlawfully [did] meet and present, support, vote for, and adopt resolutions . . . declaring their intention with force and arms and a sacrifice of life to obstruct the due administration of the law."[6] Robinson and McClatchy used their newspaper to exonerate themselves in the public eye. In the pages of the *Settlers and Miners Tribune*, they rewrote the history of the conflict in the language of anti–land monopolism. Their account of events typically portrayed Robinson and his co-defendants as aspiring freeholders, persecuted by the wealthier, more powerful Sacramento speculators wielding dubious Mexican land grants. One article criticized the legitimacy of Sutter's grant and praised the squatter-rioters: "Contrary to the wishes of a few greedy monopolists, they have manfully proclaimed the doctrine that the public domain was alike open to all."[7] The editors of the *Tribune* also culled erroneous accounts of the riot from other newspapers and corrected them, often line by line.[8] In the *Tribune*, the "affair" in Sacramento was never referred to as the "Squatter Riot" but rather as the "Land Monopolists Riot" or the "Anti-Squatter Riot," which made victims out of the riot's instigators.[9] The tactic seemed to work. Other local newspapers reported that the public favored the squatters. On November 7, when Robinson arrived at the courthouse in Benicia, throngs of supporters greeted him.[10] Israel Lord wrote in his diary:

> Most assuredly, the squatters were in the right. They had as much right to the land where Sacramento City stands as anybody (certainly more than the swindling minions of Sutter). . . . Occupancy was the only title anybody could have and Sutter has a large farm . . . and still more the 33 miles grant. Enough in all conscience for any reasonable man. . . . The squatters only claimed what they could and did then and there occupy, i.e., one or two lots at most for each.[11]

The widely held principle that use and occupancy conveyed natural rights of ownership, accompanied by the belief that natural law superseded the actual law, inspired support for the squatters, and that support became the basis of a wider political mobilization.

Meanwhile, the prosecution struggled against public sympathies to make their case. They could find no one to testify against the squatters. The defense had only one witness, John Madden, whose house McClatchy and Michael Moran had defended against the sheriff's demolition squad, but Madden did not get the chance to take the stand. On November 15, Madden was arrested for his role in the riot while waiting outside the courthouse for his turn to testify; he was taken back to Sacramento for arraignment. The *Settlers and Miners Tribune* reported the incident with indignation: "Madden had been in the streets of Sacramento for more than a month, not attempting to avoid any officer. But no one cared to arrest him till he appeared in Benicia to testify for the defendants."[12] The tactic backfired, and despite the protests of the prosecutors, who had probably arranged for Madden's timely arrest, the trial was postponed.[13]

During the period of postponement, the *Settlers and Miners Tribune* folded, a common occurrence in the volatile nineteenth-century newspaper industry, and Robinson began his term as a state assemblyman.[14] In the assembly, Robinson continued to press for squatters' rights, and he voted for legislation protecting the value of squatters' improvements and quieting claim conflicts.[15] The consistent success of the pro-squatter bills made it seem as if squatters controlled the state legislature. In one letter, Robinson reported to his fiancée, Sara Tappan Doolittle: "Neither party dares oppose us, and I expect little or no opposition in the legislature in reference to this subject [of land reform]. . . . Everyone has given up all open opposition to us and we 'damned squatters' are as much respected as anyone."[16] On May 19, 1851, Robinson's trial resumed. Still unable to produce a witness, the prosecution was forced to withdraw its case.[17] In June, Robinson left California to return to Massachusetts, where he married Doolittle.[18]

## The "Squatter Vote"

After Robinson's departure, squatter politics continued to flourish in California and the cause made inroads in the U.S. Congress. California senator William Gwin became the squatters' primary champion. Between 1851 and 1853, Gwin authored legislation that guaranteed compensation for improvements on confirmed land grants and made other efforts to liberalize California's preemption laws on unconfirmed grants.[19] The California Land Act of 1851, which established a commission to review each of the claims to Mexican land grants, was among the most important laws that Gwin authored.[20] Lawyer Henry Halleck wrote to one of his clients, Pablo de la Guerra: "The commissioners are scrutinizing the titles very closely, requiring us to prove the genuineness of each paper presented and that was signed and issued at the time it purports to be

Table 1. Ethnicity of Original Grantees and Claimants for 821 Private Land Cases Presented to the Board between 1852 and 1856

|  | Anglo | Mexican | Indian |
|---|---|---|---|
| Original grantees during the Mexican or Spanish period | 17.7% | 76.6% | 5.7% |
| Claimants before the U.S. Land Commission | 46.8% | 50.2% | 2.9% |

.... I never formed any conception of the amount of labor that would be required in this matter."[21] The U.S. Land Commission consisted of three officials, appointed by the president and assisted by interpreters fluent in Spanish and English. Claimants, seeking to prove the validity of their grants, brought witnesses, documents, maps, and other evidence of their compliance with the grants' stipulations before the commission.[22] The commissioners reviewed more than eight hundred claims between January 21, 1852, and September 14, 1854.[23] Initially, they refused to consider claims filed after that date, but in subsequent years, Congress created additional legislation to accommodate a handful of late claims.[24]

The review process revealed the diversity of the Mexican private land-grant holders.[25] While squatters were typically Anglo-American, records from the land commission reveal that Californios, Anglos, and Indians held Mexican private land grants. That diversity was not surprising; California had been a multicultural society in the decades preceding the Mexican–American War. According to Mexican law, any citizen of Mexico—native-born or naturalized—could receive a private land grant. In the 1830s and 1840s many American and European men acquired Mexican citizenship through marriage or military service. The commission's records also suggest the extent to which private land grants had changed hands from Californios to Anglos. When the commissioners reviewed a grant, they made note of who the original grantee was, and who had subsequently acquired the rights to the land associated with that grant. While Anglos only represented 17.7 percent of the original land grantees, by the early 1850s, they accounted for nearly half (46.8 percent) of all land claims presented to the federal review (table 1).[26]

Table 2. Ethnicity of Original Grantees and Claimants by Region

|  |  | Original Grantees during the Mexican or Spanish period | | | Claimants before the U.S. Land Commission | | |
| --- | --- | --- | --- | --- | --- | --- | --- |
|  | Total | Anglo | Mexican | Indian | Anglo | Mexican | Indian |
| Northern Counties | 555 | 19.3% | 77.3% | 3.4% | 55.8% | 43.2% | 1.1% |
| Southern Counties* | 266 | 14.2% | 75.2% | 10.5% | 28.2% | 65.0% | 6.8% |

*Counties below the southern Monterey County line

Residents of counties to the north of Monterey filed about two-thirds (555 out of 821) of all private land-grant cases. Of these cases, Anglo claimants filed more than half (55.8 percent), a higher incidence than the overall state percentage (46.8 percent) (table 2). The breakdown of original grantees by ethnicity in Northern California was consistent with the state overall—19.3 percent Anglo (versus 17.7 percent overall), 77.3 percent Mexican (versus 76.6 percent overall), and 3.4 percent Indian (versus 5.7 percent overall)—which indicates that a greater number of land grants had changed hands between Anglo and Mexican owners in Northern California than in Southern California. In Southern California counties, where Mexican-owned cattle ranches were predominant, Anglo claimants accounted for only about a quarter (28.2 percent) of private land-grant cases.[27]

If the commission approved the claim, the federal government surveyed the land and issued a patent. If the commission rejected the claim, the claimants could appeal the decision to the U.S. District Court and then to the Supreme Court of the United States. About one-eighth of all private land cases eventually went before the Supreme Court. Generally, the higher courts showed more leniency toward claimants than the commission did.[28] Nonetheless, this last phase could drag on for years—seventeen on average—as litigation and appeals created delays. In the meantime, squatters swarmed on unconfirmed claims and impeded the claimants' use of the land. Lawyers' fees and property taxes piled up. Squatters or

Table 3. Reasons for 225 Rejected Land Cases

|  | Percentage of total rejected claims |
| --- | --- |
| Lack of evidence | 48.4% |
| Granted by one without required authority | 8.0% |
| Conditions of grant not met | 8.0% |
| Fraud | 7.1% |
| Discontinued, withdrawn, or not prosecuted | 9.3% |
| Part of another grant | 7.6% |
| Antedating | 3.1% |
| Rejected (no reason given) | 8.4% |

other rivals often gambled that the claimants would go bankrupt or lose in a final appeal while the courts chugged along at their languorous pace.[29]

Ultimately, the review process, from the land commission to the Supreme Court, deemed one-quarter of land claims (225 out of 821) invalid. The most common reason for rejecting a claim was lack of evidence (table 3). In many cases, documents were lost or destroyed, or witnesses failed to attest to the claimant's compliance with the grant's use and occupancy stipulations. The *diseños* (rudimentary maps) accompanying each Mexican grant were insufficiently detailed to support the case.[30] Lack of evidence may have also caused plaintiffs to withdraw or discontinue their claims, but it is difficult to judge definitely because the records do not systematically note the reasons for voluntarily discontinued claims.

Nearly one-half (48.4 percent) of all claims did not have adequate documentation to convince the commission, but other factors led to rejection as well. With far less frequency, the commission rejected claims to grants issued by individuals without authority under Mexican law. During the Mexican period, only the governor of Alta California could lawfully grant land. On occasion, priests, generals, or alcaldes (the Mexican equivalent of mayors) overstepped their authority to make personal gifts of land. The commission universally dismissed these cases. A rejected claim might also have failed to comply with the terms of the original grant. Non-occupancy was a common failure; when California was part of Mexico, it was relatively remote from major population centers, and some grantees never set foot on their land. The commission also disallowed grants made by Alta California governor Pío Pico after the Bear Flag Revolt on July 7, 1846, ostensibly liberated the state from Mexican rule. Fraud accounted for only a small percentage of rejected claims, although the sensational cases received the most attention from newspapers.

When the reasons for a rejected claim are broken down by ethnicity, Anglos filed 51.4 percent of cases rejected for lack of evidence and 68.8 percent of cases rejected on the basis of fraud, which may have convinced squatters that they had more reason to distrust Anglo claimants than Mexican (table 4). For their part, Mexican claimants were more likely to be rejected for receiving a grant from an unrecognized authority or failing to comply with the terms of the grant. The most common reason for failure to comply was non-occupancy, which seemed to substantiate squatters' stereotypes of Mexican titleholders as wasteful and absent.[31]

The California Land Act (1851), with its provisions for the review of Mexican private land grants, was the most elaborate and extensive legislation addressing the state's land problems, but it did not represent the only attempt to adjudicate disputes and organize property rights. Between 1853 and 1855, the state legislature passed laws lowering the statute of limitations for landlords, speculators, and titleholders seeking action against trespassers. In 1855, State Senator William Shaw, the head of a San Francisco settlers' association, sponsored an occupancy law, which reimbursed the value of improvements to squatters evicted by a patented Mexican land grant. In a time of ill-defined property rights, the occupancy law reassured squatters that they would receive compensation for their investments and years of labor.[32]

Squatters demanding legal protections found willing supporters in multiple political parties: the Democrats, Whigs, and Know-Nothings.[33] While it was still in print, the *Settlers and Miners Tribune* had reported that squatters' associations preferred the Democratic Party over the others, and this preference grew more pronounced in the early 1850s.[34] The Democrats freely and actively courted the "squatter vote" by promising to liberalize land laws in favor of squatter claims, while their main rivals, the Whigs, found themselves torn between pursuing the squatter vote

Table 4. Reasons for Rejected Land Cases by Ethnicity

|  | Anglo Claimants | Mexican Claimants | Indian Claimants |
| --- | --- | --- | --- |
| Lack of evidence | 56 | 47 | 6 |
| Granted by one without required authority | 9 | 7 | 2 |
| Conditions of grant not met | 2 | 13 | 3 |
| Fraud | 11 | 5 | 0 |
| Discontinued, withdrawn, or not prosecuted | 20 | 1 | 0 |
| Part of another grant | 12 | 4 | 1 |
| Antedating | 3 | 4 | 0 |
| Rejected (no reason given) | 10.5* | 8.5* | 0 |

*Claim filed by two claimants, one Mexican and one Anglo

and appeasing their constituency of Mexican land-grant-holders.[35] As a result, the Democratic Party dominated California politics for most of the 1850s, holding the governorship, both U.S. Senate seats, and a majority in the state legislature.[36] In 1851 and 1853, newspapers attributed the successful gubernatorial campaigns of Democrat John Bigler to the "squatter vote."[37] In his first inaugural address, Bigler declared, "I am a firm believer in the most liberal policy towards those who lead the way in bringing into subjection the wild and unsettled lands of the wilderness." Bigler promised to act against the "establishment of monopolies, which would serve more than every thing else besides to paralyze the energies of the most enterprising and energetic class of men the world has ever seen."[38] In that promise, Bigler repeated a Jeffersonian agrarian idea that monopoly led to inefficiency and waste, while small freeholds spurred productivity and a democratic redistribution of wealth. Henry Halleck described Bigler as a "despicable ... agrarian."[39] Just before Bigler's re-election in 1853, with the federal review of Mexican private land grants in its second year, Halleck complained to his client, Pablo de la Guerra, "Bigler has thrown himself into the arms of the squatters, and if the land-holders vote for him, they ought to lose their land.... If the squatter party succeeds in electing Bigler, then farewell to land titles in California."[40]

### Challenges to Democratic Dominance

The Democrats' monopoly on the squatter vote did not last long. By the mid-1850s, squatters began to show signs of dissatisfaction with their sup-posed political champions. One source of the squatters' dissatisfaction came from Senator Gwin's Land Act of 1851. The process of reviewing the Mexican private land grants was agonizingly slow. As long as titles went unresolved, all squatters' claims and improvements were subject to con-fiscation and the land could not be sold or mortgaged. With the California economy in recession in 1854, securing property rights and investments became all the more urgent. Squatters wrote plaintive, even threatening letters to the land commissioners to speed the review process and agitated for laws to protect their interests.[41] Meanwhile, California's Supreme Court seemed to privilege the rights of large landholders. Squatters might have blamed the courts for their insecure land claims, but they did not. Instead, they pointed the finger at the Democratic officials they had elected. The case of John C. Frémont's claim to Rancho Las Mariposas was the most notorious example. Frémont purchased a ten-league grant to Las Mari-posas from the original grantee, Mexican governor Juan Bautista Alvarado. It was a "floating" grant, which gave the grantee the right to locate his claim on any ten leagues within a certain area of the Sierra Nevada foothills. In 1849, gold deposits were discovered there, and Frémont "floated" his grant over those lucrative streambeds.[42] Frémont used his connections to se-cure a place on the first docket with the land commission when it began to review private land grants in January 1852, and with the aid of his brother-in-law and lawyer, William Carey Jones, he hurried the case through the process. Frémont's claim was not strong. At that point, floating grants were not recognized by the U.S. government as valid; besides, neither he nor Alvarado could demonstrate compliance with the occupancy requirements stipulated by the grant. Despite these serious deficiencies, Frémont re-ceived a patent on February 10, 1856, a decision that amended the Cali-fornia Preemption Act of 1853, which had prohibited recognition of floating grants. The decision also overturned laws preventing preemption of mineral lands. Patent in hand, Frémont evicted the squatters at Rancho Las Mariposas without compensation for their improvements.[43]

The court's decision realized the squatters' worst fears about land monopoly and its power to attract special and unfair privileges. Some squatters already believed that surveyors favored large landowners by deliberately locating grants over the most valuable land and improvements, and the court's decision on Las Mariposas seemed to endorse the practice by permitting Frémont to claim the gold beds.[44] Two members of the Sacramento City Settlers' Association wrote to the local newspaper: "Is there, in fact, a single one, who can lie down at night, without fear lest the morning may surprise him with some before unheard of floating grant having drifted over, during his hours of rest, upon his homestead or lest he may, after all, be finally embraced within the elastic boundaries of some adjoining grant [?]"[45] A grant without set boundaries made it possible for the grantee to usurp the settler, a reversal of the usual notion that the squatter encroached on the grantee's claim.

Not only did the California Supreme Court legitimate floating grants, but it also struck at legal protections for squatters. In 1856, the court ruled the Democrat-sponsored occupancy law unconstitutional because it denied the owners rents and profits from their land until it was patented and, in effect, confiscated their property without due process.[46] John Hill McKune filed a report as a member of the state assembly judiciary committee in which he denounced the court's decision on Las Mariposas and efforts to repeal the occupancy law: "No other country ever had such a curse as these immense floating grants and doubtful titles, and to intensify the wrong, the Legislature now is asked to repeal an act by which the injured parties might be protected. The decision is so clearly erroneous that the Supreme Court must, it seems to me, reverse and change their ruling; at least the Democratic Legislature should not take away this last hope."[47] Rightly or wrongly, California Democrats bore the burden of responsibility for the state's ongoing land troubles. To many California squatters, it seemed that Democrats had failed to enact the policies and protections they had promised, and squatters began to distance themselves from the party.[48]

## The Slavery Question in California

The inability to quell land disputes was not the only challenge to the Democrats' dominance. In the 1850s, the party's association with southern slaveholders also tainted California Democrats in the eyes of the state's voters, who were predominantly antislavery. Many Californians feared that their geographic distance from the proslavery South would not shield them from the expansionist interests of slaveholders.[49] Concerns about slavery reaching into California had initially surfaced at the state's first Constitutional Convention in 1849. Although the delegates had voted unanimously to make California a free state, some worried that the prohibition of slavery would not stand against southern interests in California. Such worries led to the decision to exclude the uncultivable desert regions encompassing present-day Nevada and the Mormon-populated parts of Utah from California's boundaries. Antislavery delegates held that a smaller state was not only less likely to split in two—one free, one slave—but also easier to govern.[50] The presence of free African-Americans in California also seemed to portend the infiltration of slave labor. During and after the Gold Rush, some African-Americans immigrated to California independently, while others came with their slave masters. The latter were legally manumitted slaves who lived more or less as permanently indentured servants. California's first governor, Peter Burnett, admitted, "We have thus, in numerous instances, practical slavery in our midst."[51] Delegates to the 1849 Constitutional Convention considered whether to prohibit the migration of free blacks to the state. The debate introduced the first suggestions of a close connection between California antimonopolism and California racism.[52] Delegate Oliver Wozencraft's statement foreshadowed the antimonopolist, anti-Chinese agitation that would dominate California politics two decades later. Addressing the convention, Wozencraft invoked an antimonopolist rationale for his support of the prohibition. African-Americans, he claimed, were "living laboring machines." Capitalists exploiting the slaves' unpaid labor would have an unfair advantage over free labor industry. Prohibiting black migration would, Wozencraft believed, "protect the people of California against all monopolies." The convention had already discussed and rejected a prohibition on monopolies, specifically in the form of state-chartered banks, but the monopolies that Wozencraft cautioned against were industrial and agricultural monopolies, concentrated ownership of capital and land that eliminated opportunities for small freeholding and self-employment.[53]

In the decade after the first Constitutional Convention, as the nation's sectional crisis over slavery worsened, Democratic politicians in California faced a choice between supporting the national party's platform of slavery expansion or breaking with the party to appease antislavery voters. California Democrats also faced new competition for the coveted squatter vote from the Republicans, a coalition of northern

Whigs, abolitionists, antislavery Democrats, and former members of the short-lived Free Soil Party who had first mobilized in protest of the Kansas-Nebraska Act of 1854.[54] Republicans started from the premise that free labor could not coexist with slavery. They defined their cause as the protection of "free labor," economic independence for men who either worked for themselves or temporarily worked for wages while saving money to become self-employed. In the ideology of the Republican Party, free laborers formed both the productive and moral backbone of a healthy society with robust economic growth and a virtuous citizenry.[55] Free labor ideology fit hand-in-glove with the anti–land monopolist principles on which squatters based their claims to land rights. Both groups sought protections for the economic independence of small proprietors. The delegates to California's first Republican convention in 1856 resolved "that the future growth and prosperity of our state depends upon the speedy settlement of land titles; and we regard a law, judiciously framed, for securing to the *bona fide* settler the improvements he may have made upon private lands, in ignorance of the title, as peculiarly required in the present uncertainty of boundaries and titles."[56] The Republicans further promised to protect the value of squatters' improvements and declared their support of "a free grant to actual settlers, of reasonable portions of public lands; and also of the present system of free mining established in our state."[57]

Despite the alignment between squatters' rights and the Republicans' free soil ideology, California Republicans initially suffered for their party's association with abolition. The majority of California voters who opposed slavery were not necessarily in favor of emancipation, which they feared might encourage the westward migration of free blacks.[58] The Republicans' opponents labeled party members "abolitionists" and "negrophilists." At a public debate in May between two prominent Sacramento politicians, Republican George Bates and Democrat J. C. Zabriskie, a crowd pelted the Republican representatives with rotten eggs and set off firecrackers to disturb their speeches.[59] As the campaign continued, California Republicans struggled to keep the free white labor principles of their party at the forefront of public discussion. As the Republican Party officer, H. S. Love, claimed: "If this state or any other state is to have black slave labor placed beside free white labor; if the rights of freedom are to be interfered with, we have to fight!"[60] Republicans emphasized that a free soil regime would enact antimonopolist reforms benefiting white laborers. In Santa Cruz, Republicans declared that slavery represented a form of labor monopoly, against which white workers could not compete.[61] Republicans described free laborers as "producers." At a meeting in San Francisco, the party officer C. H. S. Williams asked, "Why is it that we are here tonight and not falling into the current of party discipline? ... It is because we have the hearts of American freemen; it is because we... are men who think, act, and produce."[62] Cornelius Cole, the principal organizer of the Republican Party in California, likened slaveholders to monopolists, calling them a "privileged class," whose every advantage came "at the expense of the independence of free white laborers."[63] Cole accused the Democrat-dominated federal government of giving preferential treatment to slaveholders: "Millions are readily appropriated for whatever purpose may promote the slave interest, but not one cent can be had to favor free labor."[64]

In 1856, the Republican Party chose John C. Frémont as its first presidential nominee. Scorned by squatters for his floating grant at Rancho Las Mariposas, Frémont did not, at first blush, seem the best representative for the interests of anti–land monopolist squatters and independent freeholders, but the Republican Party officials believed he would have broad appeal nonetheless. He was pro-Union and opposed to the expansion of slavery, but he was not, at that time, an abolitionist or a nativist, and therefore, he was palatable to conservative and immigrant voters alike. Most significantly for the squatter vote, Frémont had already earned the respect of one of the most famous California squatters, Charles Robinson. While in the state assembly in 1851, Robinson had backed Frémont's reelection to the U.S. Senate. In his memoirs, Robinson wrote: "Frémont alone of the candidates [for senator] was opposed to this division [of California into two states], and, although the proprietor of a large land grant, the squatter [i.e., Robinson himself] supported him."[65] After 142 rounds of voting, the legislature still could not arrive at the necessary two-thirds majority, which the state constitution required, and they postponed the election until the next session, by which time Robinson was no longer a state assemblyman.[66] Robinson later recalled that his support for Frémont divided his squatter constituents: "Anti-slavery squatters approved of the course taken, while a few of the pro-slavery squatters were offended."[67] For Robinson, however, opposition to slavery was an essential companion to squatters' rights. Both were means to guarantee the rights of independent, free landowners.

In the 1856 election, the Republicans attracted some Democrats who were opposed to the expansion of slavery, but they failed to make a significant dent in their rival's dominance. Democratic presidential candidate James Buchanan won the election, and Democrats swept California with 62 percent of the vote, compared to the Republicans' 13 percent.[68] But in the years thereafter, squatters' disaffection for the Democrats and support for the Republicans continued to grow.

By 1856, James McClatchy had declared his support for the free soil, free labor politics of the Republican Party.[69] McClatchy's shift in party allegiance was not surprising; he had a reputation in Sacramento not only for his opposition to land monopoly but also for his opposition to slavery. Ever since the *Settlers and Miners Tribune* folded five years earlier, McClatchy had mostly bounced from newspaper to newspaper, with one unsuccessful detour into politics. In 1851, McClatchy ran for assemblyman in Yolo County; he lost after being labeled a "violent and rabid squatter" and an "abolitionist" by the *Sacramento Daily Union*.[70] He denied the latter charge, but his history with the pro-homestead, antislavery National Reform Association and his devotion to the Republican cause suggest that there might have been some truth to the *Union*'s report. McClatchy helped Cornelius Cole launch the Republican *Sacramento Times* in 1856 and then went on to edit another Republican newspaper, the *Daily Bee*. The *Bee* was the progeny of a defunct party organ, the *Daily California American*, which dissolved with the disappointing performance of the Know-Nothing Party in the 1856 presidential elections. The *California American* had been pro-settler, antimonopolist, and antislavery in the territories. In its first edition in February 1857, the *Bee* professed its support for the same principles. The *Bee* dedicated itself to covering issues of land claims in California. Rarely a day went by without the *Bee* printing at least one, if not multiple, articles on land disputes and their impact on settlers. The newspaper concerned itself most with preemption on the public domain, Mexican land-grant fraud, and fair compensation to squatters for improvements. Working for the *Bee* as a reporter and a printer, McClatchy was in his element. Within a year, he was promoted to editor of the *Bee* and later he became its owner. Under his guidance, the newspaper became adamantly anti-Democrat, and it documented the California squatters' growing alienation from their onetime political champions.[71]

The *Bee* accused prominent Democrats of deceiving squatters by manipulating preemption laws to benefit California land speculators. At the state party convention of 1857, leading Democrats attempted to make amends by resolving "that the rights of preemption in this state ought to be as liberal as obtained in other new states, and these rights ought to be secured to settlers on all lands not actually segregated as private property."[72] They also reaffirmed the party's opposition to land monopolists who held floating grants. But the *Bee* noted that the Democratic leadership's rhetoric did not match its actions. Party nominations virtually shut out the squatter interest. With indignation, the *Bee* detailed the events of the June convention: "They [the Democratic Party leaders] nominated an anti-Settler [Colonel John B. Weller] for Governor and gave the settler candidate for Supreme Judge six votes out of three hundred and twelve, and then very complacently passed the above resolutions. Are the settlers such gudgeons as to be deceived by it?"[73] Weller's stance on preemption in California inspired the *Bee*'s contempt. According to the *Bee*, Weller was "a favorite of grant holders and monopolists" because while he was a U.S. senator, between 1852 and 1857, he had extended the time limit for Mexican land-grant claimants to submit documentation for the land commission's review.[74] Many squatters believed a disproportionate number of pro-Weller delegates were represented at the convention. In response, they assembled for a second time in Sacramento to protest the nominations and offered up their own fifty delegates for a countywide "settlers' convention." The *Bee* reprinted their resolutions, which declared that "the Democratic Settlers have been foully betrayed by the delegation from this county in the late State Convention," and that "the Americans [also called the Know-Nothings] and Republicans should unite and elect good men to office."[75]

The settlers' convention was an opportunity for California squatters to publicize their complaints against the Democrats. A delegation identified by the *Bee* only as "rural" passed a resolution denouncing the Democratic candidates for state offices. The newspaper argued that the recent nominations demonstrated how the Democratic platform worked against the settlers. Yet despite the general dissatisfaction with the Democratic Party, not all squatters were ready to support the Republicans. The "rural delegation" avoided commitment to any one political party and ultimately walked out when representatives from San Francisco tried to turn the meeting into a campaign for the Republican Party.[76] The leader of the San Franciscans, A. B. Nixon, was a prominent delegate to the first California Republican Convention in 1856 as well as the president of the Miners' and Settlers' Central Committee, a squatters' organization based in San Francisco and Sacramento, the strongholds of the California Republican Party in the 1856 elections.[77] The Miners' and Settlers' Central Committee blamed the Democrat-dominated state legislature for "defective administration" and the "neglect to provide wise and beneficent laws."[78] As a result of the Democrats' failure to protect squatters' rights, "the settlers on government lands have suffered many evils." They hoped another party—perhaps the Republicans—might remedy those evils.[79]

## Squatter Sovereignty in Kansas

Contemporaneous events in Kansas drove a deeper wedge between the Democrats and the squatters in California. Between 1855 and 1858, news of violence between free soil and proslavery settlers in Kansas gave Republicans and antislavery newspapers fodder to attack Democratic President Franklin Pierce and his successor, James Buchanan, who backed the proslavery Kansans. In an address to California Republicans, state party officer Judge F. P. Tracey asked, "The Democratic Party is in power now and what are they doing for the country and for California?" "Fighting in Kansas!" cried a voice from the audience.[80] When President Buchanan urged Congress to admit Kansas as a slave state under a constitution written by proslavery settlers in Lecompton in 1857, the *Bee* ran an article calling the policy "insane" and reported: "The mass of the people of Kansas have rejected that instrument from first to last—refused to take part in framing it, and then voted it down—yet it is to be forced upon them at the point of the bayonet! And this is Squatter Sovereignty! This is permitting the people to 'form their own institutions in their own way!'"[81] "Squatter sovereignty" was a derisive term for Senator Stephen Douglas's "popular sovereignty," and the "people" that the article referenced were a mix of proslavery and free soil settlers who converged on Kansas Territory to stake a claim for their cause and to overwhelm their opponents' vote.

The stakes of squatting in Kansas were higher than they had been in California. In Kansas, landownership was proof of residency, and in a territory governed by popular sovereignty, residency conveyed voting rights. Since purchase by preemption was a relatively inexpensive way to become a landowner, both antislavery and proslavery factions practiced squatting to secure their base of voters in the territory.[82]

Organizing documents of Kansas squatters' associations reflect the entanglement of the politics of slavery and squatting. Unlike California squatters, Kansas associations usually wrote proslavery resolutions into their bylaws. By these means, squatting in Kansas Territory became associated not only with occupancy, use, and permanence but also with the protection and extension of slavery. One of the territory's earliest squatters' associations in Salt Creek Valley, near Fort Leavenworth, provided the blueprint for the associations that followed. In the Salt Creek Valley association's resolutions, adopted June 10, 1854, the self-identified "citizens of Kansas Territory and many other citizens of the adjoining State of Missouri, contemplating a squatter's home on the fair plains of said territory,"[83] established a precedent of equating squatterism with the proslavery position. Alongside resolutions to protect "bona fide squatter sovereignty" among "actual" settlers and land limits of 160 acres, the Salt Creek Valley squatters included a prohibition on the migration of abolitionists.[84] Between June and December 1854, squatters in the Kansas towns of Whitehead, Leavenworth, and Stockbridge and those on Delaware Indian lands adopted the Salt Creek Valley resolutions.[85] Proslavery squatters initially overrode all opposing viewpoints. In July 1854, an association outside of Lawrence tried to resist the influence of slavery, but its president, John A. Wakefield, who had come to the territory from Iowa, found himself outnumbered by "people of Missouri." Wakefield attempted to exclude the Missourians from membership in the association. The antislavery settlers, whom he described as "actual settlers," gathered in secret to establish their bylaws, but the Missourians caught wind of the covert meetings and arrived en masse to force their way into the proceedings. The number of Missourians, which Wakefield estimated at between one and two hundred, compelled him to acquiesce to their inclusion.[86]

Between 1854 and 1857, the balance of power gradually shifted toward antislavery squatters like Charles Robinson, who arrived in Kansas by way of Boston (fig. 3). In 1854, the Boston abolitionist Eli Thayer organized the New England Emigrant Aid Company to support emigration of antislavery squatters from New England to Kansas. Thayer, a distant cousin of Robinson's wife, believed free soil, antislavery settlers, subsidized by New England philanthropists, stood a better chance of developing permanent settlements than the unorganized masses of Missourians migrating to Kansas Territory as proslavery settlers.[87] The company arranged for transportation for men, women, and families primarily from Connecticut, Maine, and Massachusetts to Kansas. It provided the emigrants with information on where to settle and funded the construction of hotels, mills, schools, and churches, "doing all in its power to surround the settlers, even on their first arrival, with the comforts of civilized and cultivated life."[88] These institutions, Thayer believed, would encourage free soil settlers to stay in Kansas and vote against slavery. Robinson joined the company in its first year, and in July 1854, he went to Kansas as one of two land agents tasked with scouting the best locations in the territory and coordinating land purchases.[89] Robinson looked for good agricultural land, where Indian claims had been ceded to the federal government by treaty and where a free soil settlement might avoid running into too much trouble with proslavery "Missourians."[90] In Kansas, Robinson and his partner, Charles Branscomb, determined that the land about to be given up by the Shawnee tribe along the south side of the Kansas

River was "the most eligible for settlement," partly because of the location's natural advantages and partly because of the ease with which Robinson expected settlers might acquire the land either from the government or from squatters who held quitclaims, extralegal titles on unsurveyed land customarily accepted as conveying rights of ownership. Once the Shawnee yielded the land, it would be surveyed and opened for preemption. If Robinson and his fellow settlers were already recognized as squatters on the land, they would have a head start securing prime real estate and meeting the requirements for preemption.[91]

The New England Emigrant Aid Company dispatched its first band of twenty-nine free soilers on August 1, 1854, and they settled along the south side of the Kansas River, the location Robinson had identified as ideal. The emigrants named their town Lawrence after the company's greatest benefactor, Amos Lawrence.[92] Robinson led a second group of sixty-seven emigrants from Boston on August 29, 1854, and arrived in early October. Six months later, Robinson returned to New England to guide a third group of more than 160 to Kansas.[93] To encourage stable communities, the company tried to send families rather than individual settlers, and most emigrants came with at least one relative, usually a sibling or a spouse. A handful brought children, grandchildren, and parents. The New Englanders were well equipped to build a permanent settlement in Kansas. Among the third group, approximately half identified themselves as skilled laborers, mostly from urban centers in the northeast. Thirteen classified themselves as farmers, two were teachers, and the rest were skilled craftsmen—carpenters, cabinetmakers, shoemakers, and tinsmiths.[94] They were not a population of "transient paupers" paid to vote for freedom, as many Missourians claimed.[95]

Robinson found that acquiring land was as fraught in Kansas as it was in California. Unresolved Indian claims, unsurveyed land, and floating land grants created as much uncertainty about titles in Kansas as in California. Robinson purchased a federal land grant encompassing the as-yet-unsurveyed town site of Lawrence.[96] But the grant did not prevent conflict with the other local inhabitants. On October 6, 1854, a squatter named John Baldwin delivered an angry note to Robinson: "Yourself and friends are hereby notified that you will have one half hour to move the tent, which you have on my undisputed claim and from this date desist from trespassing on said claim. If the tent is not moved within the half hour we shall take the trouble to move the same."[97] In her recollections of the dispute, Robinson's wife, Sara, claimed that Charles greeted the squatters' threat with steely defiance:

Dr. Robinson's laconic reply was returned to them: "If you molest our property you do it at your peril." The citizens of the settlement came together to witness the removal, and with praiseworthy patience waited for the half hour to expire. The time at length passed by, and no movement was made toward removing the tent. Another half hour was waning fast, and the thirty New Englanders were quietly waiting for the tent's removal. At last one of the citizens asked another if it "would be best to hit the first man who attempted to remove it or fire over his head?" The pithy reply of Dr. Robinson was, "I should be ashamed, for the rest of my life, to fire at a man and not hit him."[98]

The local surveyor sided with the New England emigrants, who were more numerous, better funded, and better armed than the squatters in Lawrence.

The run-in with Baldwin provided an important lesson for Robinson about securing his party's claim to Lawrence. In the community's first few years, he purchased dozens of quitclaims from anyone who had even the hint of the color of title.[99] By these means, Robinson did all he could to reinforce the New England emigrants' property claims and, thus, their right to vote in territorial elections. At the same time, these land deals made Robinson a large landholder and threatened to distance him from the squatter values he had bled for in California. In his memoirs, Robinson defended the resolution of the conflict between the emigrants and the other squatters by attempting to make his actions in Kansas seem consistent with those in California: "The agent of the Aid Company [i.e., Robinson] advocated the same policy as was adopted by the squatters in California, namely, let each settler be protected in occupancy till a legal decision could be had, and this policy was adopted by the Lawrence town company."[100] Justifying his actions required a contortion of memory; the law had not sided with the squatters in Sacramento. The Sacramento squatters, in fact, bore more similarities to John Baldwin and his compatriots than Robinson cared to acknowledge. The dispossessed squatters of Lawrence did not cast their quarrel with Robinson in terms of slavery versus free soil. They framed their rebuke in the traditional squatter rhetoric of antimonopoly, just as the squatters of Sacramento had done some four years earlier. When they assembled on January 11 to organize against Robinson's group, the proslavery squatters demanded protections "from

FIGURE 3. Charles and Sara Robinson in Bleeding Kansas. Spencer Research Library, University of Kansas Libraries.

all moneyed associations or influences, also the tyrannical encroachments daily made by the Lawrence Association [i.e., the emigrants from New England]."[101] To the squatters, the New England settlers were "mercenaries," backed by northeastern money. The squatters decried the emigrants as "stock-jobbers and money-getters—men of exchanges and coteries and self-interest—covered from head to foot with the leprosy of materialism."[102] These terms painted the New England men and women as non-producers, in contrast to the squatters who cultivated the land and earned their right to its rewards. But Baldwin and his group did not admit what was plain to Robinson: in Kansas, every land dispute concerned the extension of slavery because land gave its owner a vote.

Between 1854 and 1856, Robinson's encampment of abolitionists in Lawrence became a front line in Kansas Territory's battle over slavery. Robinson parlayed his work with the New England Emigrant Aid Company into a leadership role in free soil politics. Most notably, he helped draft the 1855 free soil constitution, which united the fragmented antislavery settlers of Kansas and set the stage for their comeback after devastating losses to proslavery candidates in the territorial elections.[103] When the U.S. Congress began an investigation into the "Kansas Troubles," Robinson worked closely with the Republican members of the investigation committee to represent the voice of the free soil settlers. His efforts made him a target for the opposition. On May 5, 1856, a grand jury convened by a proslavery territorial judge charged Robinson and other free soil government leaders with treason. Charles and Sara Robinson attempted to flee the territory and made it as far as Lexington, Missouri, by steamboat before a "committee" of proslavery Kansans caught up with them. The committee forcibly disembarked Charles but allowed Sara to continue on to the East, where she canvassed sympathetic northeastern politicians for support. Robinson was returned to Kansas and imprisoned first at Fort Leavenworth and later at Lecompton.[104] On May 21, proslavery settlers laid siege to Lawrence, where Robinson's supporters were clustered. The U.S. Marshal and federal troops stationed in Kansas ignored the appeals for help from the free soil enclave.[105] In response, John Brown, an abolitionist from Connecticut, took the law into his own hands and used the attack on Lawrence to justify a murderous rampage against suspected slavery sympathizers near Pottawatomie Creek.[106] The pattern of violence and retribution persisted up until the fall of 1856. On September 10, free soil settlers descended on the prison in Lecompton to free Robinson. Shortly thereafter, the newly appointed territorial governor, General John Geary, deployed U.S. troops to enforce the peace, and the violent confrontations between proslavery and free soil settlers trailed off.[107] In 1857, the migration of free-state Midwesterners gradually outpaced that of slave-state Southerners, and free soil settlers became the new demographic majority.[108] Consequently, Robinson anticipated that his side would soon prevail in Kansas. He wrote to McClatchy in June 1857, almost a year after his arrest for treason: "We think the days of fighting have passed and that the struggle now will be a political warfare. That we shall have a free state is well settled and the issue now is shall it be . . . Democratic or for freedom, alias Republican." Then, as if to underscore his freshly earned carefree confidence, Robinson jovially asked McClatchy to give his regards to "all the old 'squatters' and other friends and visit whenever you have opportunity."[109]

Robinson liked to portray his trajectory from California squatter to Kansas land speculator as an uninterrupted continuum. He claimed his goal had always been to secure land for independent, free labor landowners. In the summer of 1857, in response to a letter from McClatchy, Robinson wrote: "Your favor of May 4th . . . carried me back to old Sacramento of 49–51 when we waged war upon the Border Ruffians together. This struggle in Kansas is with the same class of men we had to contend with then, and I often wish we had your good natured wit, McKune's manly firmness, and Caulfield's fists as our allies."[110] Republican presidential candidate John Frémont reaffirmed the connection between Robinson's days as an anti–land monopolist in California and his free soil efforts in Kansas in a letter to Robinson, "You have carried to another field the same principle with courage and ability to maintain it, and I make you my sincere congratulations on your success, incomplete so far but destined to end by triumph absolutely."[111] But Robinson could not deny that his experiences in Kansas moved him away from the small free-holder ideal. Once a free soil Kansas seemed secure, Robinson took a hiatus from politics to focus on land speculation, brokering deals for himself and for the Kansas Land Trust, a group of northeastern investors and speculators that included Amos Lawrence, the New England Emigrant Aid Company's benefactor. By January 1861, when Kansas was admitted to the Union as a state and elected Robinson as its first governor, he owned dozens of lots in Shawnee and Douglas Counties.[112] To reconcile this apparent contradiction between his squatterism and newfound landed wealth, Robinson appropriated the language of squatters' rights that he had helped develop in California.[113] He described his land acquisitions as central to his ongoing struggle against "systems of oppression." While unprincipled landowners might try to deny land to others and to impose their political will—as Robinson had observed among Sacramento speculators, Missouri Border Ruffians, and legislators that "could pass laws . . . purposely to deprive one class of citizens of all legal protections"—Robinson believed himself different from that class of landowner.[114] He bought the land to make it free, to keep it in the hands of settlers like him, who upheld the politics of free labor. Perhaps it comforted his reformer's conscience to think that his squatting and his speculation could serve the same purpose.[115]

## The Panic of 1857 and the Homestead Bill of 1860

It took a severe national economic depression to sever the final ties between Democrats and squatters. The Panic of 1857, the result of overspeculation and bank failures across the United States, compelled Democratic president James Buchanan to abandon the liberal preemption rights policies his party had put in place and instead encourage quick-turnaround land sales, supplying much-needed revenue for federal coffers. Sales at public auction threatened to elevate land prices above the means of most settlers.[116] The change in policy affected both California and Kansas but in different ways. In California, 2 million acres were to be auctioned off, and the first sales were to take place in May 1858. Squatters received notice in October 1857, and they had until May to bring their preemption claims and their money ($1.25 per acre) to the land office. Most of the acreage up for sale was in the state's southern counties, where the population was still relatively sparse, so the majority of California squatters remained unharmed. Buchanan's decision, however, followed on the heels of the disastrous 1857 Democratic Convention, where California squatters walked out over the controversial nomination of John B. Weller for governor. The public-land sales and the convention controversy became the combination punch that drove California's would-be preemptors away from the Democratic Party.[117] For Kansas squatters, the new policy was much more devastating. In Kansas, squatters had enjoyed a five-year grace period between making a preemption claim and delivering payment to the land office. Buchanan planned to release almost 8 million acres of public lands in Kansas Territory, and between April 1857, when the Lecompton land office opened, and July 1858, when the first sales were scheduled, squatters scrambled to come up with $200 to preempt their 160 acres or lose their land and all improvements.[118] As Kansas Democrats tried to maintain their hold on the settler vote, they were shackled to two reviled policies: slavery's expansion into the territories and Buchanan's public-land sales.[119]

In the 1860 election year, the Democrats did nothing to reassure squatters that the party continued to champion their interests. With the presidential race approaching, the national Democratic Party split into two factions, one nominating Senator Stephen A. Douglas and the other nominating Vice President John C. Breckinridge. Neither faction mentioned preemption rights in its platform. Slavery and secession were the only concerns. The Republican Party swept up neglected squatters by placing homesteading at the center of its agenda. At the national convention, the Republicans resolved to "protest any sale or alienation to others of the public lands held by actual settlers, and against any view of the free-homestead policy which regards the settlers as paupers or suppliants for public bounty."[120] The party also professed its support for a homestead bill working its way through Congress.[121] In the first months of 1860, Republican congressmen Galusha Grow and Andrew Johnson had introduced homestead bills in the House and the Senate. The homestead debate had, as all things had at that point, devolved into a sectional issue. Northerners thought that homesteads, by promoting landownership among free laborers and small farmers, would serve as a barrier to slavery in the West. Southerners believed any liberality, be it reduced price per acre or free land, discouraged slavery's extension by promoting western migration among small, antislavery proprietors.[122] Grow's and Johnson's bills passed, but they split the Democrats' votes along sectional lines, with Northerners and Westerners siding with Republicans.[123] As

expected, Buchanan vetoed the bills, as he would have vetoed any legislation opposed by the South. With his party consumed by the interests
of expanding slavery, he could not accommodate the distractions of
squatterism.[124]

California politics largely followed national patterns in the 1860 elections, and the state's Democratic Party suffered significant setbacks. Senator William Gwin, who rode to power with the Land Act of 1851, could
not bring himself to break with the proslavery Democrats, and the California newspapers excoriated him for it. Consequently, he did not receive a nomination for reelection in 1860, and his ten-year tenure as a
senator came to an unceremonious conclusion.[125] California Democrats
divided into Douglas and Breckinridge factions: Douglas Democrats, the
party of popular sovereignty, included a cursory reference to the homestead bill in their platform resolutions; Breckinridge Democrats, the party
of slave labor's unfettered expansion, did not.[126] California, which had gone
to Buchanan in 1856, went to the Republican Abraham Lincoln in 1860.
Democratic candidates still received the most votes in absolute numbers,
but their unity and party dominance in the state were shaken by slavery. Republicans more than doubled their votes among Californians since the last
presidential election with 32 percent of the vote, demonstrating the efficacy
of a free labor platform. The split between Democratic candidates provided just enough room for the Republicans to capture the state as the
country slid toward civil war.[127]

## Squatters and Secessionists

Confederate guns fired on Fort Sumter on April 12, 1861, and the blasts
echoed on the Rancho Yerba Buena in San Jose, California. Nestled in an
agricultural valley south of San Francisco Bay, the ranch became a battle-
ground for Antonio Chabolla, a native Californian who claimed ownership under a Mexican private land grant, and squatters, who believed the
land was public and therefore open to their occupancy (fig. 4).[128] In many
ways, the encroachment upon Chabolla's property conformed to a pattern in the dispossession of Mexican land grantees after American conquest: squatters flocked to Chabolla's land, and his efforts to stave them
off resulted in near-complete dispossession. But the Rancho Yerba Buena
land troubles coincided with the outbreak of the Civil War, which endowed the ranch conflict with unique significance. The "Settlers' War," as
local newspapers and county histories would later call it, illustrated the
potency of secession anxiety in California and its ability to temporarily
but dramatically change the meanings of the land question. Between the

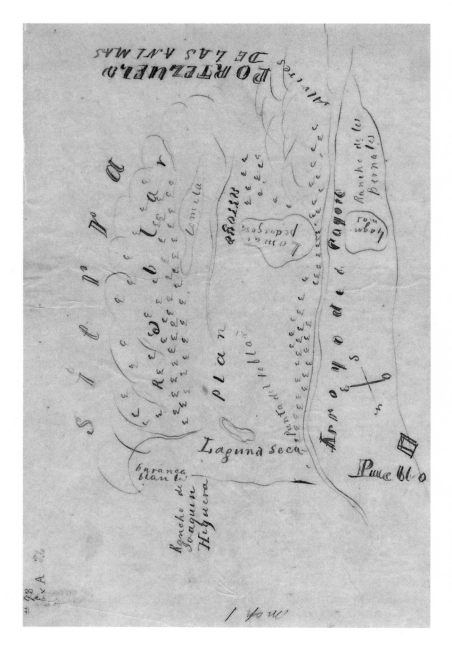

FIGURE 4. *Diseño* showing the extent of Antonio Chabolla's grant to the Rancho Yerba Buena in Santa Clara County, also known as Rancho Socayre, 1859, Land Case Map B-465. Courtesy of the Bancroft Library, University of California, Berkeley.

elections in November 1860 and the attack on Fort Sumter the following April, anxiety over whether California would leave the Union festered, and reports of secessionist organizations monopolized the front pages of California newspapers.[129] Accounts in pro-Union and pro-squatter newspapers like McClatchy's *Bee* identified the men behind the secessionist movement as Lincoln's Democratic rivals: "[The secessionists] clamored for a Pacific Republic—not that it would give us better, cheaper, or more firmer government, but that they, who were otherwise shut out from Federal office for the next four years, might in the upturning of things, have chance at the spoils."[130] Despite a few incidents of sabotage and banditry by Confederate supporters and mild skirmishes between unionists and disunionists, the attack on Fort Sumter and the secession of the Lower South seemed overwhelmingly to inspire feelings of patriotism in the Golden State.[131] On May 17, 1861, just a little more than a month after the attack on Fort Sumter, the state assembly voted forty-nine to twelve to affirm the loyalty of California to the Union.[132] The vote did not, however, dispel suspicions of a secessionist conspiracy. In 1861 when squatters resisted eviction from the Rancho Yerba Buena, accusations against them quickly escalated from resisting the law to secessionism. Fears of rebellion spreading from the South obscured the close ties between the Republicans' defense of free soil and the Rancho Yerba Buena squatters' opposition to land monopoly. Under the dark shadow of the approaching Civil War, the squatters resisting eviction from the Rancho Yerba Buena began to look like rebels and traitors. Secession anxiety forced squatters on the rancho to articulate their ideals in no uncertain terms. In their attempts to prove their fidelity to the Union through public acts and declarations, the squatters wished to make concrete the abstract connection between national loyalty and land rights and to justify the dispossession of Chabolla.

The aggrieved owner of the Rancho Yerba Buena was a longtime resident of San Jose. At least one account claimed that Chabolla, who was born around 1800, had been grazing cattle on the site that would become the Rancho Yerba Buena since 1825 or 1826, and his father and brother, Anastasio, also owned orchards and ranches in the area.[133] In 1840, Mexican governor Juan Bautista Alvarado officially granted Chabolla 24,342 acres bounded on the north by the Evergreen Hills and on the south by the Coyote Arroyo, approximately seven miles from San Jose. Chabolla and his brother were among the Californios who remained in possession of their land grants after 1848, and both submitted grants to federal review in 1852. Anastasio went before the commission with his claims to the Rancho Saujon de los Moquelemes in the San Joaquin Valley and the Rancho Tres Suertes in Santa Clara County. After his death in 1853, his heirs continued to press for recognition of their rights to the land. The land commission rejected the family's claim to Tres Suertes due to lack of evidence, but in the case of Saujon de los Moquelemes, eyewitnesses from neighboring farms verified that Anastasio had indeed continually occupied and used the land for cattle, horses, and barley. Still, the commissioners initially rejected the claim on the basis that the family failed to prove that they were, in fact, Anastasio's heirs. In an appeal, testimony by his brother, Antonio, convinced the district court to reverse the decision on Saujon de los Moquelemes.[134] So Anastasio Chabolla's heirs won their legal right to the ranch, but it was cold comfort. As with so many of his compatriots, Anastasio's will had entailed away his landholdings to pay his American creditors and lawyer, and his children never received what they saw as their rightful inheritance.[135] Antonio was more fortunate than Anastasio. Unlike his brother, Antonio Chabolla lived to see his claim to the Rancho Yerba Buena patented, but he also incurred significant costs to his estate in the process. The United States approved and patented Antonio's claim in 1858.[136] In the intervening years, he was forced to sell much of his land to pay his attorneys, John B. Hart and William Matthews. By the time he received the patent, Antonio likely held the rights to only 10 percent of the original grant, about 2,400 acres.[137]

Squatters scavenged the remnants of the estate. In 1858, Antonio Chabolla sued to evict thirteen of them. It is not clear why Chabolla named just thirteen men among what newspapers estimated to be the five hundred people unlawfully occupying the Rancho Yerba Buena. Demographically, nothing distinguished the defendants from other squatters on the ranch. The 1860 U.S. Census manuscript identified them as mostly native born—although not natives of California—or immigrants from Western Europe, who worked as farmers and farm laborers. Only one among them hailed from a slave state—Thomas B. Farnsworth of Missouri—and none came from the states that ultimately seceded from the Union. With the exception of Andrew Gehringer, born in Germany, and George Ostick, born in England, the defendants listed northern states as their place of birth. Some lived with their families while others lived with fellow farm laborers. Each of them claimed some assets in land or personal property, more or less the same as their neighbors.[138] Perhaps the thirteen squatters were occupying the unsold land that Chabolla had planned to use himself. The evidence to support that conjecture is scant, but one 1862 deed indicates that one defendant—

James W. Bottsford—had constructed a fence on Chabolla's property in some years past.[139]

Chabolla won his lawsuit on September 6, 1860, but the defendants remained on the ranch until the spring of the following year. On March 18, the county sheriff, John Murphy, made his first attempt to evict them. Murphy reported that the squatters chased him off with "arms and force."[140] Returning to San Jose, the county seat, Murphy set about mustering reinforcements. The *Bee* reprinted a *San Jose Mercury News* account of the events of April 9: "not far from 1,000 persons were present at the hour appointed . . . most of them unarmed, but a few with weapons of various sorts, such as sheep shears, old muskets without locks, wooden swords, bayonets whittled out of redwood splinters, etc., etc. One man carried an enormous cudgel, nearly as large as a fence rail on his shoulder."[141] The sheriff asked the assembled men if they would go out to Chabolla's ranch to help him execute the writ of restitution, but "a tremendous shout of 'No,' was sent up, and not one 'Yes.'" Public support apparently sided with the squatters, not with Chabolla or the law behind him. A crowd gathered at the courthouse and then descended on the ranch, where the squatters were garrisoned with provisions: "one small cannon, and perhaps 800 well armed men, besides 500 or 600 others, unarmed sympathizers." Including the men from San Jose, the *Mercury* estimated that there were 2,000 to 2,500 people assembled. When Sheriff Murphy returned to Yerba Buena on April 15, he was met by a veritable army of squatters.

It is not clear what role, if any, racism played in galvanizing public support for the squatters and against Chabolla. In the accounts of the conflict, there are no explicit or implicit mentions of what nineteenth-century Californians would have perceived as a "racial" divide between Chabolla and the defendants.[142] In their writings, the squatters rarely referenced Chabolla, and when they did, it was never in terms of his ethnicity. Instead, they referred to him as a speculator, a monopolist, and a "land shark." Alfred Doten, a Milpitas resident who was among the belligerent mass that greeted Murphy, wrote in his diary: "[The squatters] gave three groans for the land sharks—three more for the lawyer Matthews—jolly good groans."[143] Despite his diminished estate, Chabolla remained one of the largest landholders in San Jose. The "jolly good groans" expressed the conviction that "land sharks"—monopolists, speculators, and other illegitimate landowners—aided by lawyers like Matthews, threatened the squatters' right to own the land they occupied and used. In his diary, Doten described the encampment of the "squatters' army" with evident pleasure: "Several companies from a distance camped last night on the battle field—they fired salute with the cannon at sunrise—land sharks will have to stand back after this."[144]

His duties thwarted for a second time, Murphy sought recourse with the state. In a letter, Murphy appealed to Governor John Downey: "I have to inform your Excellency that I shall be unable to make service and execution of the said writ unless sufficient military force be furnished me for that purpose by the State of California."[145] Sheriff Murphy's appeal for military reinforcements reached a sympathetic ear. Downey was involved in extensive land speculation near Los Angeles, where he was married to a Californio woman, and he owned the rights to Mexican land grants for Rancho San Pedro and Rancho Santa Gertrudes.[146] The governor wrote directly to the defendants. He encouraged them to accept the writ voluntarily: "As I am sincerely desirous that a conflict with the authority of the state should not occur, and that the blood of our fellow citizens should not be spilled, I am thus anxious to give you every opportunity to yield an obedience to the edicts of the courts as this will be your own safety." But he concluded his letter with an ominous warning: "If you persist in the course you have thus inaugurated, I will be under the painful necessity of responding to the requisition of the sheriff and of using the power of the state to enforce the law. Let the consequences be what they may."[147] The governor sent the letter and then dispatched a commissioner, William G. Morris, from Sacramento to San Jose to arbitrate a peaceful resolution to the dispute.

William Raymond, a forty-six-year-old woodchopper from Connecticut, wrote back to Downey on behalf of the Settlers' Council, which was composed mostly of defendants in Chabolla's case.[148] He reiterated the rhetoric of anti–land monopolism that California squatters had rehearsed repeatedly during the previous decade. Raymond claimed that the squatters were engaged in battle to protect a higher law, which mandated the occupant's natural rights of ownership and perpetuated small freeholding in California: "We do most sincerely regret with you that we as good, law-abiding citizens are forced by circumstances beyond our control to defend ourselves and our homes against a grasping monopoly of land speculators." Raymond accused Chabolla of being a land monopolist, whose purpose was to dispossess small farmers of their claims. Since small farmers were popularly believed to be the moral backbone of the American republic, Chabolla's attempts to evict them undermined the democratic foundations of California society. To reinforce the connections between the squatters' anti–land monopolism and a defense of democracy, the Settlers' Council composed a "Declaration of Settlers'

Rights," an appeal to what "the intelligent citizens of this State know to be true.... Live or die, sink or swim, we will by the help of our own strong arm ... defend our rights and homes and our families as best we can."[149] References to home and family reinforced the squatters' claim to be upholding patriarchal traditions of agrarian democracy.

Raymond gave the letter to Morris, who opened it and relayed its contents to Downey: "It needs no comment save you are openly defied."[150] Nonetheless, Morris remained determined to mediate a peaceful agreement, and it seemed as though things were moving along in that direction.[151] On April 25, Chabolla drafted a set of propositions from which to begin negotiations with the squatters. He offered to rent the land to them at one dollar per acre and to extend limited rights to cut timber for their personal use.[152]

At another time, the conflict might have ended there, in a fragile détente forged between a horde of squatters and an outnumbered Mexican land grantee, but in April 1861, the Yerba Buena squatters had the misfortune of sharing newsprint with increasingly dire reports from the southern states. The news from the South primed Californians to read rebellion into every defiant act. Although official notice of the April 12 attack on Fort Sumter did not reach the West Coast until April 24, California newspapers had been monitoring the mounting tensions at the fort throughout the month of April, and they commented daily on the growing popularity of secessionism in the southern states. By April 22, the *Alta California*, a San Francisco newspaper, had reported that there was "very little doubt that hostilities have already commenced."[153] The public preoccupation with the approaching Civil War inspired a new interpretation of squatterism on the Rancho Yerba Buena. "Squatter" became synonymous with "secessionist."

The California press played a large part in applying the new vocabulary of war to local land disputes. Newspapers propagated rumors of secessionism among the Yerba Buena squatters. By doing so, they elevated the stakes of the land dispute between Chabolla and the squatters, exacerbated tensions between the squatters and state authorities, and perpetuated a baseless secession anxiety in California. On April 17, the *Bee* reported that a delegate from the Settlers' Council had traveled to the state capital to "ascertain whether the Governor had ordered out the troops to eject the settlers from the valley." The article claimed that the delegate threatened to retaliate against state coercion: "They will remain at peace with the world if let alone, but if interfered with they will fight. They claim to be independent of the State Government in this matter, just as South

Carolina is of the National Government in her little affairs."[154] The article positioned the defense of squatters' rights within a framework of states' rights, which invented a connection between squatting and secession.

Within a few days, rumors began to spread that "secessionists" had joined ranks with the Yerba Buena squatters. The *Sacramento Daily Union* reported that seventeen hundred people, "armed and mustered," had assembled in San Jose to show their support for the squatters.[155] Given that there were only thirteen defendants in the Chabolla case, the *Union* conjectured that a secessionist conspiracy accounted for the multitudes. "It would seem but natural to look to some other source than mere sympathy with the Settlers for the secret of this powerful organization. Painful as is the suspicion, a variety of circumstances point to the discontented element at work in our midst for the overthrow of the Government."[156] Excerpting from the *Union* article, the *Bee* disputed that theory and accused the *Union* of sensationalist reporting: "The settlers in adjoining counties—Santa Cruz, Monterey, and Alameda—act in sympathy with those upon the Chabolla grant, and it is those who swell the numbers to the amount named."[157] An assemblyman from San Jose chimed in to defend the Yerba Buena squatters in a letter to the *Union* that "denied the charge that the show of force the Settlers of that county have made was in any way augmented by Secessionists—on the contrary, they are against secession."[158]

On April 22, the *Alta California* printed a letter from the squatters' purported attorney, William Carey Jones, the son-in-law of Missouri senator Thomas Hart Benton and the brother-in-law of John C. Frémont. In 1849, Jones had infamously sided with Mexican land grantees in California, but he believed that Chabolla had secured the right to his grant by "fraud." Jones was also, according to the anti-squatter *Sacramento Daily Union*, "the author of some of the most violent secession articles that have appeared in print."[159] The *Union* took the letter, which asserted the squatters' right to rebel, as proof of the squatters' intent to incite a civil war: "If the writer represents the sentiments of any considerable portion of the Settler party, the suspicion of a revolutionary element menacing to the peace of the State may be entertained."[160] The *Bee*, ever the squatters' defender, refuted the *Alta California*'s interpretation and declared that Jones "represents nobody but himself."[161] The Yerba Buena squatters, the *Bee* insisted, were working with the authorities to resolve the conflict peacefully.

After news of the attack on Fort Sumter reached California on April 24, the hope for peaceful arbitration at Yerba Buena seemed lost in a flurry of secessionist conspiracy theories. On April 29, Chabolla withdrew his propositions for negotiation and again demanded that Sheriff Murphy evict the squatters. Murphy wrote to the governor requesting three thousand troops to aid in executing the writ.[162] The governor, in turn, asked the state legislature for an appropriation of $100,000 to defray the costs of sending militia to Santa Clara County.[163]

The threat of force compelled the Yerba Buena squatters to prove their allegiance to the Union. They staged an elaborate public demonstration of their patriotism. They unfurled an enormous American flag, measuring six by ten feet and made of silk. The *Bee* described the flag: "The blue field contains thirty-four stars and on one side of the field is an American eagle bearing the escutcheon of the Union, around which, in gold letters, reads 'Evergreen Home Guards No. 2.'"[164] Evergreen was the name of the district in which the Rancho Yerba Buena lay, and by dubbing themselves the "home guards," the Yerba Buena squatters assumed the mantle of a noble militia, defending family, hearth, and home. The opposite side of the flag, the *Bee* reported, read "Settlers' Rights and Union Forever." The *Bee* applauded the squatters' display: "This national ensign is the best reproof to those who have designedly set the report afloat that the Settlers are Secessionists."[165] The performance was intended to remind the public of the traditional connection between the squatters' agrarian ideals and the survival of the American republic.

In a letter to the *Sacramento Daily Union* printed on April 30, Chauncey Barbour, one of the thirteen defendants in the Chabolla case, explained that the squatters' opposition to land monopoly expressed their ardent, unshakable Unionism. Identifying himself as a "settler" on the ranch, Barbour wrote of his fellow squatters: "A more loyal, union loving people can nowhere be found. As for secession, they will hardly tolerate its discussion, much less suffer themselves to be inveigled into its support. There is as little sympathy with this movement here as in any part of the State."[166] Barbour described the squatters on the Rancho Yerba Buena in terms borrowed from the American agrarian tradition, wherein cultivation enhanced the laborer's virtue. He insisted that, on the Rancho Yerba Buena, "it is not true that the Settlers . . . are a mere rabble or mob, consisting of transient or turbulent persons determined on a forcible resistance to all legal authority." Barbour portrayed the squatters as yeoman patriarchs and cultivators. "They are all permanent," Barbour insisted. "Many of them old residents and heads of families. . . . They are farmers and without exception men of quiet and pacific habits, never having been engaged in any acts of violence and very few of them ever having kept firearms about their premises prior to the present difficulties. In fact, they have been as a community, distinguished for their industrious habits and orderly conduct." Without the bonds of Union, federal preemption laws would not have been extended to California. Squatters depended on federal governance to secure their homesteads. Such men, Barbour reminded his readers, could not wish for disunion.

Between May 1 and May 6, rumors of impending military intervention on the Rancho Yerba Buena ran wild. In a panic, William Raymond again wrote to the governor: "We feel ourselves again compelled to address you in the subject of our land trouble in order to settle by a firm and distinct denial the rumor that our settlers' league is an organization initiated for political purposes and favorable in the dismemberment of the Union."[167] The accusations of secessionism were not only unfounded but also dangerous: "This rumor appears circulated by parties antagonistic to a peaceable solution of our difficulties and who wish to impress you with the seeming necessity of military coercion to crush out our treasonable projects, thus forcing this state into a civil war within itself and during the anarchy and confusion which would doubtless reign, carry out their own designs and raise the secession banner in our midst." Raymond implored the governor to refuse military aid and acknowledge that the squatters were not secessionists.

In his appeal to Downey, the vocabulary of agrarianism mingled with the new language of union and secession. As he had in his first letter to Downey, Raymond insisted that the squatters' cause was anti–land monopolism and the defense of small freeholding: "We have banded ourselves together for what we consider justice and rights and have merged every other consideration into the leading ideas of defense of our homes and our country."[168] Raymond insisted that the squatters' loyalty to the United States ran so deep that even if Downey unleashed troops upon them, they would still defend the Union: "To call upon the military to enforce this writ of ejectment no matter what the end may be should our homes be burned, our [crops] destroyed, our families dispersed, and ourselves treated as outlaws, that then even then we or so many of us as may survive will be ready to throw all other considerations aside and if necessary combine with our persecutors in proving to the world at large the loyalty of Californians to the federal laws and Constitution." The promise to fight with the Union was another demonstration of the squatters' patriotism. Raymond concluded his letter imploring the governor for assistance in bringing about "a peaceable solution of all our squatter difficulties."

A "peaceable solution" did present itself, but no thanks to the Yerba Buena squatters, Downey, or anyone else directly involved in the conflict.

The appropriation from the legislature did not materialize, which effectively diffused tensions on the ranch. On May 7, Morris returned to Sacramento with a bill charging the government $250 for his time in Santa Clara County. By the end of May, Chabolla had given up. He decided not to exercise his writ of restitution, and Murphy ended the standoff on the Rancho Yerba Buena when he withdrew his request for three thousand soldiers on May 24.[169] California's secession anxiety proved to be fleeting. By the summer of 1861, concerns that local land disputes would escalate into a new civil war seem to have largely evaporated. In the following year, armed confrontations between squatters and Mexican land grantees erupted in San Joaquin, San Mateo, Solano, and Sonoma Counties, and while the conflicts roughly mirrored the events on the Rancho Yerba Buena, they did not inspire theories of secessionist conspiracy, and they did not provoke (or nearly provoke) military intervention by the state.[170] Perhaps, as the Civil War gathered steam in the East, Californians realized their place in the Union was more secure and the state's secessionist movement less potent than they had imagined it to be. Or perhaps the Yerba Buena squatters had succeeded in reminding Californians of the bond between anti–land monopolism and the American republic.

Local newspapers and county histories remembered the Settlers' War of San Jose as a colorful but ultimately harmless event in California's history. Indeed, for the defendants in Antonio Chabolla's lawsuit, there seemed to be no negative repercussions. At least two of them went on to become prominent members of the community. Thomas B. Farnsworth became a trustee of the Evergreen School District in 1866, and John Aborn amassed a large estate south of the Rancho Yerba Buena where a street is now named after him. A map of the ranch and its subdivisions from the turn of the twentieth century shows that four of the original defendants, Farnsworth, Aborn, William McClay, and Andrew Gehringer, remained in residence as owners and tenants.[171] The conflict was not, however, harmless to Antonio Chabolla and his family. Legal battles with squatters sapped Chabolla of his energy and resources, and, as many other native Californians had, he found himself with no choice but to seek a peaceful coexistence with the trespassers on his land. He died in November 1865. But amid this story of dispossession, there is also evidence of the resilience of the Californio family. A 1900 map of the Rancho Yerba Buena shows that Chabolla's children and grandchildren continued to own 2,200 acres in the northeastern part of the ranch, which suggests that, forty years later, the Chabolla family retained control of nearly all

FIGURE 5. Photograph of Antonio Chabolla's descendants on the Rancho Yerba Buena, 1903. Courtesy of Evergreen Valley College Library.

the land that their patriarch, Antonio, had possessed at the end of his life (fig. 5).[172]

## Conclusion

In the 1850s, squatters' rights to land in Kansas and California took on new significance. Land tenure, which had always been critical to American concepts of independence, became central to debates over slavery's expansion into the West and the organization of political parties. As the squatters' support for the Democratic Party disintegrated, the Republican Party rose to power by highlighting the compatibility of the defense of the "settler" and the "homesteader" with its ideology of free soil and free labor. As the conflict on the Rancho Yerba Buena demonstrates, the trauma of secession temporarily obscured the bond between squatters' rights and the Republican Party, the party of Unionism. The outbreak of the Civil War and the spread of secession anxiety in California lent a new urgency to defining and defending anti–land monopolism as a central ideal of the American republic. In 1861, the Rancho Yerba Buena squatters believed they were the arbiters of Jeffersonian democracy in California, and when they trespassed against a "land monopolist," they upheld the promise of the agrarian republic. In that way, they justified the dispossession of Californios as vital to the perpetuation of American ideals.

The irony of the Settlers' War was that the victors ultimately became the vanquished. While the squatters prevailed in their battle over whose land rights would receive precedence and protection in postconquest California, they eventually lost the war over whose ideals would shape the American political economy and culture. Initially, it seemed that the secession of the southern states removed the opposition to the homestead bill and, by extension, the last impediments to the squatter's republic. The Republican-dominated Congress rewarded western squatters for supporting the cause of free soil, free labor Unionism with the passage of the Homestead Act of 1862, which gave settlers essentially free gifts of 160 acres of public land. President Lincoln imagined that the act would "settl[e] the wild lands into small parcels so that every poor man may have a home."[173] The Homestead Act was a public declaration of the government's commitment to land rights for small, independent cultivators. Yet for all its good intentions, the Homestead Act never fulfilled its promise.[174] While the cost per acre was low, homesteaders still required significant funds to migrate to western lands and start up farms, and very few wageworkers could cover those expenses.[175] The Homestead Act did not replace other modes of public-land disposal. The government also continued to dispose of the public domain through private sale, public auction, and large grants, most famously to railroad corporations.[176] Thus, reserving public lands for bona fide settlers remained an unanswered call for anti–monopolist reformers in the post–Civil War years. The true legacy of the Republican Party turned out to be its agenda of national economic activism, which propelled the country toward large-scale industrial capitalism and away from the agrarian ideals that James McClatchy, Charles Robinson, and the Rancho Yerba Buena squatters so ardently defended. The problem of industrial monopoly in the post–Civil War era would eventually revive the interparty rivalry for the squatter vote.

With their raucous days behind them, Robinson and McClatchy settled into middle age and the next phase of their careers as anti–monopolist reformers. McClatchy preached squatters' rights from the pulpit of his Sacramento newspaper, the *Bee*, while Robinson championed small farmers and producers in Kansas. Although Robinson was, by 1885, one of the wealthiest men in the state, with 2,100 acres of improved land, he always identified himself foremost as a small farmer, running a

1,600-acre farm outside of Lawrence.[177] He became a vocal member of the Farmers' Alliance and participated in the Greenback and Populist movements, antimonopolist organizations that promoted paper currency, bank reform, and debt relief for farmers and small producers in the 1880s and 1890s.[178]

In the last decades of their lives, Robinson and McClatchy became the curators of their own histories. Robinson devoted himself to "correcting" public accounts of territorial Kansas as president of the state historical society. He also wrote his memoirs, *The Kansas Conflict*, to emphasize the role his nonviolent tactics played in securing the state for freedom.[179] After his death, Sara Robinson enlisted the aid of her husband's devotees to write laudatory biographies. In California, McClatchy found his own revisionist historian in a printer from Philadelphia named Henry George, who imbibed McClatchy's stories about squatters in California and rewrote them for a new industrial era.

## CHAPTER THREE

"ROOT THE WHITE RACE IN THE SOIL": HENRY GEORGE,
LAND MONOPOLY, AND CHINESE EXCLUSION

James McClatchy spent the summer of 1866 in San Francisco overseeing the launch of a newspaper, the *San Francisco Times*. One day,
a typesetter from the printing office approached him and asked for
a tryout as a writer. Always scouting for new talent, McClatchy dispatched the man to Oakland to cover a reunion of a California pioneers'
club. The resultant article convinced McClatchy to offer the typesetter a
job in the editorial department. Thus, Henry George became a reporter
for the *San Francisco Times*.[1] In November, McClatchy quit the newspaper after arguing with the company's owners, but George stayed on.[2]
Writing was the bridge that took George from typesetting to land reform
and politics, and from an 1866 article on a club reunion in Oakland to one
of the best-selling books of the nineteenth century, *Progress and Poverty*,
first published in 1879.[3] Although George's career as a writer and reformer began two decades after McClatchy participated in the Sacramento squatter riot of 1850, George's vision for California and the nation
took its inspiration from McClatchy's era of antimonopolist land politics.
George never credited McClatchy with his ideas or with his success, but
strains of the squatter's anti–land monopolism were evident in George's
attitudes toward public-land policy, wealth, and opportunity.[4]

Living in California in the wake of the Civil War, George confronted
issues unknown to McClatchy's earlier generation of squatters. In the absence of Democratic rivals during and just after the war, the Republican
Party pushed through an agenda that accelerated the industrialization of
the nation and the incorporation of the Far West. Most significantly
for California, the Republican-dominated Congress and state legislature approved the subsidization of a transcontinental railroad, which
terminated in Oakland.[5] George watched as the railroad introduced
California to a set of problems that would become characteristic of
post–Civil War America: more frequent cycling of boom-and-bust

economies, underemployment, and a new scale of corporate monopoly, which was sustained by foreign laborers from China. Making sense of new industrial monopolies and communicating the imperatives of antimonopolist reform to American producers required an able and articulate interpreter; Henry George volunteered for the job. George used the squatters' preindustrial language of anti–land monopolism, with its associated images of republican independence and preemption rights on public land, to make sense of Gilded Age industrial monopolies and their effect on the individual producer. He looked back to McClatchy's generation of squatters, who seemed to embody the liberal ideal of landownership, who claimed natural rights to the land they worked and occupied and no more than that.

Not only did George articulate the problems of new monopolies in an older language of agrarian reform, but he also connected land monopoly to the emerging "problem" of Chinese immigration. George feared that land monopoly, if left unchecked, would corrupt the American republic. It would crowd out small, independent producers, the backbone of democratic values, and replace them with cheap, unassimilable foreign labor. The Chinese, who had come to California first to mine for gold and then, in increasing numbers, to build the railroads, gradually expanded into other jobs in manufacturing, construction, and farming. George rallied behind white workers, who felt displaced by nonwhite labor competition, and promulgated a virulent, anti-Chinese racism. To George, Chinese laborers were racially fit and culturally inclined to be tools of large-scale industrial monopoly. The presence of Chinese laborers increased monopoly's power by lowering labor costs, raising profit margins, and enabling a few capitalists to use the profits to acquire a greater monopoly on land, the basis of production and wealth. Such conditions would stifle the spirit of opportunity that brought productivity and vitality to American life. And then, George wondered, "What sort of a republic will this be?"[6] For George, independent land tenure became the solution to problems created by the new monopolies and Chinese labor competition. George believed that land reform and Chinese exclusion were two necessary steps to eliminate monopoly, restore independence to small producers, and democratize opportunity in Gilded Age America. As George looked back to California's Gold Rush history for a model of a free labor society, the squatter's republic became the ideal for his industrial age.

## George's Early Career

George did not develop his attitudes toward monopoly or the Chinese until he went west. Raised in Philadelphia, he dropped out of school at age thirteen. Two years later, in 1855, he joined the crew of a ship captained by a family friend and sailed to Australia and India. After a year at sea, George returned to find work in Philadelphia. His father, a onetime printer of religious pamphlets, arranged for George to take up that trade.[7] George had no special predilection for printing, but he deferred to his parents' wishes, unaware that it would become the foundation of a lifelong career.

The comforts of home soon made George long for the deprivations of a life at sea. He attempted to rejoin his old crew but was dismissed by the captain, who wrote, "Take my advice and never go to sea. You know of the troubles of a sailor's life before the mast. It never gets any better."[8] Nonetheless, a year of adventure had seasoned the teenager for more freedom than was possible under his parents' roof, and his wanderlust continued to grow. He kept up an enthusiastic correspondence with some family friends who were on a sea passage from the East Coast to Oregon. He wrote, "Your feelings in passing over the Isthmus I can well imagine having experienced the same myself in passing up the Bay of Bengal and River Hoogaly [Hooghly] and first sighting the shores of India. Is there not a 'magical charm of foreign lands with their shadows of palms and shining sands?'" From the noisy, stifling confines of the job room of his latest employer, King and Baird's Printing House, the teenager longed for some fresh adventure "to raise the soul for a time above the common monotonous every day life and open to the view for a time a vast but undefined world of beauty and glory."[9] But George temporarily set aside those longings and remained in Philadelphia, where he worked when there was work available and passed the rest of the time drinking and carousing with friends. The eighteen-year-old George complained of persistent unemployment and general boredom:

> The times here are damned hard, and are practically getting worse and worse every day, factory after factory suspending and discharging its hands. There are thousands of hard working mechanics now out of employment in this city. And it is to the fact that among them is your humble servant that you owe this letter. . . . We have had but little excitement lately, saving a drink on last Saturday night, when Jeffries laid down in the street and had to be carried home and put to bed.[10]

Through his friends in the West, George learned that a printer could earn as much as four dollars a day in Oregon, and so, he sought out a position as the steward of a coast-surveying steamer bound for San Francisco.[11] Upon arriving in California in May 1858, he received word that the job opportunities in Oregon had dried up, and his friends cautioned him against going there.[12] Instead, he traveled to the Fraser River in British Columbia and tried his hand at gold prospecting. The experience introduced him to both the presence of poverty amid wealth and the presence of Chinese competition. He later recalled:

> Sitting on the deck of a topsail schooner with a lot of miners on the way to the [Fraser] River; and we got to talking about the Chinese, and I . . . ventured to ask what harm the Chinese were doing here, if, as these miners said, they were only working the cheap diggings? And one old miner turned to me and said, "No harm now; but it will not be always that wages are as high as they are to-day in California. As the country grows, as people come in, wages will go down, and some day or other white men will be glad to get these diggings that the Chinamen are now working."[13]

On the Fraser River, George first learned what would become the core of his reform philosophy: more wealth did not necessarily create more opportunities for white wageworkers: "And I well remembered how it impressed me, the idea that as the country grew in all that we are hoping that it might grow, the condition of those who had to work for their living must grow, not better, but worse."[14] He also learned that he had no skill in gold mining. He returned to San Francisco to renew his endeavors as a typesetter.[15]

Printing work in San Francisco was as inconsistent as it had been in Philadelphia, and George became personally acquainted with poverty when he married and started his family in 1861. His journals from these years reflect his growing distress. The near-daily entries between 1864 and 1868 were often little more than records of jobs won and lost, money earned and owed, and the days when there was no work to be had at all (fig. 6). "Did very little in office," George wrote the day after Christmas in 1864. "Tried at 6 places to get work, but failed. . . . Have not done all nor as well as I could wish."[16] Two months later, to stave off creditors, he sold his interest in a printing business in which he had invested:

> I am starting out afresh, very much crippled and embarrassed, owing over $200. I have been unsuccessful in everything. I wish to profit by my experiences and to

FIGURE 6. Henry George at age 26, 1865. Courtesy of
the Bancroft Library, University of California, Berkeley.

cultivate these qualities necessary to success in which I
have been lacking. I have not saved as much as I ought
and am resolved in future to practice a rigid economy
until I have something ahead. 1st to make every cent I
can. 2nd to spend nothing unnecessarily. 3rd to put
something by each week, if it is only a five cent piece,
borrowed for the purpose. 4th, not to run in debt for
one cent if it can be avoided.[17]

His resolutions proved difficult to keep, but he continued to hunt for work
at various San Francisco–area newspapers. After George met McClatchy
at the *San Francisco Times*, the older newspaperman assisted the younger
one when he could, with loans of $70 on one occasion, $100 on another,
and employment for George's family members and for him.[18]

George blamed himself for these hard times. In his journal, he scolded
himself for being idle and unfocused. "Was not prompt enough in rising,"

he wrote. "Have been walking around a good part of the day without definite purpose, thereby losing time." But he was also beginning to think about larger forces that contributed to his poverty. He wrote, "Went to the library in the evening. Thinking of economy."[19] In 1865, he wrote a letter to the editor of the *Journal of the Trades and Workingmen*, praising the journal for voicing the interests of the working class:

> At a time when most of our public prints pander to wealth and power and would crush the poor man beneath the wheel of the capitalist's carriage; when one begins . . . to have quick reprobation for any effort of mechanics or laborers to obtain their dues, but nothing to say against combinations to deprive them of their rights, I, for one, feel that your enterprise is one which we all should feel the necessity of.[20]

In the letter, George beseeched San Francisco laborers to engage with political and social issues and "to check the tendency of society to resolve itself into classes who have too much or too little."[21] George was, at heart, a producerist, who believed that producing classes—laborers and farmers—had natural rights to the wealth their labor created. In the 1860s, ideas about the power of combinations (or monopolies) to interfere with the rights of producers were percolating in George's mind.

During the years of sporadic employment, George earned money writing about California issues for journals and newspapers that had access to national audiences, and in these articles, he began to articulate the questions that would define his career. In an 1868 article for the *Overland Monthly*, George weighed the possible effects of the nearly completed transcontinental railroad for California. Historians have typically identified the article, "What the Railroad Will Bring Us," as George's inaugural moment as an antimonopolist. It introduced what would become the common refrain in George's work—namely, that monopoly, with its privilege and power, robbed laborers of their independence. Although George acknowledged that the railroad was stimulating speculative activity, industrial development, and population growth, particularly in the cities, he also feared that the railroad would bring monopoly to California, and its harmful effects would outweigh any benefits of increased prosperity:

> She will have more people; but among those people will there be so large a proportion of full, true men? She will have more wealth; but will it be so evenly distributed?

> She will have more luxury and refinement and culture;
> but will she have such general comfort, so little squalor
> and misery; so little of the grinding, hopeless poverty that
> chills and cramps the souls of men, and converts them
> into brutes?[22]

Republicanism had long identified luxury as the enemy of virtue, a relationship that seemed evident in old-world Europe, where money and power seemed to concentrate in the hands of an indulgent, corrupt aristocracy, ruling a beleaguered, degenerate peasantry. It was apparent to George that maximizing wealth would not necessarily maximize the conditions that led to equality and independence for all citizens.

George made his warning intelligible to readers by equating the speculation spurred by the railroad with that of land monopolists in the Gold Rush era. They both diminished opportunities for settlers to preempt inexpensive government land and become economically independent proprietors. George looked back to the earlier era of squatterism and anti–land monopolism for inspiration in confronting the crisis in his time. McClatchy's Gold Rush generation of squatters and placer miners seemed to have laid a foundation for democracy. The squatters' legacy for San Francisco was, according to George, a "larger proportion of . . . homesteads and homestead lots than in any other city of the United States" (302–3). When land values rose, a wider segment of the population stood to gain: "The product of the rise of real estate will thus be more evenly distributed, and the great social and political advantages of this diffused proprietorship cannot be over-estimated" (303). George also celebrated the era of the placer miner as a model for the free labor society he envisioned: "Than the placer mining," he wrote, "no more independent business could be conceived" (301). George made placer mining his perfect example of a free labor economy, where workers owned their own labor and could claim only as much land as they could use: "The miner working for himself, owned no master; worked when and only when he pleased; took out his earnings each day in the shining particles which depended for their value on no fluctuations in the market, but would pass current and supply all wants the world over" (305). George's depiction of placer mining had little to do with the realities of labor in the gold fields. As the historian Malcolm Rohrbough has demonstrated, after the first flush year or two, miners found that "the Gold Rush had generated a complex and highly competitive economy that conferred advantages on those with capital and luck and that ignored men who possessed neither."[23] But George was not one to let history get in the way of making a point. He regretted that placer mining had disappeared in the increasingly industrialized landscape of California: "If [placer mining] could have been united with ownership of land and the comforts and restraints of home, it would have given us a class of citizens of the utmost value to a republican state" (305). When placers gave out, and the more capital-intensive practice of quartz mining took over, George claimed that independent miners moved away. He ignored the fact that many failed placer miners actually stayed in California and went to work in agriculture and commerce. But George was less interested in accurately describing the Gold Rush era than he was in using squatters and placer miners to explain the transition from republican utopia to monopolistic dystopia.

He did concede that the reality of land ownership in San Francisco was not as democratic as he wished it were. In his adopted hometown of San Francisco, the squatters' legacy of diffused proprietorship had not endured. By the 1860s, San Francisco squatters were embroiled in a land-grant conflict with the city, which claimed about eighteen thousand acres under a Mexican pueblo grant. As part of that grant, the city had declared in 1866 its ownership of seven thousand acres of "Outside Lands," an oceanfront expanse to the west of the city's incorporation boundary. The area, mostly sand dunes, was sparsely populated with dairy farms and squatters, who protested their evictions from what they believed to be public domain. The federal courts sided with the city, which sold off large tracts of the land to private real estate developers.[24] George lamented the court decision. The "princely domain which San Francisco inherited as the successor of the pueblo" should have been "appropriated to furnishing free, or almost free, homesteads to actual settlers, instead of being allowed to pass into the hands of a few, to make more millionaires." If the Outside Lands had remained open to preemption, George imagined, "the great city of the future [San Francisco] would have had a population bound to her by the strongest ties—a population better, freer, more virtuous, independent and public spirited than any great city the world has ever had" (303). Monopoly and the laws that permitted it imperiled the tradition of democratic land distribution that California squatters had established.

Despite his nostalgia for the independent placer miner and home-steading squatter, George did not long to return to the past as much as he tried to imagine how industrial progress could re-create the egalitarian society he thought once existed in California: "A great change is coming over the State. We should not prevent it if we could and could not if we would, but we can view it in all its bearings—look at the dark as well as the bright side, and endeavor to hasten that which is good and retard or prevent that which is bad" (306). When George wrote "What the Railroad Will Bring

Us," the banking crises and economic depressions of the 1870s had yet to rock the American faith in the industrial economy. His cautionary words anticipated a swelling wave of opposition to railroad monopoly in California.[25] Later generations of George disciples and scholars have identified the *Overland Monthly* article as laying the groundwork for what would become his signature reform idea, the "single tax," which aimed to strip monopolies of income they earned from rent through taxation. The article was not yet an articulation of that answer, but it did indicate that he was beginning to ask questions about the social costs of monopoly.

## "The Chinese in California"

In "What the Railroad Will Bring Us," George had only gestured at Chinese immigration when he described how the transcontinental railroad would introduce a new "labor question, rendered particularly complex by our proximity to Asia" (306). But George believed that Chinese workers were the lifeblood of monopoly in California, and that a reformer could not address the problem of monopoly without addressing the problem of the Chinese. George first learned to associate the Chinese immigrants with monopoly because they dominated the jobs in quartz mining and railroad construction, both large-scale industries. In the 1860s, opportunities in mining and railroad construction began to diminish, and the Chinese moved to California's agricultural valleys to work as tenant farmers and sharecroppers, or they moved into western, urban centers, especially San Francisco, to work in light manufacturing, construction, and other trades.[26] In San Francisco, where there was already a surplus of unskilled labor, white workers found themselves increasingly underbid and displaced by their new Chinese competitors. In 1867, unskilled white workers organized the first anti-coolie leagues to protest the hiring of Chinese "coolies," a pejorative term used to describe involuntary contractual, usually "imported" laborers.[27] Among California workers, the Chinese were the largest nonwhite ethnic group. The historian Alexander Saxton has estimated that although they comprised less than 10 percent of the state's population, they accounted for more than 20 percent of its waged labor force by 1870.[28] In the 1870s, anti-Chinese racism grew up out of these working-class clubs and infused state, regional, and eventually national politics. George sensed an opportunity to place himself and his anti–land monopolist reform agenda in the center of a growing anti-Chinese movement. In articles for the *New York Daily Herald* and the *New-York Tribune*, he developed the close connection between the Chinese and monopoly. It was his writing on the Chinese, not antimonopolism, that first garnered him notoriety. His first anti-Chinese article preceded the *Overland Monthly* article by a year. In March 1867, George wrote and sold a piece on the Chinese to the *New York Herald*, receiving twenty dollars.[29] The sale coincided with an attack by four hundred white laborers on Chinese construction workers in San Francisco, one of the first large-scale expressions of "anti-coolie" violence in the United States.[30]

In a subsequent article for the *New-York Tribune* in 1869, "The Chinese in California," George explained anti-Chinese sentiment in the West to eastern readers, and he attempted to dispel sensationalist images of anti-Chinese violence on the West Coast while simultaneously justifying the motivation for it.[31] As a San Francisco resident writing for a national audience, George asserted the authority of an insider's perspective, but he mostly reiterated common prejudices and fears about the Chinese in the United States.[32] George repeated a popular assumption that the Chinese were an unassimilable group in American society. He reported that the Chinese were "as cruel as they are cowardly" and apt to "practice all the unnamable vices of the East." He wrote: "Infanticide is common among them; so is abduction and assassination." George found offense in their customs, religion, and smells: "Their quarters reek with noisome odors and are fit breeding-places for pestilence." The description reinforced the widely held belief that the Chinese represented not only a wholly different race from whites but also an inferior one. George attributed the Chinese immigrants' inability to assimilate to their transience and lack of loyalty to the United States. He portrayed the Chinese as sojourners who brought "no women with them . . . except those intended for purposes of prostitution, and the children of these, of whom there are some hundreds in California, will exercise upon the whole mass but little perceptible influence, while they will be in all respects as essentially Chinese as though born and reared in China" (2). Anti-coolie clubs described the almost all-male Chinese enclaves as George did: "Chinatown" seemed "unnatural" in its gender imbalance, "dirty," and "diseased," qualities that reinforced notions of Chinese otherness and nonassimilability.[33]

At the same time that George described Chinese laborers as intellectually and physically inferior to white workers, he noted the many western industries that had been infiltrated by Chinese employees while white workers were forced out. The Chinese takeover of white jobs created a puzzle for George: if the Chinese were, in fact, inferior intellectually, morally, and physically, how could they constitute a threat to white labor? To resolve this puzzle, George argued that the characteristics that rendered Chinese inferior to whites made them ideal for work in the new industrial environments:

> The great characteristics of the Chinese as laborers are
> patience and economy—the first makes them efficient
> laborers, the second cheap laborers. As a rule they have
> not the physical strength of Europeans but their steadi-
> ness makes up for this. They take less earth at a spade-
> full than an Irishman; but in a day's work take up more
> spadesfull. This patient steadiness peculiarly adapts the
> Chinese for tending machinery and for manufacturing.

The purported frugality of the Chinese supposedly enabled them to sub-
sist on less food, live in smaller spaces, and wring the last golden flakes
out of long-exhausted placer mines. "The great recommendation of Chinese labor is its cheapness. There are no people in the world who are
such close economists as the Chinese," George wrote. "They will live and
live well according to their notions, where an American or Englishman
would starve" (1). According to George, it was that abnormal capacity for
economy that allowed monopoly to flourish. "While making enemies of
the workmen with whom they come into competition, they have made
friends of the employers who found a profit in their labor. . . . A very large
and powerful class, rapidly becoming larger and more powerful, is directly interested in maintaining their right to avail themselves of Chinese
labor." Capitalists used cheap labor to lower production costs but not to
lower consumer prices: "It is evident that the laborer's gain as a consumer
would be less than his loss as a laborer. . . . The whole benefit would . . . go
to employers in increased profits. . . . So long as China can furnish a supply of labor equal to demand, wages will not rise again." In that way, Chinese workers constituted a "potent force, more potent than any of those
now operating, to accelerate the prevailing tendency to the concentration
of wealth . . . to substitute, if it goes far enough, a population of serfs and
their masters for that population of intelligent free men" (2).

In "What the Railroad Will Bring Us," George described how monopoly made economic independence less attainable for the average California family, but in "The Chinese in California," he took it a step further
and developed what amounted to a twin menace. Chinese labor competition threatened not just the independence but also the very survival of
the white race in California. Without immigration reform, the Chinese
would eventually become the demographic majority: "If the increase of
the white population is checked, so long as no check is imposed on Chinese immigration . . . the only effect will be the substitution of a Mongolian for a Caucasian population" (2). White labor faced a difficult choice:

"In every case in which Chinese comes into fair competition with white labor, the whites must either retire from the field or come down to the Chinese standard of living" (1). To compete with the Chinese, white labor had to behave like the Chinese. The consequence would be fatal. George believed that if the white family, the basic unit of the American republic, could not sustain itself, neither could the nation: "For this increase of production we must pay a high price, one of the smallest items of which, in my opinion will be (if the substitution of Mongolians for Anglo-Saxons goes far enough), the utter subversion of republicanism upon the Pacific, perhaps upon the continent" (2). Decisions made about the exclusion of Chinese in the West thus could determine the fate of the republic itself.

The article created a flurry of interest among San Francisco Bay area newspapers and earned George a position as the "special correspondent for the *New-York Tribune* in California."[34] George then successfully orchestrated the nineteenth-century equivalent of a publicity stunt by sending a copy to the British philosopher John Stuart Mill and requesting his thoughts on the matter of Chinese immigration. Mill replied to George in a letter that was published in the *Oakland Daily Transcript.* "Concerning the purely economic view of the subject," Mill wrote, "I entirely agree with you . . . that the Chinese immigration, if it attains great dimensions, must be economically injurious to the mass of the present population; that it must diminish their wages, and reduce them to a lower stage of physical comfort and well being, I have no manner of doubt."[35]

Mill was reluctant, however, to concur with George's portrayal of the Chinese as wholly unassimilable. He interpreted Chinese norms not as signs of racial difference but as signs of their less-developed civilization:

> Is it justifiable to assume that the character and habits of the Chinese are unsusceptible of improvement? The institutions of the United States are the most potent means that have yet existed of spreading the most important elements of civilization down to the poorest and most ignorant of the laboring masses. If every Chinese child were compulsorily brought under your school system, or under a still more effective one, if possible, and kept under it for a sufficient number of years, would not the Chinese population be in time raised to the level of the American?

Mill assumed the number of children in question would be very few, and the burden of educating them low. Because Chinese immigrants came

as single men and not as families—as sojourners and not as settlers—
Mill claimed that the most extreme predictions of a Chinese colonization
of American society were unfounded: "I believe, indeed, that hitherto the
number of Chinese born in America has not been very great; but so long
as this is the case—so long (that is) as the Chinese do not come in families and settle, but those who come are mostly men, and return to their
native country, the evil can hardly reach so great a magnitude as to re-
quire that it should be put a stop by force."[36] The real "evil" for American
society according to Mill's logic was the rooted foreign population that
failed to assimilate, not the rootless. The rootless population would come
and go, leaving an economic but not a social or cultural footprint.

In his rebuttal, George asserted that the return migration of Chinese workers did nothing to neutralize their social effect: "We cannot
see that the fact that the Chinese do not settle here permanently sets
any bounds to the limits which the Chinese population in this country
may attain. With four or five hundred millions of people to draw upon,
the supply is practicalbly [sic] inexhaustible, and though the individuals who compose our Chinese population may be changing, that population in the aggregate will be permanent." The rootless population
threatened to become "rooted" so long as monopoly created demand
for its labor. "The only practical difference," George continued, "will be
that it will maintain its native character—will be composed continuously of fresh barbarians, with everything to forget and everything to
learn."[37] San Francisco Bay area newspapers printed the complete exchange between George and Mill, which won George the attention of
state Democrats.

## The Reconstruction of the Democratic Party

George became a Democrat just as the party was making its post–Civil
War comeback in California. In the 1850s, the Democratic Party had been
the dominant political power in the state, but changes in the national
party's position on public-land distribution and its association with
slaveholders had tarnished the party's reputation among voters. By 1863,
a majority of California Democrats had moved into a newly organized
Union Party and remained there until 1867.[38] Appealing to the popularity of antimonopolism and Chinese exclusion among industrial workers
and farmers, California Democrats secured a broad base of workingmen's
support, which enabled them to sweep the 1867 elections, taking the governorship, two out of three seats in the state senate, and an overwhelming majority in the state assembly.[39] Having returned to state dominance
and recommitted themselves to squatter antimonopolism, the Democratic

Party set about restoring land rights for small producers and placing limits on corporate, industrial capitalism.

After the publication of "The Chinese in California," George's career in social reform took off, due in large part to his alliance with California's Democratic Party. In the 1870s, George received financial support for his writing and speechmaking from Democratic governors and anti-monopolists Henry Haight and William Irwin. Haight also put George at the helm of the party organ, *The Reporter*, in 1870.[40]

Anti–land monopolism remained as much a part of California's public discourse in the 1870s as it had been in the 1850s.[41] About half of the Mexican land-grant cases still languished unresolved in the federal courts. Meanwhile, between 1862 and 1875, news spread about corrupt California land office agents, who were "missing" receipts for public-land sales, and the greed of tax assessors who had been bribed by wealthy wheat growers. State legislators responded with calls for investigative committees, limitations on landholdings, and reforms to tax laws governing property value assessment.[42]

In Sacramento, James McClatchy continued to be California's voice of anti–land monopolism and squatters' preemption rights through the *Bee*. For George and McClatchy, the fate of freehold tenure, which was the fate of republican independence, depended on perpetuating public-land policies that favored squatters. Both men wanted to ensure that the distribution of public land created a large base of freeholders, who were true cultivators and occupants. In 1871, George published a pamphlet on the monopolization of public lands in California. The pamphlet, *Our Land and Land Policy*, is best known as the first explicit articulation of George's single tax. George's journals indicate that he began work on the pamphlet on March 26, 1871, not long after a dinner with McClatchy.[43] The journals do not detail what they discussed over dinner, but the fingerprints of McClatchy's anti–land monopolism and experiences with California public-land disputes are evident in *Our Land and Land Policy*. The pamphlet espoused the squatters' side of California history and proposed the same limitations on public-land distribution that McClatchy had consistently advocated in his newspapers. George claimed that land monopoly displaced white laborers and prevented them from owning the land that they worked, and he attributed the spread of monopoly and the degradation of white labor to federal public-land policy. The policy, George argued, favored speculators and monopolists and not settlers, the true "cultivators": "We have been liberal, very liberal, to everybody but those who have a right to our liberality.... This growing liberality to the settler has been accompanied by a still more rapidly growing liberality to speculators and corporations."[44]

Many economists and historians have rightly challenged George's observations and analysis in *Our Land and Land Policy*. For his statistics on land ownership, George seems to have taken a raw average of census bureau data on the size of landholdings, which meant that extremely large holdings skewed the mean upward and obscured the actual diversity of landholding in the state. A closer look at the *1870 Census of Agriculture* reveals that 40 percent of farms in California were less than one hundred acres, and 92 percent were less than five hundred acres. Moreover, although California boasted the largest average farm size of any state, its numbers had actually dropped off precipitously from 4,466 acres in 1850 to 466 and then 482 in 1860 and 1870, respectively, which was likely due to the dismantling of large Mexican land grants.[45] Later historians showed that George's portrayal of tenancy and itinerancy among white and Chinese farmers was also without firm empirical grounding. For George, tenantry was a debased form of landholding, but for many farmers—white and Chinese alike—it was an effective strategy for acquisition and use.[46] Yet, however faulty it may have been, George's analysis of California land policies became the core of a land ethic adopted by an immense following that included unionists, tax reformers, immigration reformers, horticulturists, and conservationists.

George believed that the U.S. government "squandered" the public domain in sales and grants to individuals or corporations that intended to use the land for speculation. Over time, their monopoly created an artificial scarcity, driving up the price for the common man. Countless farmers and small-scale manufacturers—those who would actually make the land productive—were denied access (22–23). According to George, the economy suffered, immigration dwindled, and the promise of free men and free land in the West vanished.

To identify the cause of these conditions, George first considered the legacy of the Mexican land-grant system. In doing so, he resuscitated the squatters' interpretation of land rights and conquest from the 1850s. Squatter protests echo in his claim that the original source of monopolization in California was the Mexican land-grant system. George argued that the Treaty of Guadalupe Hidalgo, by protecting land rights bestowed by Mexican private grants, failed to protect American settlers and permitted vast tracts of land to remain in the hands of just a few individuals. The United States should have placed limits on the property that Mexican land-grant-holders could claim (25). Yet, like McClatchy, George believed that while the Mexican grants were the original source of land monopolization in the state, American land policy institutionalized and entrenched monopoly: "For the injuries which these Mexican grants have done to California, the Mexican land policy is not responsible. That merely furnished the pretext under cover of which *our* policy has fostered land monopolization" (31). George argued that the state legislature behaved irresponsibly by passing legislation that permitted, if not encouraged, land monopolization. This legislation removed protections to squatters while railroad grants and private entry by large speculators extended land monopoly rights beyond Mexican grantees (38). George made railroad grants a modern extension of the monopolistic practices of the private Mexican land grants. "The railroad grants have worked nothing but evil to California," he wrote. "Though given under pretext of aiding settlement, they have really retarded it," by allowing corporations to hold the land for speculation (33). George deliberately ignored the fact that private railroad corporations sold their land to individual settlers to raise revenues and create a customer base for their services. Acknowledgment of such practices would have contradicted the portrait he wished to paint of the railroads as usurpers of land more productively employed by actual settlers.[47]

Land monopoly, George argued, caused myriad social maladies—chief among them, the proliferation of landlordism and tenantry:

> [The landlord] boards at the San Francisco hotels, and drives a spanking team over the Cliff House road; or, perhaps, he spends his time in the gayer capitals of the East or Europe. His land is rented for one third or one fourth of the crop, or is covered by scraggy cattle, which need to look after them only a few half-civilised *vaqueros*; or his great wheat fields, of from ten to twenty thousand acres, are ploughed and sown and reaped by contract. (47)

George believed that large landholders brought the worst of the European caste system to California. They were the new American aristocracy, awaiting an exploitable class of renters. There were two possible sources for this situation. The first was among California farmers, who, as George observed, did not own the land they worked. The second source of tenants came from China, and in this way, George blended anti-Chinese racism with anti–land monopoly:

> The division of our land into these vast estates derives
> additional significance from the threatening wave of Asi-
> atic immigration whose first ripples are already break-
> ing upon our shores. What the barbarians enslaved by
> foreign wars were to the great landlords of ancient Italy,
> what the blacks of the African coast were to the great
> landlords of the Southern States, the Chinese coolies
> may be, in fact are already beginning to be, to the great
> landlords of our Pacific slope. (51)

Land monopoly threatened to reorganize society into two castes: white landlords and Chinese tenants.[48] Meanwhile, small, white freeholders found themselves confined to a restricted and vanishing space. Whites competed unsuccessfully with the Chinese, not for wages, but for rented farm shares, which George considered an even more debased form of labor than wage work.

George's convergence with McClatchy on the land question did not lead to convergence on the race question. Although McClatchy was far from racially progressive and believed the Chinese to be inferior to whites, he did not share George's anti-Chinese attitude. Editorials on Chinese immigration published during his tenure as editor-in-chief of Sacramento's *Daily Bee* suggest that McClatchy felt at most ambivalent about exclusion. One typical editorial on the Chinese in California stated: "They cannot be driven out of the State—they cannot be prevented from coming into it—public sentiment will not allow them to be murdered though the courts might, and they must live and live by labor."[49] Another editorial encouraged white laborers to get out of wage labor if they suffered from Chinese competition:

> There are millions of acres, fertile as the sun, in his diur-
> nal course around the world shines upon us, wanting
> hands to cultivate them. They can be had, if public land,
> for next to nothing, in fact, and many of those who begin
> to feel the pressure of Chinese labor would improve their
> condition and the country's prospect by going upon them
> [the public lands]. But this, few if any of them, will do.
> They prefer to bang about the cities, drudging continu-
> ally, and fighting in the battle of life eternally.[50]

McClatchy's anti-land monopolism, formed before mass immigration from China, did not change with the times.

George, on the other hand, updated the history of land disputes to explore the deep, entangled roots of California's present problems with monopoly, white poverty, and Chinese immigration. Unable to secure a freehold or compete with Chinese immigrants where monopoly prevailed, white freeholders would become itinerant laborers, George believed, or in nineteenth-century terminology, *tramps*: "Over our ill-kept, shadeless, dusty roads...plod the tramps, with blankets on back—the laborers of the California farmer—looking for work, in its seasons, or toiling back to the city when the plowing is ended or the wheat crop is gathered" (47). The man "on the tramp" was a fixture of the wheat economy, which depended on a large, seasonal labor force. The tramp was also, by the early 1870s, associated with industrial labor and poverty in cities where social reformers and charitable organizations noted the growing masses of underemployed men, searching for work and moving by rail between rural and urban areas.[51] George linked speculators to monopolists and tramps to squatters. Monopoly produced the squatter and the tramp; both were landless men, differing only in that one was a victim of Mexican land grants and the other was a victim of industrialization. They were men utterly alienated from the republican ideal of independence because land monopoly prevented them from becoming freeholders. Instead, they roamed from place to place in search of wages, or they worked land they did not own in shares. Speculation by monopolists drove up the value of land without contributing to the economic or social capital of a community. It not only gave profits to those who produced no wealth but also ate away at republican equity, "for high priced land means luxury on the one side, and low wages on the other. Luxury means waste, and low wages means unintelligent and inefficient labor" (54–55). In traditional conceptions of republicanism, luxury was the enemy of virtue.

Like the squatters of the Gold Rush era, George asserted that the only true title to the land was its occupation and use (59). He called for the cessation of land grants on the public domain until a complete survey might be undertaken and "actual" settlers located on homesteads: "We have no right to dispose of them except to *actual settlers*—to men who really want to use them; no right to give them to railroad companies or to grant them for agricultural colleges; no more right to do so than we have to sell or to grant the labor of the people who must someday live upon them.... And to actual settlers we should *give* them. *Give*, not sell" (69). George also called for a tax on rent, which became the basis for what would later become his signature reform idea, the single tax. He imagined a tax on rent would make monopoly unprofitable and thus break up large estates of unused land (74–75). This was George's strategy to populate western lands with independent landowners who were capable of regenerating and perpetuating American democracy. As it was, however, a perverted public-land policy destroyed the promise of the West by populating it with monopolists, Chinese, and tramps.

In 1873, a crisis in New York City's financial market provoked a severe national depression, which gave substance to some of George's worst predictions.[52] California's geographic isolation from the rest of the country initially shielded the state from the earliest waves of the depression, but in late 1874 and early 1875, dramatic fluctuations in mining stocks signaled its arrival. By the fall of 1875, the crisis had descended on California, spurring local bank failures, unemployment, and labor unrest. Despite a brief rebound early in 1876, a drought in the winter of 1876–77 deepened California's economic woes. Another series of events in 1876 and 1877 exacerbated conditions: the Texas and Pacific Railway Company decided not to extend its line westward, thereby diminishing the prospects of farmers in the state's southern counties. Finally, in January 1877, the Consolidated Virginia Mining Company on the Comstock Lode reported that it could not pay its monthly dividend of $1 million, an announcement that set off another panic in the stock market. Thousands of Californians who had speculated in mining stocks saw their paper fortunes plummet.

The state's economic crisis bolstered antimonopolist sentiment and motivated the legislature to consider the problem of land monopoly anew. Between 1871 and 1877, the state legislature organized three special committees to investigate public-land distribution in California. The committees acknowledged fraud in the system and reaffirmed the state's desire to grant land to "actual" settlers rather than "speculators" or "monopolists." According to one report, false rumors that all good land in California was monopolized drove away potential white migrants: "There are millions of men of the same race as ourselves in other and older States and countries who would gladly own, occupy, mine, and cultivate our mountain lands that are open to them under government and State laws, if aware of what Californians affect to despise and regard as not worth taking up." It was imperative that these rumors be corrected so that the best class of immigrants might settle in California:

> The frugal Germans, Swiss, and Italians, who understand the culture of the vine, the mulberry, and the fruits that our mountains produce in such great perfection, the nurture of the silk worm, the reeling, spinning, and

manufacture of silk, and the making of raisins and wine, would not be deterred from coming by the statement that "the vine and mulberry take several years to mature before they become productive," if at the same time assured that they could indeed become the owners of the soil in which to plant them in a climate where success in the culture is an assured fact. The neglected but well watered and timbered portions of our mountains would afford happy homes for thousands of industrious Welshmen, Swedes, and Norwegians, if only we could invite them here and facilitate and encourage their settlement.[53]

Attracting white settlers to cultivate California remained the focus of the antimonopoly efforts.

The ideological challenge of antimonopolism was that it forced two "sacred" principles to compete. On the one hand were the rights of small producers and proprietors to own land, and on the other were the rights of private property. None of the legislature's efforts went beyond investigating the problem and making minor reforms to land taxation and limitation laws. For all their antimonopolist rhetoric, California legislators were reluctant to upset large landholders. An 1874 special committee report suggested that the state assume a passive resistance to land monopoly and allow a full generation for it to die out naturally:

We would not propose to disturb anyone in his possessions—permitting each to hold whatever land he may possess at the date of the Act taking effect while he lives if he so choose and after his death allowing five years for his heirs to dispose of the surplus. Thus in a generation, land monopoly would be extinguished without injury to any, and with benefit to all. These large possessions now such an incubus upon the energy and prosperity of the State would crumble away, from day to day, gradually, as men die, until, in say 25 years, there would be scarcely one land monopolist within our borders.[54]

Ultimately, the legislators failed to take decisive, radical action, which meant that land-reform initiatives languished in committees.

The legislature's inaction did not stifle public interest in anti–land monopolism, and George capitalized on that interest to launch a professional public-speaking career in 1876. Stumping for Samuel J. Tilden, the

Democratic presidential candidate running against the Republican Ruther-
ford B. Hayes, George gave speeches that began as campaign rallies only to
morph into lectures on monopoly.[55] George associated the Republican
Party with the "money power" and transitioned seamlessly from a speech
about party politics to a speech about monopoly.[56] "Look around you in
this campaign," he gestured. "Is not aggregated capital everywhere on the
side of the Republican Party[?]"[57] In reality, Tilden was a corporate lawyer
backed by wealthy industrialists and railroad investors, and the Republican
Party still contained a strong antimonopoly wing, as it had from the days
of its founding in the 1850s. But acknowledging these contradictions
would have served neither George's argument nor his Democratic pa-
trons. George played on the racist sympathies of white Westerners and
white Southerners to rally support for the Democrats. Monopolists,
George argued, had an "instinctive ability to combine, to seize opportunities, to secure ends by intelligent choice of means, to take advantage of
the trade winds of prejudice in the shifting gusts of passing, to enlist out-
standing forces which are characteristic of aggregate capital."[58] The "out-
standing forces" that George described were the nonwhite laborers that
fueled monopoly: African-Americans in the South and the Chinese in
the West. He described African-Americans and the Chinese as laborers
racially conditioned for subhuman treatment, which allowed large-scale industrialized monopoly to flourish. Backed by the party that emancipated
African-American slaves, monopolies substituted a new slavery for the old.
George accused the Republicans and monopolists of bringing the Chinese
to California over the protests of white workers. "Do you suppose this
power will spare you when you tell it that the Chinese are heathen, cheap
laborers?" George asked rhetorically. "Why, gentlemen, you might as well
as tell the wolves to prohibit the importation of sheep on the ground that
they are animals too fat to run, too ignoble to fight. Cheap laboring heathen are the very things it wants."[59] Invoking the names of Leland Stanford
and Charles Crocker, Central Pacific Railroad tycoons who had profited
from the cheap labor of Chinese immigrants, George paired mentions of
Stanford's Nob Hill mansion and the "Duke de Crocker's" predatory real estate practices with descriptions of their California Republican backers,
parading through the street with their way alit by "Chinese lanterns."[60] It
was a malevolent image of corporate monopoly's wealth powered by political favoritism and Chinese labor. George reiterated the argument he had
made six years earlier in the *New-York Tribune* that, wherever monopoly
existed, the Chinese were better adapted than whites to work under its
conditions. The successful settlement of American lands by the white race
was not a foregone conclusion; George lamented that "a conflict is going

on as to whether this soil shall breed Caucasians or Mongolians, a conflict in which under present conditions the Mongolian must win by reason of what political economists style lower standard of comfort."[61]

Working out the connections between anti–land monopoly and Chinese exclusion led George to the question that would define his career: what explained the persistence of white poverty in an age of material progress? In a Fourth of July lecture in 1878, George said: "Go out in this fair land today and you may see estates tilled by Chinamen, while citizens of the Republic carry their blankets through dusty roads begging for work."[62] Wherever he looked, George saw monopolists, the Chinese, and the tramp: "Look at the social conditions which are growing up here in California. Land monopolized, water monopolized, a race of cheap workers crowding in, whose effect upon our own laboring classes is precisely that of slavery, all the avenues of trade and travel under one control, all wealth and power tending more and more to concentrate in a few hands."[63] Throughout the early years of his speaking career, George employed an older language of land monopoly associated with agrarian republicanism to make sense of the new industrial system and the places of white and Chinese labor within it. The Chinese became the negative example for white workers, their opposite in every respect, and a warning of what white workers might become without land reform.

### Land and Race

Although he never flagged in his support of Chinese exclusion, by 1878, George had recalibrated his message about antimonopolism and exclusionism. He was beginning to think that exclusion was only a "half measure" in resolving the problem of land monopoly. In a lecture given on March 26, 1878, in San Francisco's Metropolitan Temple, George explained: "It is not only more important to abolish land monopoly than to get rid of the Chinese; but to abolish land monopoly will be to make short work of the Chinese question. Clear out the land-grabber and the Chinaman must go. Root the white race in the soil and the millions of Asia cannot dispossess it."[64] Exclusion without land reform would not restore economic independence.[65] White families had to be supported in establishing residences and putting down roots in the land where they worked.

This shift in argumentation was due at least in part to his distaste for the new leader in anti-Chinese politics, Denis Kearney, whom George called "a rude, uncultured drayman."[66] Kearney, the owner of a hauling business in San Francisco, entered anti-Chinese politics when he joined the 1877 railroad strikes that swept into San Francisco from the East.

Strikers in San Francisco vented their frustrations with their employers by attacking Chinese workers.[67] A militant, theatrical leader, Kearney sharpened and politicized the Sinophobic elements of the Workingmen's Party of California. In his assessment of Kearney's leadership, George surmised, "The style of his oratory, the prominence he attained, his energy, tact, and temperance, gave him command of the floating element which will travel around to the most meetings and do the loudest shouting. And, commanding this, he commanded his party."[68] Between 1877 and 1880, the Workingmen's Party successfully wooed away members of San Francisco Democratic clubs with its anti-Chinese, antimonopolist, pro-labor platform and stole the Democrats' base out from under them.[69]

Given its platform, one might have expected George to be a card-carrying member of the Workingmen's Party, but there were two insurmountable barriers between George and Kearney. First, George was on the payroll of the California Democrats, who saw the Workingmen's Party as a rival. More than a decade after the Civil War, the state's Democrats were still struggling to hold their party together. They had withstood the temporary alienation of a number of key members who were attracted to the antimonopolist Independent Party, in its brief lifespan from 1873 to 1875, but they worried that the Workingmen's Party would draw away the less conservative Democrats and more dramatically diminish the party's base.[70] George also had ideological problems with Kearney's movement, which he saw as shortsighted and detrimental to the anti–land monopolist cause. He believed that Kearney did little more than stir up white workers without offering a real, lasting remedy for their problems: "What seems to me ominous in all these events is that they show how easily our political struggles may pass into all the bitterness and dangers of excited class-feeling without calling forth any principle of improvement or reform."[71] The Workingmen's Party was "desirous of doing something for the laboring classes without the slightest idea of how to do it."[72] George's response to Kearney foreshadowed a shift in his aspirations. Chinese immigration was a vital issue for Californians and other Westerners, but, by the end of the 1870s, the West no longer contained the ambitions of Henry George. He did not recant his anti-Chinese racism—in fact, he remained committed to Chinese exclusion up until the end of his life—but he began to downplay its significance to his reform agenda.[73] As he turned to address a wider audience, George spoke less about the Chinese and more about the monopolist. The Chinese mostly clustered in the Far West, but the monopolist was everywhere. Monopoly was a problem that translated more easily across regional lines.

## Conclusion

Biographers and historians have remarked that George's racism toward the Chinese seemed incongruous with a land-reform agenda that emphasized the democratic distribution of wealth and opportunity.[74] But racism toward the Chinese was an essential part of how George understood the rights of American producers. Monopoly was destructive not only because it eliminated opportunities for small producers and proprietors to become independent but also because it forced them to live like the Chinese. Monopoly displaced white workers and made them squatters, tramps, and sojourners in their own country. For George, the suffering and deprivation of Chinese immigrant workers portended the fate of white labor under monopoly. George became a land reformer to protect white producers from becoming like the Chinese. He understood anti–land monopolism and exclusionism as linked remedies for the same social malady: the erosion of liberal, agrarian ideals in industrialized economies. In the coming years, other issues overshadowed the problem of Chinese immigration, but these issues did not obliterate the close connection between the Chinese problem and land monopolism. The racial logic of antimonopolism persisted and eventually resurfaced as George scrambled to join the leagues of major industrial reformers.

The example of Henry George suggests the way in which racism was constitutive of antimonopolist reform. It not only identified the deserving beneficiaries but also suggested what was at stake: the survival of the white race. By racializing the squatter's republic, George affirmed a definition of whiteness at a moment when it seemed most threatened by emancipated slaves and immigrants.[75] To be white was to be a small, independent proprietor, or at the very least, to protect small, independent proprietors from monopolists and coolie laborers. Anti–land monopolism, allied with anti-Chinese racism, became the foundation of George's career in labor politics as well as the reform ideal that united him with Terence Vincent Powderly, who, under the title of Grand Master Workman, led the Knights of Labor, one of the most important labor organizations of the late nineteenth century.

## Labor and the Land Question: Henry George, Terence Powderly, and Industrial Labor Reform

T he land is the heritage of God!" Grand Master Workman Terence Powderly declared in his address to the general assembly of the Knights of Labor in 1882. "He gave it to all his people. If He intended it for all His people, then no one man or set of men has a right to monopolize it."[1] It was as if Powderly were calling Henry George's name. The close tie between land and labor reform in the Gilded Age is nowhere more apparent than in the alliance formed by George and Powderly. George joined the Knights of Labor in 1883 because he believed the Knights had the potential to succeed where other labor unions had failed, to "force their issues into politics," and to transform the relationship between labor and capital. That potential came from their opposition to land monopoly. In a letter to Powderly, George wrote: "The pointing out of a great primary wrong, the proposal to strike at its root, will arouse and combine men as nothing else can."[2] George's anti–land monopolism, cultivated in California, became a means for him to forge common ground with Powderly and to propel himself into the inner circles of organized labor.

George and Powderly's ability to connect anti–land monopolism to industrial labor reform reflected the enduring power of agrarian ideals, even in an age characterized by large-scale industrialization. In the 1870s, and increasingly in the 1880s, antimonopolism became a rallying cry of American workers. Unions spearheaded campaigns against monopolies on land, railroads, and other industries. In doing so, organized labor joined forces with farmers and merchants in a movement toward antimonopolist reform and politics in the Gilded Age.[3] Between 1872 and 1896, five national political parties, drawing support from workers, farmers, and small businessmen, organized on the principles of antimonopolism to compete with Republicans and Democrats.[4] Although the Greenback Party and the Populists would become the most enduring and the best remembered, the National Labor Union, the predecessor to the Knights of Labor, was the first to organize a national antimonopolist political party, the Labor Reform Party. Campaigning in the 1872 elections, the Labor Reform Party advocated what would become typical of the antimonopolist reform agenda: a nationalized currency, reservation of public lands for "actual" settlers, regulation of railroad and telegraph rates, and Chinese exclusion.[5] After the National Labor Union dissolved in the midst of the economic downturn in the 1870s, the Knights of Labor took up its crusade. With the organization's national reach and unprecedented number of members, it became the most important and influential of the Gilded Age's antimonopolist labor unions. In the first half of the 1880s, anti–land monopolism still resonated with workers who believed in the sanctity of free competition, the virtues of the small freeholder, and the villainy of the monopolist and speculator.

### "Progress and Poverty"

Henry George's road from land reformer to labor leader began in 1879 with the publication of *Progress and Poverty*. This book of political economy introduced him to an international network of labor reformers and, eventually, made him world famous. In *Progress and Poverty*, George attempted to solve the puzzle of why industrialization fostered disparities of wealth and power, why land monopolies developed, and what social remedies might reverse those trends. The book marked a subtle but important shift in George's thinking about land monopoly. In his earlier work on California land reform, he was concerned primarily with the size and scope of land monopoly, the number of acres of public land that monopolists claimed and withheld from "actual settlers."[6] In *Progress and Poverty*, he focused less on the physical scale of monopoly and more on its ability to diminish wealth by withholding land from production. Poverty, George argued, was not a moral failing but the result of "human greed," "social maladjustments," and "unjust laws" that permitted "the rent-receiving classes"—speculators, landlords, monopolists, and middlemen—to unfairly appropriate the wealth created by production.[7] By accumulating, withholding, and controlling land, "the source of all wealth" and "the foundation of the industrial structure," the rent-receiving classes created an artificial scarcity of land and elevated the cost of using it: "When labor cannot satisfy its wants, may we not with certainty infer that it can be from no other cause than that labor is denied access to land?"[8] In short, land monopoly caused poverty.

To illustrate his theories, George employed examples from California and, in this way, attempted to draw universal lessons from his experience there. His romanticized depiction of the Gold Rush era served him in *Progress and Poverty*, as it had served him in earlier writings, as a model of natural distribution, where laborers had access to land and received the wealth their labor produced. George claimed that the prevalence of placer mining in the early years of the Gold Rush led to a rediscovery of "first principles" of landholding: in other words, limited landholding, based on use, the essence of the antimonopolist ideal. George explained: "If this work were not done, any one could relocate the ground. Thus, no one was allowed to forestall or to lock up natural resources. . . . All had an equal chance."[9] George looked to California's recent past to derive a model for the social and economic values he wanted to preserve in the nation's growing industrial system.

Early indicators of the book's success were not encouraging. George's mentor, James McClatchy, wrote a positive review in his newspaper, the *Daily Bee*, as did one other newspaper in San Francisco.[10] Meanwhile, George's opportunities for career advancement in California vanished with the unseating of his patron, the state's Democratic governor, William Irwin, in the 1880 election. George consequently lost his appointment as state inspector of gas meters, a position that had provided him with an income and time to work on his speeches and publications. Unwilling to return to newspaper work and hoping to find a wider audience for his reform theories, George borrowed money from a friend, and in the fall of 1880, he moved his family to New York City.[11] Only then did *Progress and Poverty* really take off.

George arrived in New York at a propitious time. Nearly thirty years after the dissolution of George Henry Evans's National Reform Association, antimonopolist land reform was making a comeback among northeastern workers. The renewed interest was due largely to a land crisis in Ireland that captured the attention of American laborers—many of whom were Irish immigrants or their descendants.[12] In Ireland, a severe drought in the 1870s had crippled the economy. English landlords, who controlled much of the countryside, began raising rents and evicting their Irish tenants. To keep the tenants on the land they worked, Irish journalists organized the Irish National Land League in 1879.[13] The league's leaders toured American cities giving speeches and courting sympathy among first- and second-generation Irish workers.[14] In California, McClatchy—Irish immigrant, erstwhile American squatter, and land reformer—energetically devoted himself to fundraising for the Irish National Land League. The images of displaced peasants oppressed by the wealthy, powerful landlords outraged McClatchy, and in 1879, he was quoted as saying, "Land monopoly is the greatest curse that could ever fasten itself upon any people."[15] *Progress and Poverty*, with its emphasis on reserving land rights for cultivators and eliminating landlordism and monopoly, resonated with the Irish situation and gave George a voice in an international dialogue about land reform. In a letter to McClatchy, George happily reported his progress and mentioned his growing involvement in Irish land reform.[16] That involvement won the attention of William Jay Youmans, an editor at *Popular Science Monthly*, and with Youmans's assistance and the backing of the publisher, W. H. Appleton, George began to promote *Progress and Poverty*.[17]

Land reform brought George into the orbit of Patrick Ford, the publisher of *The Irish World and American Industrial Liberator*, a New York City daily newspaper. As reflected in the title of his paper, Ford, an Irish immigrant, believed that land monopoly and the problems of industrial labor were inextricably connected. Ford used the newspaper to rally support for land reform in Ireland and to speak for Irish peasants and American laborers alike. He supported the nationalization of Irish lands and, like George, thought that land was a natural gift from God to the people, and thus, no one should have to pay rent to work on it. Ford also believed land and social reform in Ireland could serve as a model for the United States. The lengthy subtitle to one editorial on the "land question" outlined Ford's land-reform philosophy: "Rack-Rents and Evictions Quite as Possible and Common in America as in Ireland. Private Ownership the Evil. May One Human Creature Rightfully Claim as His Own That on and from Which Others Might Live?"[18] Ford shared George's conviction that land reform was the key to empowering wageworkers: "Is not a peaceable solution of the INDUSTRIAL PROBLEM more to be desired than railroad riots, strikes, rebellions, a chronic war of classes, and general devastation?"[19] If workers could command higher pay, improve their living conditions, or escape wage work altogether and become landowners, class conflict would cease to exist.

California continued to serve as George's intellectual springboard, even as he joined Ford's Auxiliary Land and Industrial Leagues of America and began to write for the *Irish World*. George's first publication in the newspaper was a reprint of an 1880 article he wrote for McClatchy's *Daily Bee*, entitled, "The Irish Question." The article likened the peasants of Ireland to the squatters of Sacramento. According to George, "There is really nothing peculiar to the Irish land question. It in no wise essentially differs from the English land question, or the Scotch land question, or the American land question. It is Simply the Land Question—the question whether land may rightfully be treated as private property—the question whether one human creature may rightfully claim as his own that element on which and from which other human creatures must live if they are to live at all."[20] George compared the evictions of Irish peasants to the evictions of California squatters by land monopolists: "Any landowner among us may invoke the power of the law—the whole force of the State if necessary—to put out a tenant *as readily as he can in Ireland.* In many parts of California you may see the blackened ruins of the little homes from which settlers have been evicted by the sheriff at the instance of some rich thief or blackmailing lawyer, who by fraud and perjury had obtained title to their lands." George hoped that the Irish land question might force Californians to interrogate their own land policies: "Possibly some of our California Irishmen, in attempting to pick the mote out of the eye of Irish landlordism, may discover what a big beam there is in their own."[21] In the *Irish World* article, George grafted the history of California squatter conflict onto an international dialogue about industrialism and labor reform. He accomplished this juxtaposition by collapsing the categories of *squatter* and *tramp*, just as he had in his 1871 pamphlet *Our Land and Land Policy*, but George knew well that squatters and tramps were not necessarily the same men. In antebellum California, squatters were typically settlers who sought to preempt public land from the government. Tramps, in the late nineteenth-century vernacular, were underemployed, often itinerant laborers, and they were the iconic image of industrial poverty.[22] By making squatters synonymous with tramps, George made mid-nineteenth-century California mirror conditions in Ireland and presage the situation in the late nineteenth-century United States:

> Ireland is an agricultural country, and a well-populated country, and a country where the ownership of the land is in the hands of a clearly defined class, and hence the connection between Irish famine and Irish Landlordism is clearly seen. But the same relation exists between English pauperism and English Landlordism; between American tramps and the American Land System; between the gradual fall of wages which we have seen in California and the gradual monopolization of our land.[23]

The common bond between squatters and tramps was their landlessness, which made Californian antimonopolism relevant to an audience of American industrial workers and Irish National Land Leaguers. George emphasized the shared circumstances of tramps and squatters to draw attention to what he believed to be the fundamental cause of industrial poverty: land monopoly.

In the fall of 1881, George left New York for a lecture tour of England and Ireland. *The Irish World* underwrote some of the costs by paying George as an overseas correspondent.[24] By the time George returned to New York in 1883, he had cemented his credentials as a champion for the impoverished, displaced, and landless working class. Chapters of northeastern labor unions invited George to speak on land and industrial reform.

Back in California, McClatchy pitched in to promote *Progress and Poverty*. In March 1883, he received 134 copies of the book and distributed them to interested parties.[25] A few months later, in October, he suffered a stroke and died. The obituary printed in the *Daily Bee* noted that McClatchy kept on his office bookshelf, alongside the Bible and a history of California, a copy of *Progress and Poverty*.[26]

## Terence Powderly, Land Reform, and the Knights of Labor

Terence Powderly also came to land reform via the Irish National Land League (fig. 7). The son of Irish immigrants, he, too, was a member of Patrick Ford's Auxiliary Land and Industrial Leagues of America, and he donated funds for the legal defense of Irish National Land League leaders in Dublin.[27] A longtime resident of Scranton, Pennsylvania, Powderly served as president of that city's branch of the Irish National Land League, and he continued in that role after he became a member and, later, the grand master workman, of the Knights of Labor. In 1881 and 1882, Powderly's early years as grand master workman, the Knights were a secret society, and he used his affiliation with the Irish National Land League to recruit Knights. Prospective Knights attended league events under the cloak of Irish land reform and became inducted into the order. Powderly continued to hold a leadership position with the Irish National Land League until 1883, when the Knights of Labor shed "the garb of secrecy" in order to expand more rapidly.[28] Thereafter, he shifted his attention from Irish to American land reform.

Powderly's opposition to land monopoly was one part of the Knights' broad antimonopolist agenda, which aimed to combat the "tendencies toward centralization of power in the hands of those who control the wealth of the country."[29] In an address to the general assembly, Powderly declared:

FIGURE 7.  Terence Vincent Powderly in 1879. Terence Vincent Powderly Photo-
graphic Prints, The American Catholic History Research Center and University
Archives, The Catholic University of America, Washington, D.C.

> Combinations, monopolies, trusts and pools make it
> easy for a few to absorb the earnings of the workers, and
> limit their earnings to the lowest sum on which they can
> sustain life.... Natural opportunities are being con-
> trolled, monopolized, and dwarfed by artificial means.
> ... To free the earth and its treasures, and allow man to
> have free access to his natural rights, is the aim of organ-
> ization today.[30]

The Knights' constitution resolved to oppose private monopolies in all
industries essential to production—transportation (most notably, the
railroads), communication, and energy.[31] Powderly and the Knights demanded public ownership of these industries to guarantee unfettered access to their services. The logic was that private monopolies could force
the public to pay the rate they set, however exorbitant, and drive up costs
for producers or stymie production, whereas a democratically elected
government, with the public interest at heart, would keep rates low. In an
address to the general assembly, Powderly explained the danger of such
monopolies: "Is it not true that the individual who controls the telegraph
and railway lines of the nation also controls the people of the nation?"[32]

Antimonopolist land reform was Powderly's pet cause. Ardently and
sometimes mulishly, he believed that land monopoly, among all forms of
monopoly, created the greatest and most pressing problems for industrial
labor:

> Give me the land, and you may frame as many eight
> hour laws as you please, yet I can baffle them all and
> render them null and void. Prohibit child labor if you
> will, but give me the land, and your children will be my
> slaves. Make your currency of what material you choose;
> but if I own land, you cannot base your currency upon
> the wealth of the nation, for that wealth is the land. You
> may make the laws and own the currency, but give me
> the land and I will absorb your wealth and render your
> legislation null and void.[33]

Powderly's anti–land monopolism had less in common with the Gilded
Age land reform of Henry George and more with the antebellum land
reform of George Henry Evans. Powderly believed, as Evans had, that
land ownership was synonymous with agricultural labor. Neither Evans

nor Powderly could imagine what a landowner might do other than farm.[34] Although Powderly admitted that "the majority of men who live in large cities are not adapted to the life which a farmer must lead," he contended that many workingmen had the aptitude and desire but not the funds necessary to become farmers: "There are in all of our large cities and towns a number of men and families who would make excellent farmers if they were provided with sufficient means to give them a start in agricultural life; but if they are deficient in means . . . they must remain to compete with others in our crowded centers in the race of life."[35] Repeating a demand made forty years earlier by Evans and the National Reform Association, Powderly called for Congress to extend financial assistance "to all who wish to leave the cities and adopt agriculture as a calling."[36] The farm represented the escape from wage work and the fulfillment of the republican promise. Powderly clung to his belief in the redemptive power of agrarian independence. In the early, heady days of the early 1880s, his followers believed in it, too.

The land crisis in Ireland and the perceived plight of American farmers piqued the Knights' interest in antimonopolist land reform. Many Knights had rural roots and belonged simultaneously to the Knights and to the Farmers' Alliance.[37] Not surprisingly, the two organizations espoused many of the same principles, including land rights for actual homesteaders. When the Farmers' Alliance urged Congress to democratize the distribution of public land, to eliminate land grants to corporations and speculators, and to make the U.S. General Land Office function more fairly, the Knights of Labor echoed that call in their constitution.[38] One resolution called for the "reserving of the public lands—the heritage of the people—for the actual settler; not another acre for railroads or speculators."[39] Between 1882 and 1886, articles addressing "the land question" regularly appeared in the *Journal of United Labor*, the Knights' official newspaper. The journal covered the antimonopolist canon of thought, from land rights for true cultivators to the problems of tenantry on public lands.[40] Powderly did his part to encourage the trend by printing and distributing relevant sections of his past general assembly addresses. In 1883, Powderly put *Progress and Poverty* on the official Knights of Labor recommended reading list, and every one of the local assemblies' reading rooms held a copy.[41] Although George first wrote a personal letter to Powderly in April 1883, the two men did not likely meet until August of that year. George was, by that point, a member of the Knights of Labor, and by 1885, he had ascended the ranks to become a lecturer.[42] In 1885, the *Journal of United Labor* began publishing advertisements for George's pamphlet *The Land Question* in each of its semimonthly issues.[43]

George was a more nuanced thinker than Powderly. Although George drew his vocabulary from an idealized preindustrial, agrarian past, he did not seek to reinstate a preindustrial, subsistence economy. As he professed in *Progress and Poverty,* no social remedy was "worth considering that does not fall in with the natural direction of social development, and swim, so to speak, with the current of the times."[44] Like his earlier writings on California land reform, *Progress and Poverty* freely referenced Thomas Jefferson and relied on agrarianism to explain the problems of large-scale industrialization. Nonetheless, George rejected moving back toward an economy of subsistence farming.[45] In a speech before the Burlington, Iowa, assembly of the Knights of Labor, George said:

> [Men] seem to think, when you talk of land that you always refer to farms; to think that the land question is a question that relates entirely to farmers, as though land had no other use than growing crops.... Whether a man is working away three thousand feet under the surface of the earth, or whether he is working up in the top of one of those immense buildings that they have in New York; whether he is plowing the soil or sailing across the ocean, he is still using land.[46]

The problem with land monopolies was that they controlled not only natural resources necessary for production but also the very space in which production occurred. Coming from a liberal tradition, George upheld the sanctity of private property and associated socialism with "government repression." But he also opposed the limitless accumulation of property that monopolistic capitalism pursued.[47] George called for a new attitude toward land ownership, one that protected free competition among small proprietors: "Let the individuals who now hold it still retain, if they want to, possession of what they are pleased to call *their* land. . . . *It is not necessary to confiscate land; it is only necessary to confiscate rent.*"[48] Confiscating rent in a tax became the basis of George's signature reform proposal, the single tax. He imagined that confiscating rent would enable industrial laborers to escape wage work and become economically independent landowners. In that way, his anti–land monopolism did not propose to distribute wealth equally among producers. Rather, it established "natural" conditions of free competition for that wealth by removing the "artificial" restraints of monopoly.[49] In the absence of monopoly, land would become less expensive and more accessible to wageworkers.

What united George's and Powderly's antimonopolism was a fundamental belief in democratizing and protecting independent proprietorship. They both thought that the 1862 Homestead Act, which promised gifts of essentially free land to American citizens, had failed, and that railroad corporations and speculators stole the best acreage from bona fide settlers.[50] In an address to the Knights' general assembly, Powderly stated: "I sincerely believe that for every acre of the land which God designed for man's use and benefit that is stolen another link is riveted to the chain with which the land and bond lords hope to finally encircle us."[51] George argued that prohibiting land monopoly and speculation would "open opportunities to labor and enable men to provide employment for themselves."[52] As antimonopolist reformers, George and Powderly aimed to protect and restore a small-scale capitalist economy, dominated by independent proprietors and producers.

## Antimonopoly and Chinese Exclusion

George and Powderly also shared the belief that monopolists and Chinese laborers went hand in hand. Powderly and the Knights railed against the "importation" of inexpensive Chinese labor by monopolists as a tactic to diminish wages and undermine American workers' bargaining power with employers.[53] Anti-Chinese racism and a commitment to Chinese exclusion were inscribed into the order's foundational documents. The preamble to the Knights' constitution called for an end to the importation of "servile races"—namely, the Chinese.[54] Like George, the Knights saw Chinese exclusion as a means of protecting labor against the forces of monopoly: "The basic principle on which the Order was founded was protection, not protection from the manufacturer or employer alone, but from our own avarice, our weakness, and from cheap workmen also."[55] Anti-Chinese sentiment was particularly strong among Knights in the western states, where assemblies were often instrumental in the most vicious attacks on Chinese workers. Adherents of nonviolent protest, Powderly and the general assembly condemned brutality against Chinese laborers, but they tended to lay the blame not on the Knights but on the employers.

Such was the case with the notorious massacre of Chinese coal miners in Rock Springs, Wyoming. For the Knights, the coal mines at Rock Springs became a site for the twinned problems of monopoly and Chinese labor. The mines were owned by the Union Pacific Railroad Company, which contracted with white and Chinese workers. The Knights of Labor had already declared their opposition to large, consolidated mine ownership by throwing their support behind small mine operators in an 1884 strike in Colorado and New Mexico.[56] At Rock Springs, competition between white and Chinese miners over wages and the right to work particularly productive coal pits exacerbated preexisting antipathy toward the Union Pacific's monopolistic control of coal production and distribution. On the morning of September 2, 1885, long-brewing tensions reached their boiling point when a group of ten white miners, members of the Knights of Labor, found that they had been assigned to the same pit as Chinese miners. The ensuing argument quickly escalated; white and Chinese miners swung picks and shovels at one another. Later that day, the brawl became a massacre when a mob of white men and women, wielding firearms, assembled and descended on "Chinatown," the Chinese miners' camp. Chinese workers and residents of Rock Springs later recounted to the Chinese Consul in New York what transpired:

> Some of the rioters would let a Chinese go after depriving him of all his gold and silver, while another Chinese would be beaten with the butt ends of the weapons before being let go. Some of the rioters, when they could not stop a Chinese, would shoot him dead on the spot, and then search and rob him.... Some of the rioters would not fire their weapons, but would only use the butt ends to beat the Chinese with.... Some, who took no part either in beating or robbing the Chinese, stood by, shouting loudly and laughing and clapping their hands. There was a gang of women that stood at the "Chinatown" end of the plank bridge and cheered; among the women, two of them each fired successive shots at the Chinese.[57]

When investigators arrived on the scene, they discovered the bodies of Chinese who had burned to death in their homes or had been slain in the foothills, where they had attempted to flee.

By the evening of September 2, the white mob had dispersed, and the Chinese survivors escaped, following the railroad tracks to the town of Green River, fourteen miles distant. The Union Pacific telegraphed its conductors to pick up any Chinese laborers they found alongside the tracks and transport them to nearby Evanston, the company's second-largest coal-mining site after Rock Springs. If the Union Pacific thought Evanston might be a safe harbor for its Chinese employees, it underestimated the pervasiveness of anti-Chinese racism. On September 5, the white residents of Evanston threatened to kill the Chinese taking refuge there. U.S. troops were ordered into Evanston to protect the Chinese, and four days later, the troops escorted them back to Rock Springs.[58] One can hardly imagine the fear that the Chinese workers must have felt as they returned to the very place where they had escaped a savage slaughter just a week earlier.

Thousands of miles away in New York, Powderly commented on the Rock Springs massacre when he addressed the general assembly of the Knights of Labor the following month. While he did not condone the cruelty perpetrated against the Chinese miners, he expressed sympathy with the motivation behind it and blamed the outbreak of violence on the failure of Congress to enforce the Chinese Exclusion Act:

> The recent assault upon the Chinese at Rock Springs is but the outcome of the feeling caused by the indifference of our law-makers to the just demands of the people for relief. No man can applaud the act by which these poor people were deprived of their lives and homes. They were not to blame. They were but the instruments in the hands of men who sought to degrade American free labor.[59]

By overlooking violations of the act, Congress permitted the continued "importation" of Chinese labor and, by extension, the "degradation" of white laborers, who were forced to compete with the so-called servile race. Powderly's address pointed to what he saw as Congress's more significant failure: the failure to check the power of large-scale corporate monopoly like the Union Pacific. It was monopoly that created demand for Chinese labor. The men at Rock Springs, said Powderly, "destroyed the instrument; the hand and brain by which it was guided still remains."[60]

Widespread public support for miners allowed western Knights to promote Chinese exclusion in the *Journal of United Labor* and other publications. Western assemblies made their anti-Chinese crusade part and parcel of the organization's campaign against monopoly and, thus, secured a place for their regional concerns in the national agenda. W. W. Stone, a delegate from District Assembly 162 in San Francisco, wrote an article for the *Overland Monthly* in which he asserted that Chinese exclusion protected American labor: "With Caucasians only to confront on this point, we enjoy a reasonably sure prospect of eventually gaining a triumph; but with a horde of people in our midst whose education from the cradle unfits them to mingle with us as equals in industrial marts, the outcome is not so encouraging."[61] Repeating a common stereotype, he claimed that Chinese immigrants derived their competitive advantage from their supposed bachelorhood, which subverted white norms of patriarchal families. Prohibiting immigration of the Chinese shielded labor from "the greed of the avaricious in the hunt for subsistence for his wife and family."[62] The contrast between the "Chinaman" with "no family to support" and the Caucasian's "wife and family" made anti-Chinese racism part of a larger defense of independent, white families. Powderly expressed his unqualified support for the western Knights' "crusade against a race." In a letter to Stone, he wrote, "The General Board is heart and soul with you in your struggle, and will do all in its power to assist you."[63]

## The United Labor Party and Antimonopolism

In 1886, the Knights of Labor joined forces with New York's Central Labor Union and formed the United Labor Party. The Central Labor Union had originally organized to support Irish tenant farmers in the late 1870s, and its philosophy blended producerism with anti–land monopolism and European socialism. The combination attracted a mixed following of Irish land radicals and German socialist trade unions.[64] In the 1886 New York City mayoral election, when the United Labor Party decided to field a candidate to run against the Democratic and Republican prospects, it chose Henry George. George's racial, social, and economic theories came together in a vocabulary that made sense to the New York working class. These images were culled from various social-reform traditions that were familiar to the city's working-class population—Irish nationalism, liberal and agrarian land reform, and antimonopolism. Accepting the nomination, George linked the United Labor Party platform with the tradition of Jeffersonian ideals. The "workingmen's party," he said, would be "a party that shall reassert the principles of Thomas Jefferson in their application to the questions of the present day." At the New York Labor Conference in August 1886, he described his reform agenda in a language of rights that recalled the Declaration of Independence. New York City, "the American city where monstrous wealth and monstrous want make their most shocking contrast," was "a fitting place to begin a movement which shall aim at the final assertion of the natural and unalienable rights of man." George promised that anti–land

monopolism would eliminate the nonproducing classes and make all producers equals: "Where all men stood on an equality with regard to the use
of the earth and the enjoyment of the bounty of their Creator, all men
would belong to the working-class." George declared his intent to break
up concentrations of wealth and power that denied labor the wealth it
created: "I see in political action the only way of abolishing that injustice
which robs labor of its natural rewards . . . that monstrous injustice which
crowds families into tenement rooms of our cities and fills even our new
states with tramps."[65] George's campaign attracted a broad spectrum of
supporters. Irish-American organizations including the *Irish World*, the
Irish-American Independent Democrats, and dozens of New York
Catholic parishes endorsed George's candidacy and organized campaign
clubs. Working-class German-American, black, and Jewish groups also
formed clubs. The United Labor Party also attracted middle-class supporters, who were professionals and businessmen interested in George's
antimonopolist protections for small proprietors. Some labor leaders
worried that middle-class participants would distract the party from its
working-class agenda, but for the 1886 election season, the United Labor
Party maintained its focus on industrial issues and drew its leaders from
New York trade unions.[66]

George's primary opposition in the race was Abram S. Hewitt, a former U.S. congressman and one of the founders of the iron and manufacturing firm Cooper, Hewitt, and Company. The other candidate was
Theodore Roosevelt, an upstart Republican member of the state assembly and, unbeknownst to all, the future president of the United States.
George and Hewitt knew one another well enough not to like one another. While in Congress, Hewitt had undertaken a review of federal land
policy, and he had hired George in 1880 to write a report. George quit
when they squabbled over compensation. During the campaign, Hewitt
exposed their former relationship and claimed that he had fired George
for "running the land tax into everything."[67] If Hewitt expected working-
class voters to see George as a land reformer and not as a labor leader, he
failed to understand the significance of land among New York's workers.
For the unions that nominated him, campaigned for him, and voted for
him, land reform was labor reform.[68]

In the final count, Hewitt had 90,552 votes and George had 68,110.
Roosevelt came in third with 60,435. Years later, George's son recalled
that the campaign faltered because of a simple matter of logistics. New
York municipal election law required each party to print its ballots and
to have its representatives at the polling stations to distribute the ballots

and count the votes. George's party did not print enough ballots, nor did they have representatives at every polling district. Many of George's contemporaries believed that he could have won the election if his party had been better organized on voting day. George was bitterly disappointed and felt as though he had been "counted out" of the election.[69]

Even though George did not win the New York mayoralty, his strong second-place finish represented a significant moment in the history of industrial labor in America. The *Irish World* and other New York labor newspapers celebrated the near victory of the labor ticket as a step forward in transforming the industrial system. The United Labor Party and George's campaign also inspired the proliferation of other independent labor parties across the country.[70] The 1886 New York City mayoral election was the pinnacle of George's career in labor reform. Never again would a third-party candidate running on an anti–land monopoly platform come so close to winning a major municipal election as George had.

## *"A Fight in the Dark"*

George's strong showing in the New York mayoral race was one event in a tumultuous year that American labor historians have dubbed the Great Upheaval of 1886. Workers organized politically in new labor parties and mobilized mass strikes for higher wages and shorter workdays. The strikes revealed ideological divisions between antimonopolist labor leaders and rank-and-file union members. These divisions ultimately led to the decline of land reform as labor reform in the Gilded Age. George and Powderly refused to support the strikes, which they believed undermined their goal of cooperation among small, independent proprietors and laborers. They doggedly continued to promote anti–land monopolism as the only true, long-term solution to the problems of the industrial system. Their position ultimately alienated them from the mainstream of organized labor and marginalized anti–land monopolism as an industrial labor-reform movement.

George never concealed his disdain for striking. When the United Labor Party nominated him for New York mayor, he had declared that "the ballot is the proper means of protest, and the only instrument of reform."[71] After the New York mayoral election, George began to publish a weekly newspaper entitled *The Standard*, which addressed the problems of labor and promoted anti–land monopolism, but the strikes of 1886 and 1887 seemed to steal the spotlight from his work. In February 1887, the *New York Herald* asked George for his opinion on a strike by New York longshoremen and freight haulers, and George dismissed it as a "fight in the dark, the blind push of men squeezed past endurance."[72] As far as George could see, the only purpose striking served was to mitigate the "petty tyrannies" of long work hours or low wages. He continued to believe that the only significant tyranny was land monopoly. George complained, "I have constantly endeavored in every way I could to throw light into the darkness; to induce men to revert to first principles and think of these questions in a large way; to convince them that the evils which they feel are not due to the greed or wickedness of individuals but are the result of social maladjustments, for which the whole community is responsible, and which can only be righted by general action."[73] George repeated his standard refrain: breaking up land monopolies would increase wages and create opportunities for laborers to escape wage work. "Nothing can prevent these labor troubles and nothing can prevent them becoming wider and more violent," George opined in the pages of *The Standard*, "save the acknowledgment of the right of all men to the equal use of nature's bounties." He continued, "Striking can at best secure only temporary advantage. . . . The root of all labor difficulties is to be found in the land question."[74] Although George identified the New York District Assembly of the Knights of Labor as some of his most loyal supporters, his position on strikes drove the first wedge between him and the majority of unionists.

Powderly similarly believed that striking undermined the larger anti-monopolist goals. When rank-and-file Knights asked Powderly and the general executive board to support a general strike for the eight-hour day, Powderly, with what was becoming characteristic tone deafness, suggested that they organize a letter-writing campaign instead.[75] Yet for all his obstinacy, Powderly could not deny that when strikes succeeded, the Knights benefited. In 1886, the order had local assemblies in every state, and membership in the Knights of Labor surged to approximately seven hundred thousand, which, according to historian Kim Voss's estimation, represented 8 to 12 percent of the American industrial labor force.[76]

The Haymarket Riot, one of the most infamous events of the Great Upheaval, brought the tension building between Powderly and the other Knights to a crescendo. On May 4, 1886, a crowd assembled in Chicago's Haymarket Square to protest police action against a factory strike that had begun just a few days before on May 1. As the police broke up the demonstration, a bomb went off, killing seven policemen and four protesters and wounding many others. The police arrested eight anarchists, only one of whom had attended the demonstration, and as he had been a speaker, he clearly had not thrown the bomb.[77] Nevertheless, the jury indicted the eight anarchists for murder because their propaganda had influenced the unknown bomb-thrower. The fear of anarchy and its connotations with social subversion justified the indictment, conviction, and sentencing.[78] Many Knights sympathized with the anarchists arrested in the Haymarket Riot. At the general assembly meeting in October 1886, delegates proposed a resolution defending the anarchists involved in the Haymarket Riot, but Powderly rejected it:

> The world regards all labor societies in the same light since May 1; and had it not been for the imbecile act which afforded the anarchists the opportunity to do an evil deed while the eyes of the world were upon the men of labor, we would not be regarded with suspicion by all who are beyond our sanctuaries.... Under no circumstances should we do anything that can, even by implication, be interpreted as identification with the anarchist element.[79]

That year, Powderly's address to the general assembly described the two enemies of labor: monopoly and anarchy. "Anarchy is the legitimate child of monopoly," Powderly declared. Monopoly brought "uneducated, desperate men to this country." Disaffected, immigrant laborers, whose opportunities had been diminished by monopoly in their homelands and in the United States, had no choice but to retaliate with violence. Powderly promised to eradicate the anarchist element in the United States through antimonopolist reform: "When monopoly dies, no more anarchists will be born unto this country."[80] In the midst of the Haymarket anarchists' trial in 1887, Powderly beseeched the Knights to distance themselves from anarchy. "This organization among other things is endeavoring to create a healthy public opinion on the subject of labor," he said. "How can you go back to your homes and say that you have elevated the Order in the eyes of the public by catering to an element that defies public opinion and attempts to dragoon us into doing the same thing?"[81] Powderly denounced anarchy thus:

> As an order we are striving for the establishment of justice for industry. We are attempting to remove unjust laws from the statutes, and are doing what we can to better the condition of humanity.... At every step we are handicapped by the unwarrantable and impertinent

interference of these blatant, shallow-pated men, who
affect to believe that they know all that is worth knowing
about the conditions of labor.[82]

Ultimately, Powderly's fears about the riot's effect on the reputation of
organized labor were borne out. In the riot's wake, employers became
less willing to tolerate unionization among their employees. The historian James Green has lamented that the Haymarket bombing and trial
"ushered in fifty years of recurrent industrial violence, a period when
workers, especially immigrants, often found themselves at war with their
employers, the courts, the policy, and the armed forces of their own government."[83] Increased intransigence on the part of employers drove some
workers to more radical action. Socialism's emphasis on class conflict attracted those impatient with George and Powderly's more conservative
approach to industrial reform. By the mid-1880s, socialists dominated
the general assembly of the Knights of Labor, and Powderly was careful
to profess his support of socialism: "Those who assert that socialism is
destructive of law and order do not know what socialism is." He wrote,
"Government would not disappear, but a more equitable form of government would prevail. The aim of socialism, in a word, is to make the
world better."[84] Yet he observed that as labor unrest spread in 1886, the
meaningful differences between socialism and anarchy seemed to lessen.
If the two ideologies became synonymous in the public mind, then Powderly could not defend one without implicating the Knights in the other.[85]

    In contrast with Powderly, George refused to approve of socialism in
any form. In *Progress and Poverty*, George dismissed communalism and
cooperation, the hallmarks of socialist thought, with a single adjective:
*fashionable.* He deemed them impractical for a modern, industrial society. In *Progress and Poverty,* he wrote, "We have passed out of socialism
of the tribal state and cannot reenter it again except by a retrogression
that would involve anarchy and perhaps barbarism."[86] In an 1889 debate
with the British socialist H. M. Hyndman, George declared that "socialism begins at the wrong end.... Its dream is simply of a benevolent
tyranny." He believed that the socialist criticism of capitalism was misplaced: "Give labor access to land and the power of the capitalists to grind
the masses must disappear.... It is the poverty of the laborers, not the
wealth of the capitalist, that is the evil to be removed."[87] American socialist leaders like Daniel De Leon acknowledged antimonopolist land
reform as one step toward the larger goal of eliminating private ownership of capital, but they refused to accept George's signature reform

idea—the single tax—as a panacea.[88] Powderly agreed. He conceded that George's single tax theory would "come the nearest to the remedy for the evils of the present system,"[89] but he would "not believe, with many advocates of a single land tax, that it will prove a 'cure-all' for every ill that industry is heir to."[90]

George further alienated himself from the mainstream of organized labor by opposing two popular forms of labor protectionism: the tariff on manufactured goods and restrictions on immigration from southern and eastern Europe. The Knights' support for tariffs seemed pointless to George. In a *Standard* article addressed "to Workingmen," George declared that "labor cannot be hurt by freedom. The only thing that can be hurt by freedom is monopoly.... What labor needs is freedom, not protection; justice, not charity; equal rights for all, not special privileges for some."[91] Free trade fit with George's antimonopolism, which sought to remove all unnatural restraints on competition. George made repeated attempts to convince Powderly of the fallacy of tariff protection for labor. In a personal letter, George wrote:

> Will you allow me, in the most paternal spirit, to say to you a word on a matter as to which we differ? If you will pardon the seeming presumption, I would like to ask you not to further identify yourself with "protection" until you have time to more carefully think over the matter.... That the great injury done by the protective theory seems to me to be that it sets workingmen to "barking up the wrong tree," "it draws" as the Irish would say, "a red herring across the true trail." What Labor wants, it seems to me, is not protection but justice.[92]

By "justice," George meant the just rewards of producers. As he had argued in *Progress and Poverty*, the key to eradicating poverty was restoring the natural distribution of wealth through unfettered competition.[93]

George also believed that restrictions on southern and eastern European immigration distracted from the genuine danger of Chinese immigration: "To talk of immigration as though that were the cause of scant employment and low wages is at once to make a pretense of devotion to the interests of labor and to turn the attention of the laboring masses in a direction that will not threaten 'vested interests.'" George denied the claim that European immigration drove down wages by increasing the supply of labor: "Surplus population! What does the general master workman of the world instructing order mean by the phrase 'surplus population' which he uses so glibly? Does he mean a greater population than there are natural resources to support—a greater population than the Creator, in whom, as a Catholic, he believes intended to exist?"[94] George argued that European immigration could not threaten wages under conditions of free trade and anti–land monopolism. Breaking up land monopolies would increase demand for labor by bringing more land into production. Workers would disperse themselves accordingly and thus relieve overcrowded cities.[95] George's comparison between Chinese immigrants and southern and eastern European immigrants revealed his assumptions about whiteness. Nineteenth-century Americans often racialized Catholics as non-whites and were inclined to do the same with Jewish immigrants as well as the darker-complected eastern Europeans, but George, with his large base of support among Irish and Irish-Americans, defined the white race in a way that elided religious and ethnic differences among European populations:

> The people who are coming to us from Europe belong to the same great family of mankind as we ourselves, have the same religious beliefs that exist among us, speak for the most part different variations of what philologists tell us is the same mother tongue, and when not massed together as are the French in Canada, become in a generation indistinguishably blended with the rest of our people.[96]

George believed southern and eastern European immigrants might be assimilated into American society because they already shared the basic racial characteristics of Anglo-Saxon Americans. European immigrants would not compromise the racial integrity of the American population as George believed Chinese immigrants would. Unlike the Chinese, southern and eastern Europeans were not racially fit for cheap labor: "The Italian, the Hungarian, or the Pole does not work for low wages because he likes to, but because he has to."[97] Whereas the Chinese survived in degraded living conditions, George observed no unnatural personal economies lurking among the European immigrant populations: "These immigrants like to lodge well and fare well, whenever they can; that as soon as they can afford it their scale of living improves, and that their children when they have opportunities for education and contact are growing up Americans."[98] George described European immigrant families as virtuous republicans in the making, altogether unlike the Chinese, who raised their children to stand apart and to maintain loyalties to China. That difference between the "infusible" Chinese and the "indistinguishably blended" Europeans shaped George's stance on immigration restriction, but such distinctions had less meaning to most northeastern laborers, who rarely encountered Chinese workers but knew well, and feared, their Polish and Italian neighbors.

In 1887, George ran for New York secretary of state on the United Labor Party ticket, but his position on strikes, labor radicalism, the tariff, and immigration had distanced him from working-class voters. The contentious and ultimately unsuccessful campaign reflected a larger fracture developing within the United Labor Party. At the summer convention, the antiradical party leadership ejected all socialists on the grounds that their membership in the Socialist Labor Party (SLP) disqualified them from belonging to any other political party. Although the initiative had come from the newly elected leader of the United Labor Party, John McMackin, several delegates blamed George for the decision because he supported the expulsion in *The Standard*.[99] In response, the SLP members banded together with trade unionists and organized themselves into the Progressive Labor Party to field their own candidates.[100] Meanwhile, McMackin further denounced all anarchists, Greenbackers, Irish nationalists, and German nationalists as radicals, which alienated no small number of working-class union members from the party.[101] The United Labor Party soon found itself almost entirely composed of middle-class devotees of George's single tax on rent.[102] To make matters worse, in September, when the Illinois Supreme Court denied the Haymarket anarchists' appeals and upheld the death sentence, George publicly declared his support of the court's decision. Trade unionists labeled George a "class traitor," and he lost the November election for secretary of state in a landslide.[103] Writing about the loss on the front page of *The Standard,* George tried to portray the outcome in the best light: "Our seventy-three thousand votes seem small compared with the Democratic 480,000 and the Republican 450,000, but they represent a nucleus of intelligent and determined men." He blamed his loss on the labor radicals: "This year a vote for me was . . . a vote for a naked principle . . . made so clear and plain, and so uncompromisingly and unhesitatingly asserted as to drive off not only the socialists, anarchists, and cranks who constituted the 'progressive labor party.'"[104] The quotation marks around "progressive labor party" underscored the contempt George felt for the socialist organization. The 1887 election ended George's political career as a labor leader.

George's punishing defeat was not the only blow to antimonopolist labor reform in the wake of the Great Upheaval. Strikes and the Haymarket Riot initially grew the ranks of the Knights, but they also marked the beginning of its decline. Although the Knights of Labor had originated as an organization of skilled trade unions, by 1886, it embraced not only skilled but also semiskilled and unskilled labor unions. The changing membership of the Knights resulted in an uneasy collaboration between skilled trade unionists, who tended to be more politically and socially conservative, and semiskilled and unskilled workers, many of whom were more radical.[105] In the mid-1880s, a group of socialists assumed control of the general assembly and began to espouse anti–trade union policies. In response, trade unionists defected from the order and signed on with its rival, the American Federation of Labor.[106] By the summer of 1887, the Knights' membership numbered just over five hundred thousand, having dropped from its high of seven hundred thousand. One year later, their ranks had plunged to 221,618.[107]

After a power struggle among the Knights forced Powderly to resign as grand master workman in 1894, he continued his crusade against land monopoly as the U.S. commissioner-general of immigration, striving to expand opportunities for both native-born and foreign workers to escape wage work and own a farm.[108] Near the end of his life, in 1924, Powderly reflected on his experiences as grand master workman with disappointment and defensiveness: "The Knights of Labor did not tell me to advocate land reform in the way I advocated it but they approved of my course by not opposing me. I still regard a solution of the land problem as the one above all others."[109] The elderly Powderly continued to believe that anti–land monopolism could transform the American working class, but he lived with the fact that he had failed to persuade the Knights to his way of thinking.

After 1887, George's antimonopolism, with its emphasis on eliminating land monopoly through targeted government intervention, was not wholly discredited among the working class. It continued to attract followings in smaller manufacturing centers like Cleveland, Ohio; Portland, Oregon; and Everett, Washington. At the same time, echoes of his call to restore land rights to producers reverberated in the efforts by charitable organizations and trade unions to "colonize" unused land with the unemployed in the wake of the depressions of the 1890s.[110] Nonetheless, by 1890, George's supporters were mostly members of the middle class. They called themselves "single taxers."[111] George did not care much for the name, which he thought placed too much emphasis on the mechanism of taxation and too little on the sweeping social reformation it implied, but he still employed it in speeches and articles.[112]

Up until the end of his life, George remained committed to using government to break up land monopolies and to achieve liberal and agrarian republican ideals. "Jefferson was right," George wrote to Louis F. Post, a prominent single taxer, in 1891, "the secret of a healthy society of a stable state of national peace and plenty and virtue and happiness, lies in the practical application of the Golden Rule. In the recognition by all of the rights of each."[113] In an 1893 speech before the House of Representatives, he defined the single tax as "really democracy—nothing more and nothing less. Democracy—what is its essence? It is 'equal rights to all and special privileges to none.' That is what we aim at by the Single Tax, to carry forward to full expression the principles upon which this republic was founded; to carry forward to reality the ideas expounded by Thomas Jefferson."[114]

Yet George invoked the rhetoric of "inalienable rights" in ways that Jefferson himself would not have imagined. Under the category of "inalienable rights" and "natural freedoms," George included free trade and society's right to appropriate rent through taxation. The future of the republic, George asserted, "cannot be secured by dividing land out; it cannot be secured by giving every man a faro or every man a town lot. If equality could for a moment be secured in that way it could not be continued."[115] In his age of industrialization and consolidation, George expected that the equal distribution of land would be impossible. But he hoped that the equal distribution of land *value* would remain possible: "What is necessary to secure equality and to preserve equality is to give to all not an equal piece of land, but an equal share in the value of land. . . . The state should appropriate for the benefit of all, that unearned increment which political economists call rent, as well as all other unearned increment."[116] When the single taxers encouraged him to run a second time for the New York mayoralty in 1897, he did so under the banner of the "Jeffersonian Party." By that time, George had grown feeble due to the stroke he had suffered in 1890, and the physical rigors of campaigning took their toll. He died just two weeks before the election.[117]

## Conclusion

As George and Powderly receded from the center of labor reform, so did the opposition to land monopoly. Antimonopolist land reform had never fulfilled its promise to restore freedoms to industrial workers, but more importantly, its ideals of small, independent landownership ceased to resonate with a rising class of permanently entrenched wage laborers.

At the time of his death, George was one of the world's most famous public intellectuals. *Progress and Poverty* was a best-selling book of the nineteenth century—by some accounts, second only to the Bible—and George was revered as a political economist and social theorist, all despite his two and a half unsuccessful bids for elected office. His middle-class followers continued to promote the single tax, and they claimed some victories in reforming land-value taxation overseas, particularly in Australia, New Zealand, and Great Britain. In the United States, however, they met with little success. George Raymond Geiger's 1933 biography of George identified more than two dozen campaigns to introduce assembly bills or put a single tax referendum on the ballot in eleven states between 1892 and 1921. In 1911, Everett, Washington, passed a tax exemption for property improvements, which Geiger claimed as the sole example of single tax–inspired legislation to be enacted. The single tax as George imagined it, however, never became law in the United States.[118]

Middle-class reformers still clung to their belief that consolidated wealth and power would unravel the fabric of American democracy. In their minds, the opposition to land monopoly remained a useful framework for thinking about the industrial economy, its most efficient organization, and just regulation. In the 1880s, antimonopolists continued to rely on anti–land monopolism to decry the overweening power of corporate monopolies, but they also began to run up against the limits of the land question. Even the most strident antimonopolists could not ignore the fact that the late nineteenth century's industrial monopolies—the railroad, the telegraph, and others—had, for better or worse, become integral and desirable parts of the American economy. Eliminating them was not an option. Thus, antimonopolist reformers in the 1880s began to reformulate stories about the squatter's republic to find a new way of living with monopoly.

## CHAPTER FIVE

TELLING STORIES ABOUT SQUATTERS:
REPRESENTATIONS OF SQUATTERS IN HISTORY AND FICTION

Early in the morning on May 11, 1880, a decade-long land dispute ended in bloodshed. Seven men died in an armed confrontation between squatters and representatives of the Southern Pacific Railroad Company in Mussel Slough, an agricultural district in Central California's San Joaquin Valley. The seeds of the conflict were first sown in 1867 when the Southern Pacific petitioned Congress to move its land grant from the coast to the valley, where it intended to locate a rail line from San Jose to Southern California. Squatters nervously kept watch over the proceedings. Settlement along the Mussel Slough, a branch of the Kings River, had begun in the 1860s and increased throughout the 1870s after the federal government confirmed the change to the Southern Pacific's grant. Many of the Mussel Slough squatters were commercial hay and wheat farmers, some drawn by the prospect of a railroad to connect their product to widening markets, others enticed by the escalating land values that connectivity might bring. The Southern Pacific encouraged settlement of the district and, despite its reputation as a land monopolist, promised to sell land to the squatters at the low price of $2.50 per acre. Land sales generated revenues and customers for rail services, and the company's policy toward settlers in Mussel Slough was consistent with its policies toward settlers on its other reserved lands. In 1877, the company began construction of its rail line. To the would-be buyers' dismay, the company then demanded $8 to $20 per acre. Some squatters chose to buy their claims from the railroad even at the new price, but many resisted because they believed that the Southern Pacific had overvalued the land. They sent plaintive letters to Congress, appealed directly to the leaders of the Southern Pacific, and, when those tactics proved unsuccessful, organized a militia and committed acts of arson and intimidation against railroad representatives and their sympathizers. This pattern persisted for three years until that morning in

May, when a U.S. marshal arrived to evict a handful of Mussel Slough squatters. He was accompanied by a land surveyor and two other men, Walter J. Crow and Mills Hartt, who had purchased titles from the railroad. A group of squatters rode up on horseback to confront the party of four. The men argued, drew their guns, and exchanged fire. Crow, an expert marksman, killed five squatters while the squatters managed to fatally wound Hartt. Crow then fled, only to be shot and killed in a wheatfield a mile and a half to the south.[1]

The conflict at Mussel Slough reminded Californians that land troubles were as much a part of their present as their past (fig. 8). In the two decades after the "battle," California writers began to tell stories about squatters. They recounted and reimagined what had transpired at Mussel Slough, and they revived stories about the 1850 riot in Sacramento and other land disputes from the Gold Rush era.[2] Stories about squatters belonged to a new category of popular writing that emerged with the economic depressions of the 1870s. As authors tried to explain the causes of the rising numbers of "wandering poor" in Chicago, New York, and other northeastern cities, they churned out fictional and nonfictional accounts of "tramps" and "bums." The terms were used interchangeably to describe the able-bodied and underemployed, many of whom were white, male, and native born. According to nineteenth-century notions that conflated whiteness, manliness, and independence, these people were not supposed to exist at the margins of society. Gilded Age writers explained such unexpected circumstances by characterizing "tramps" and "bums" either as criminals or as victims of economic forces beyond their control.[3] On the West Coast, writers in California explored the same themes, but they substituted the squatter for the tramp.

Substituting the squatter for the tramp reasserted the traditional connections between anti–land monopolism and widespread prosperity, independent freeholding and democratic order. In an age characterized by industries that were ever larger and cities that were ever more impersonal, squatter stories maintained the centrality of agrarian ideals to the culture of the American political economy. As Henry George had before them, California writers in the 1880s linked the national problem of industrial inequality with the state's history of land conflict. They believed that the freedom to own land and to access natural resources could fix what ailed California. Unlike George, however, they no longer saw land monopoly as the sole source of the state's maladies. Nor did they see anti–land monopolism as the panacea. The lessons that Gilded Age antimonopolists drew from squatter stories had less to do with agrarian land rights and more to do with the dangers of corporate capitalism. Their stories reflected a shift, which began in the 1880s, in antimonopolist reform, a shift away from the unfettered veneration of small freeholders and toward a new, uncertain relationship with land monopolists.

## Squatter Histories

In California, Anglo-American migrants wrote their history as it happened. The state's first historical society, the Society of California Pioneers, was founded in August 1850 to commemorate the Gold Rush, not even two years after it had begun. That same year, John T. Frost published the first history of California. Between 1858 and 1900, more than 150 state and county histories rolled out of publishing houses to meet a growing public appetite for stories about California.[4] Reigning supreme over California history was Hubert Howe Bancroft, who came to California in 1852 and, within a few years, owned the largest book and stationery store west of Chicago. In the 1860s, Bancroft began amassing a trove of California ephemera, and he hired a Dartmouth-trained librarian, Henry Lebbeus Oak, to catalogue the collection. Between 1881 and 1890, Bancroft's team of librarians, writers, editors, and salesmen put out thirty-nine volumes of *The History of the Pacific States of North America*, which featured eleven volumes on California alone. Although Bancroft's name appeared as the author of the series, his staff did most of the writing while he managed production, promotion, and sales.[5] The multivolume history of California was the most comprehensive source on the state and the first to give significant attention to squatters.[6]

In the Bancroft series, squatter history became a means of explaining Anglo-American settlement and its consequences for Californios. His books followed the formula of a progressive historical narrative. Each wave of occupation—"Indian," "Mexican," and "American"—elevated the state's level of civilization and productivity: "As the savages faded before the superior Mexicans, so faded the Mexicans before the superior Americans."[7] Anglo-American settlers supposedly brought an energy and industry lacking among Mexicans, who were "spoiled by bountiful nature" and "lived for the enjoyment of the hour, in reverie or sport, rejoicing in bull-fighting and bear-baiting, eager for the chase as for the fandango."[8] The Bancroft histories naturalized the process of conquest and characterized Mexican Californians as childlike, "simple-minded," and "indolent" by nature: "They were not a strong community in any sense, either morally, physically, or politically."[9] According to the historian Phoebe S. K. Young, Bancroft used Californio histories "merely as props for his argument about

FIGURE 8. Edward Keller, "Impending Retribution," cartoon of Mussel Slough victims from *The Wasp*, October 7, 1882. Courtesy of the Bancroft Library, University of California, Berkeley.

the inevitable and proper ascent of Anglo-Americans to dominance in the state."[10] Bancroft's histories drank from the well of Manifest Destiny and declared that innate differences between conquering and conquered races made the dispossession of Californios inevitable.

The doctrine of Manifest Destiny may have made it easy to explain how an "industrious" race triumphed over the "inferior" Mexican Californians. It was more difficult to account for the discrepancies of character and conflict among white settlers. Anglo-American squatters and their extralegal, occasionally violent actions wreaked havoc on the narrative of naturalized conquest. Yet, to condemn the squatters, who contested Mexican land grants, was to defend the Californio landowners, who held the rights to those grants. Thus, Bancroft's histories scrambled to reconcile squatterism with the narrative of Anglo-Saxon progress and supremacy. They drew a line between the "honest" settler and the "land-hungry" squatter. The settler, as one volume described him, "was contented with what land he could use ... he did not oppose monopoly in another while practicing it himself; he was not unjustly agrarian, but ready to respect the rights and titles of others, as he would have others respect his."[11] The description of the "settler" implied that the squatter was in fact a species of land monopolist. The squatter "was a professional gull, ever hovering about some broad-acred pelican, which had dived into the depths for its possessions, and held them rightfully. He it was who speculated in town lots, staked off farming lands, jumped mining claims, and stole the nest of another rather than build one of his own."[12] Squatters impinged upon the freedoms of other settlers by asserting the supremacy of preemption rights. The squatter in the Bancroft histories was not a bona fide settler but a land thief, stealing the fruit of another man's labor. Anti–land monopolism, as a positive force for democratization, was still central to Bancroft's progressive narrative, but squatters were no longer part of its legacy. The effect was to write the squatters out of the history of conquest. Their efforts to secure an alternative property regime were regrettable obstacles on the otherwise unobstructed march toward civilization, law, and order in California.

The Bancroft histories were unable to accommodate shades of moral complexity, and their account of the 1850 riot in Sacramento ran up against an empirical challenge. One volume conceded that "there was good ground—in the belief of the squatters that the Alvarado grant [to Sutter] did not extend to [Sacramento]," and that the squatters' protestations might have been justified, as "Sutter was playing into the hands of a set of soulless speculators, who used the pretence of a grant for securing paper titles to the best portions of [California]."¹³ Unsure of how to explain the conflict within the context of a progressive narrative, the *History of California* referred its reader to another California history: Professor Josiah Royce's "able" presentation of the riot in an 1885 article for the *Overland Monthly.*¹⁴

The article was Royce's first stab at writing a squatter story. A California native and a professor of philosophy at Harvard University, Royce wrote about California history not only because it was familiar to him but also because it seemed to answer the philosophical questions that puzzled him most (fig. 9). His early work in the 1880s reflected a preoccupation with questions about how communities arrived at a common set of ethics and how bonds of mutual loyalty were forged. Scholars of philosophy and its history categorize Royce as a "temporalist," meaning that he interpreted all human choices as expressions of past experiences, present circumstances, and future expectations.¹⁵ In this way, Royce reflected the influence of William James, whose philosophies emphasized the contingent nature of human knowledge. Royce studied the evolution of knowledge over time and came to believe that it emerged from experiences with the "essential," that which is unchanging through time and space, and the "accidental," that which is unique to an era and a community.¹⁶

Many of Royce's biographers have traced his fascination with community and loyalty to his youth in Grass Valley, California. His parents migrated west with the Gold Rush. After a string of failed ventures in Sacramento—where they missed the 1850 riot by just a few months—and San Francisco, they settled in the bustling mining community of Grass Valley, about fifty miles north of Sacramento, in 1854. A year later, Royce was born.¹⁷ Financial difficulties meant that Royce's father, a merchant and fruit peddler, was often absent, seeking out new business opportunities in California and Nevada mining towns, and Royce was largely raised by his mother, a devout Christian, and his three older sisters.¹⁸ Christian fellowship was the center of his young life, and he knew California not as a rough-hewn frontier but as a safe, domesticated landscape. Even when the family moved to a dairy farm outside of Grass Valley, they were never far from the city center. In 1865, the family relocated to San Francisco, where Royce completed his primary education and then, at age fifteen, enrolled in the second class of the new University of California at Berkeley. After college, he went on to a PhD and, eventually, a faculty position at Harvard.¹⁹ He was, by all accounts, a cerebral child who became an even more cerebral adult, and, according to his sister Ruth, was utterly without "mechanical tastes and [with] little bodily agility."²⁰ Asthmatic and rheumatic, Royce hardly embodied the image of the robust frontiersman who populated western stories. It is, perhaps, unsurprising that the "great men" stories that filled the Bancroft tomes held little interest for Royce. He opted instead to devote his early career to the study of community bonds, what he called "social devotion."

As a newly minted philosopher in the 1880s, Royce examined what he called the "harmonization" of different ethics within a community.[21] In an 1882 lecture, he said, "We . . . must see ourselves as little members of a vast body, as little fragments of a mighty temple, as single workers whose work has importance only by reason of its relations to the whole."[22] Royce saw this subjugation of personal desires, ambitions, and interests as achieving a state of social devotion, which represented a community's essential leap out of a state of nature, a state characterized by constant insecurity and conflict, and into a state of civilization, characterized by law and order.[23] Like John Locke, Royce believed that individuals invested power in government to protect property rights.[24] But where Locke was most concerned with the relationship between government and citizen, Royce focused on the relationship among citizens and the decision to embrace or reject a common set of laws, even when they seemed to violate personal rights. For Royce, the 1850 riot in Sacramento seemed like an apt illustration of that decision.

In the summer of 1884, Royce began his research in Bancroft's massive warehouse of California ephemera in San Francisco. With the assistance of Bancroft's main librarian, Henry Lebbeus Oak, Royce began to compile the details that would inform a book on the history of California.[25] To publicize his forthcoming work, Royce published an article for the *Overland Monthly* entitled "The Squatter Riot of '50 in Sacramento," which Bancroft would later recommend to his readers. Royce described the riot as "a most helpful exercise in social science." He hoped it would reveal to his readers the difficult process of subjugating self-interest to community interest. He wrote: "The Squatter Riot in Sacramento is significant not because bloodshed was unknown elsewhere in California land quarrels, but because nowhere else did any single land quarrel come so near to involving an organized effort to get rid, once and for all, of the Spanish titles as evidences of property in land." American law had validated Mexican land grants under the Treaty of Guadalupe Hidalgo in 1848, and, according to Royce, the squatters sought an "abrogation" of those land rights. "Had they been successful," Royce claimed, "a period of anarchy as to land property would probably have followed."[26] For Royce, the Sacramento riot represented a moment when California might have abandoned civilization, a moment of choice between anarchy and social order in a new community.

FIGURE 9. Josiah Royce in an undated photograph. Josiah Royce Memorial Collection (Collection 253), Department of Special Collections, Charles E. Young Research Library, UCLA.

Like Bancroft, Royce drew a line between illegitimate squatters' rights and legitimate settlers' laws. Royce used adjectives like "rapacious" and "predatory" to characterize squatters' attitudes toward Mexican land grants. In the article, he called Sacramento squatters "gold-seekers" and "discontented idlers," who valued wealth over social order. Royce lamented "the moral mischief done to the country by the encouragement offered to thriftless and disorderly squatters and by the exclusion of a great number of the best sort of farmers' families, who left the state early, or never came to it at all because of the uncertainty of land-titles."[27] Royce distinguished squatters from the "best sort of farmers' families," who were "settlers," community-builders, and arbiters of agrarian democratic values. The categories defied historical evidence, which indicated that squatters were no more or less land hungry, disorderly, or undemocratic than any other settler, but the distinction, however unsubstantiated, was more useful to his moral argument.

For Royce, history was a morality play, and the squatters were the villains because they failed to demonstrate "social devotion." Royce argued that the squatters used anti–land monopolism as a "pretense" for land grabbing and the overthrow of institutions that governed a healthy society.[28] Squatters may have defended their self-interest in a language of natural rights, but Royce insisted they were deluded by an idealism that was, in fact, destructive to society. He used Charles Robinson, the president of the Sacramento City Settlers' Association, to explain the fallacy of the squatters' position. Robinson, Royce wrote, led the squatters according to "grand abstract formulae." "The complex and wearisome details of Spanish law plainly do not interest him [Dr. Robinson], since he is at home in the divine Higher Law," wrote Royce, in a tone dripping with sarcasm. "Concrete rights of rapacious land speculators in Sacramento are unworthy of the attention of one who sees so clearly into the abstract rights of Man. God is not in the Sutter grant; that is plain. It is the mission of squatters to introduce the divine justice into California: no absurd justice that depends upon erroneous lines of latitude and establishments at New Helvetia."[29] For Royce, this "mission" reflected self-interest and individualism, which weakened community. Social order depended on its members' participation and mutual acceptance of the rules and laws of society. By seeking the abrogation of private property laws, the Sacramento squatters failed to follow the true path to harmony and order, the path of social devotion.

In 1886, Royce published the full monograph, *California: A Study of American Character*, which expanded on his claim that self-interest and self-aggrandizement undermine social order. California, in the first ten years after American conquest, exemplified a "new" society in the throes of this struggle between individual and community: "What we have here to do is to understand what forces worked for and against order in this community of irresponsible strangers."[30] The world that Royce portrayed in *California: A Study of American Character* did and did not reflect the reality of California in the 1850s. Royce exaggerated the degree of social complexity, capital investment, and industrial organization that Gold Rush–era California experienced. The result was that California of the mid-nineteenth-century began to seem more like his own times, and this resemblance was critical to the moral lesson Royce sought to impart to his Gilded Age readers. Royce believed that economic consolidation and mechanization helped to build a healthy society. He reasoned that if individuals were more involved in collective endeavors and ownership, then they were more invested in upholding law and order.

Whereas other California writers and reformers of the Gilded Age were fond of locating the origins of California's democratic institutions in placer mining, Royce insisted that it was in fact the subsequent development of sluice mining that democratized the new state (244).[31] Collaborative labor and growing mechanization of gold mining in California, he wrote, "was destined to render far more stable and responsible this roving mining life of 1849" (242). In the first years of the Gold Rush, 1848 and 1849, the dominant method for extracting gold was placer mining, wherein a miner would swirl riverbed gravel in water, separating the sand from the heavier gold particles. It was work accomplished by a single miner, and it was labor-intensive, not capital-intensive, since a miner needed only a pan, a spoon, or a shovel and a spot along a watercourse. As gold seekers multiplied, the opportunities to find significant mineral deposits by this method diminished, and between 1849 and 1851, more complicated means of gold extraction replaced placer mining. In that change, Royce saw a great opportunity for moral progress: "The pan as sole instrument for gold-washing was . . . sociologically and morally, as well as economically considered, a great evil for the mining life; and one can be glad that its time of more extended use was so short. Already in 1848, many men and some whole camps, were desiring and using 'machines' as they are at first rather vaguely called in the accounts" (226). The "machines" were really just long boxes with sieves. Miners ran water through the boxes— called cradles, rockers, or sluice boxes—to separate gold flakes from gravel. Because this type of mining required group labor of between three and nine miners and more equipment than placer mining, it compelled men to work together. Thus, Royce claimed, "this accidentally primitive society had passed from a state of 'nature' in the old sense of the word (this state of 'nature' being indeed here a state of unstable peace, not of general war) and had become a collection of mutually more or less independent, but inwardly united bands" (227).

Herein was Royce's defense of industrial organization in his own time: "At all events, men found in the advance of the industry to its more complex forms, in the formation of the necessary great partnerships, and in the organization of labor, the thing that all men need: namely, something to give a sense of mutual duties and of common risks" (246–47). Complex industries required all community members to adhere to laws and to protect private property and investments: "The better part of every such mining community learned...that their stay in California was to be long, their social responsibility great, and their duty to devote time and money to rational work as citizens unavoidable" (295). Squatters, Royce claimed, failed to participate in California's changing economy and society. His descriptions of squatters in *California: A Study of American Character* likened them to the most negative portrayals of underemployed tramp laborers in the late nineteenth century. He described the squatters as "landless, idle, and disappointed wanderers" and "complaining idlers" who "sought wealth and not a social order" (217, 370–71).[32] Royce emphasized the squatters' resistance to becoming permanent or productive members of the community. In his theory of social order, squatterism represented all forces aligned against community building: "Their early quest was at all events an unmoral one; and when they neglected their duties as freemen, as citizens, and as brethren among brethren, their quest became not merely unmoral, but positively sinful" (218).

Themes of industrialization and modernity also led Royce to cast an eye on Californio land grantees and to question the role they might play in the new state's economy and society. Royce defended the land rights of Mexican Californians against incursions by Anglo-American squatters, but he did so based on the sanctity of private property, not racial egalitarianism. Mexican Californians were legal titleholders, and for the health of the community and out of respect for the law, they deserved protection (368). Nonetheless, for Royce, the dispossession of Mexican Californians was an inevitable consequence of the social development of California under American rule. Reiterating commonly held prejudices against Mexican Californians, Royce described them as "moderately charming and innocent," "gay and jovial," "happy and unprogressive" (25–26). This characterization of Californio culture as backward and simple underscored Royce's belief that Mexican Californians could not exist in modern, industrial America: "The poor Californians, no business men to begin with, were thus forced into the most wearisome sort of business. They must, as it were, gamble for their own property, under the rules of an alien game, which they found largely unintelligible" (382–83). Both squatters and Californios were out of step with California's increasingly complex, large-scale industrial society. Royce believed land titles would eventually come under the control of Anglo-American "settlers" (as distinguished from "squatters") because they were more capable of adaptation to the new order.[33]

As with Bancroft, Royce used the squatters and Mexican land grantees as foils to the modernizing settlers of Gold Rush California. Royce did not discuss what happened to the squatters in the 1850s—how they organized politically and influenced legislators to codify their "abstract" land rights.[34] In the *Overland Monthly* article, he dismissed the aftermath of the Sacramento land troubles by saying that they eventually dissipated in the "torrent" of California life.[35] As for the fate of the Californios, Royce did not account for the enduring political power of the Mexican Californians in state government or their demographic majority in the southern counties up until the 1880s, nor did he explain why they represented more than half of the successful land-claim cases between 1860 and 1890.[36] These facts would not have served the moral of his story, in which the "healthy" elements of society prospered while the "unhealthy" perished. The false distinction between "squatters" and "settlers" supported a narrative that began in wilderness and chaos and ended in civilization and order. By writing squatters out of history, Bancroft and Royce denied the significance of their anti–land monopolism to California's political institutions and society. More significantly, they also naturalized consolidated, private landownership within a story about law, order, and industry in California. It would take nearly a century for historians to recover the contested nature of California's conquest and to grapple with the long-term consequences of uncertain land rights.[37]

## Squatters in Fiction

While Bancroft and Royce made the Gold Rush–era squatter represent forces working against progress, California novelists tended to craft more sympathetic portrayals. Many novelists took their inspiration from the events at Mussel Slough, and what happened there seemed altogether different from earlier land disputes. When Gold Rush squatters attacked land monopolists, they attacked individuals, often famous pioneers like John Sutter. The image of the pioneer occupied a sacral space for many Californians. In the late nineteenth and early twentieth centuries, they were enshrined in public statuary, ceremonial art, and city and state seals.[38] Writers understood Mussel Slough as a battle between squatters and a corporation. It was easier to hate the corporation than to hate the pioneer.[39] Bancroft and Royce had made Gold Rush–era squatters represent antimodern impulses, but the Gilded Age corporation, with its impersonal power, seemed like a modern perversion. Antimonopolist sentiment—in particular, anti-railroad sentiment—was riding high in California politics and society in the 1880s, and, for some writers, the conflict between the Southern Pacific and the Mussel Slough squatters confirmed that monopoly, embodied by the railroad, besieged small landholders and drove them to destitution or even death.[40]

The most straightforward example of this literary turn was C. C. Post's 1884 novel, *Driven from Sea to Sea*. The book had a simple message: Gilded Age squatters were Jeffersonian agrarians reincarnate:

> These men were not speculators, not gamblers by nature. They were men who loved best the quiet of home and the peaceful pursuits of agriculture. Farmers and farmers' sons back in the States, a brief experience in mining had satisfied most, and all had tried it until they were satisfied. What they wanted was an opportunity to earn their living and make homes for themselves and families in obedience to nature's laws and their own inclinations, by the cultivation of the soil, and the gathering of its ripened fruits and grains.[41]

While Bancroft's *History of California* and Royce's *California: A Study of American Character* separated squatters from the honest stock of pioneers and settlers, Post made no distinction; squatters were heroic pioneers who tamed the wilderness of California by the sweat of their brows. "They were not cowards," Post wrote. "The cowards went out later, when the wilderness had been, in a measure, subdued; when braver men had proven the immense resources of the country; had bridged its torrents; had opened its mines; had driven out the Indians; had laid the foundation for private fortunes and national wealth."[42] The description emphasized images of manliness, home, and family to make the squatter seem more sympathetic, stable, perhaps noble, and therefore more worthy of society's admiration and protection.

The cowards, in Post's novel, were the land monopolists, both Mexican land grantees and railroad corporations. He presumed that these landholders did not work the land and decried the injustice of landownership by individuals or corporations "that never struck a blow, nor turned a sod, nor put up a shanty."[43] At the same time, he lamented the dispossession of the "brave" men who did work the land. With land monopolists denying true cultivators their natural rights, the antimonopolist refrain resounded in Post's novel. *Driven from Sea to Sea* concluded with a call for antimonopolist reform of land legislation: "The people themselves are to blame, as a mass, for tolerating a system of laws that turns the larger portion of the fruits of honest labor into the hands of the shrewd schemer, leaving the toiling millions of real producers to suffer for the very things which they have produced."[44] Like Henry George, Post demanded state intervention to restore and to protect the land rights of small proprietors and producers.

Post's approach was pure and untrammeled anti–land monopolism, and it was, by 1884, out of step with its time. Antimonopolist reform novels of the 1880s tended toward more complex attitudes about monopoly. Whereas Post pitted small freeholder against land monopolist, other authors were beginning to blur the categories. This shift was nowhere more evident than in two novels inspired by the Battle of Mussel Slough: Josiah Royce's *The Feud of Oakfield Creek* (1887) and María Amparo Ruiz de Burton's *The Squatter and the Don* (1885).

Royce, who had condemned squatterism as antisocial in *California: A Study of American Character*, was more sympathetic to the squatter in his subsequent work, *The Feud of Oakfield Creek*.[45] While Royce enthusiastically embraced the collective enterprise engendered by industrialization, his feelings toward corporations were more ambivalent. What happened at Mussel Slough seemed to prove that corporations concentrated power in a distant, socially disconnected way. Corporate ownership severed the interpersonal relationship necessary to align interests and engender feelings of mutual responsibility. Corporations recklessly sacrificed social devotion to serve the interests of their shareholders, who resided outside the community. Royce worried about the consequences if corporations had the legal but not the moral right to land. In such a case, how could community bonds survive? At "Oakfield Creek," the stand-in for Mussel Slough, squatters encounter a corporate land monopoly. The ensuing conflict and ultimate compromise outline the possibilities for achieving social harmony in an era of consolidated corporate capitalism.

Royce endowed the Oakfield Creek squatters with social devotion. He described them—and by extension the Mussel Slough squatters—as "families" in search of free or inexpensive land on which they could make a "home" (36). Royce explained that the Oakfield Creek squatters' moral right to land ownership was based on natural rights: "Their presence and hard labor . . . had much increased the value of all the surrounding real estate" (38). In his earlier work, Royce had never considered the possibility that the Sacramento squatters similarly occupied and improved their lots, nor did he make much of the dubiousness of the Sutter grant. The Sacramento squatters were enemies of the law, while the Oakfield Creek/Mussel Slough squatters were victims of it. In the plot's climactic moment, the Oakfield Creek squatters arm themselves against the Land and Improvement Company, a fictitious corporation standing in for the Southern Pacific, but they do so with "no real desire to begin war against the national government. . . . All must be done . . . decently and in order" (458). All of the characters in the novel recognize the settlers' moral right to the land, even Alonzo Eldon, the president of the Land and Improvement Company. Royce describes Eldon as a "merciless" monopolist who "had for years gone about to destroy the settlers at Oakfield Creek." Yet over the course of the novel, Eldon seeks an "escape from his own undertakings against them" (359). The distant, faceless corporation blocks any escape. "There are more interests than mine over there," Eldon explains. "There's more capital invested than mine. When, as its president, I defend the legal rights of the Land and Improvement Company, I'm acting not alone for myself, but for the capital of innocent shareholders, invested in those undertakings" (258). Nonetheless, once Eldon recognizes the cost of his inaction to the community, he knows he must devise a plan to resolve the land dispute without bloodshed. He will buy out the shareholders of his corporation and then sell the land at the low rates initially promised to the settlers at Oakfield Creek, thus exercising his sense of individual responsibility and community loyalty (267–68). The plan is a costly expedient, not a systemic reform, but it promises to honor the squatters' natural rights to land while working within the existing legal and social institutions. It harmonizes conflicting ethics and maintains order.

By the end of the story, the protagonists wind up dead, disillusioned, or in exile from California—not because Eldon's plan fails, but because shortsighted, self-interested characters impede its execution. *The Feud of Oakfield Creek* was not just about the constraints of decision making under corporate ownership. It was a tragedy about the human weaknesses that disrupt social order, prevent compromise, and keep ideals at a distance from reality. Royce implies that if the sole impediment were the shareholders, the plan would have worked. The failure of the compromise was thus a choice, not an inevitable outcome. But, his message as a philosopher and reformer nonetheless remained a hopeful one: squatters and corporations might peacefully and productively coexist if each individual applies himself to the practice of social devotion.

## Squatters and Californios

The Battle of Mussel Slough also inspired María Amparo Ruiz de Burton, although her antimonopolist novel, *The Squatter and the Don*, did not cleave as closely to the tragedy's details as did *The Feud of Oakfield Creek* (fig. 10). Literary critics have mostly remembered *The Squatter and the Don* as an early example of Chicano literature and hailed Ruiz de Burton as the nineteenth-century voice of *la raza*, or the people.[46] But what begins as a story about conflict between Anglo squatters and Californio landowners evolves into an exploration of interclass and interethnic alliances against corporate monopoly and a plea for political economic reform.

Ruiz de Burton's experiences provided her with ample fodder for *The Squatter and the Don*. Over the course of four decades, from the time of her marriage in 1849 until her death in 1895, Ruiz de Burton acquired several large tracts of land in San Diego and Baja California. Squatters and other rival claimants—often members of her extended family—contested her property rights. Navigating the vagaries of American and Mexican land laws required her to assume many roles during her lifetime. Some roles were legitimate; others were pretended. She was a landowner, by dint of California's community property laws; she reinvented herself as a Mexican land grantee, which she was not; and she was a homesteader and a squatter, depending on which tactics best secured her land rights. In the 1870s and 1880s, she took up writing—two novels, two plays, and a smattering of newspaper articles—but it was always a distant second to her first career as a landed proprietor, speculator, and capitalist.[47] Writing offered her a little extra income, an entertaining diversion from her legal and family woes, and an outlet to express her discontent with the politics of her adopted homeland, the United States.

Born in 1831 in Baja California, Ruiz de Burton adopted the last name of her maternal grandfather, Don Jose Manuel Ruiz, who was a prominent local politician and former military leader in possession of a large land grant in Ensenada. Taking her grandfather's name in place of her father's gave Ruiz social capital but not actual capital. It enabled her to move in the upper echelons of Mexican and, later, American society, but she was never a wealthy woman. With the end of the Mexican–American War in 1848, Ruiz de Burton relocated with her sister's family to Monterey, California. A year later, she married an American, Captain Henry S. Burton, with whom she had first become acquainted in 1846 when he led the oc-cupying forces in Baja California during the war between the United States and Mexico.[48] Shortly after their marriage, the couple moved to San Diego and made their first forays into railroad and land speculation. In the 1850s, San Diego boosters, including the Burtons, endeavored to make their city the western terminus of a transcontinental railroad along the thirty-second parallel. In 1854, Burton became a director of the San Diego and Gila, Southern Pacific and Atlantic Railroad Company, which commissioned a survey for a potential rail line between San Diego and Yuma, Arizona. Ultimately, the Civil War quashed the city's hopes of a southern route.[49]

The Burtons also devoted themselves to amassing acreage in San Diego. The purchase of Rancho Jamul in San Diego County had the most profound effect on Ruiz de Burton's consciousness as an American land-owner. The Mexican government made the original grant to the ranch in 1831 to Pío Pico, who would later gain notoriety as the last Mexican governor of Alta California. Pico installed his mother and sisters on the Rancho Jamul while he lived primarily in Los Angeles. In 1846, John Fré-mont's Bear Flag Revolt ousted Pico, who fled to Mexico and left his brother-in-law, John Forster, in charge of his affairs, including the Ran-cho Jamul. Forster subdivided and sold the land to four buyers for a de-posit of $2,000, but the sale was contingent upon Pico's final approval. Pico had no intention of turning over the deed to Forster's buyers. When he returned to the United States in 1848, he was no longer on good terms with his brother-in-law. The deal remained unresolved until 1854, when Burton purchased the rights from the four buyers for half of the land's es-timated value and moved his wife and two young children to the adobe home once occupied by Pico's mother and sisters. As with all private Mexican land grants, Pico's claim to the Rancho Jamul came under the scrutiny of the board of land commissioners and was rejected in 1858. Even without a formal title, the Burtons assumed responsibility for ap-pealing the decision, and their case slowly moved through the federal courts. In 1859, the U.S. military relocated the Burton family to the north-east, and Ruiz de Burton left her mother and brother in charge of the Rancho Jamul. From three thousand miles distant, while her military hus-band was occupied by the Civil War and its aftermath, Ruiz de Burton continued to press for confirmation of their rights to the ranch. She doggedly pursued Pico's title until he finally relented and sent it to her in 1870, a year after Captain Burton passed away.[50]

In 1870, Ruiz de Burton found herself living in New York, widowed and supporting herself and her two unmarried teenage children on a

FIGURE 10. María Amparo Ruiz de Burton, n.d. Courtesy of Arte Público Press.

widow's pension and a meager allowance from Burton's estate. Even with the deed to the Rancho Jamul in hand, Ruiz de Burton still confronted the problem that the United States did not recognize the original land grant and, by extension, her ownership. Moreover, the ranch was beset by squatters and had been since the Burtons' departure from California in 1859. Ruiz de Burton relied on her lawyers to represent her interests on the ground in San Diego and in Washington, D.C., but her letters reflected a deep distrust in their efforts. To her longtime friend and confidante, Mariano Guadalupe Vallejo, Ruiz de Burton fretted that her Los Angeles–based lawyer would fail to file an appeal with the state supreme court in the time allotted. As squatters on Jamul moved forward with their petition to receive 160-acre allotments on the ranch, she implored Vallejo to speak with the lawyer on her behalf and urge him to give her case the proper attention. Bitterly, she complained that the lawyer habitually neglected her requests.[51] Communications from another of her lawyers in San Diego had grown worryingly infrequent, and she began to suspect that Rancho Jamul squatters had enlisted him to work against her. Her suspicions were confirmed in November 1870 when the lawyer wrote to his colleagues in Washington, D.C., to challenge Ruiz de Burton's case on behalf of the squatters.[52] Distance and dependence on others made Ruiz de Burton feel powerless and adrift. To Vallejo, she lamented, "It is terrible to be in this state of uncertainty, in a Limbo of doubts and anxieties."[53]

In May 1870, Ruiz de Burton returned to San Diego, where she could better oversee her affairs in California and Mexico. Her children joined her six months later. The family moved back into the adobe house on the Rancho Jamul and set to work fighting rival claimants to the land. To her friends and lawyers, Ruiz de Burton complained that the squatters cut down her trees for fuel and "ruined" the ranch, and she persisted in a long legal struggle to evict them from the property, or, at the very least, to rein in the damage they were causing.[54] The ongoing litigation sapped her resources. By 1872, she owed her principal mortgagor, Maurice Dore, $10,000. To raise money, she pursued a number of avenues on the Rancho Jamul, including oil works, waterworks, cement works, and, more conventionally, farming and stock raising. Ruiz de Burton also investigated the possibility of becoming a landlord to tenant farmers or sharecroppers. But these efforts failed to relieve her indebtedness. At the same time, she struggled to manage her Baja California property holdings, which remained woefully underdeveloped and failed to produce badly needed returns. She had not successfully attracted investors to her mining ventures, nor had she lured commercial farmers to the Ensenada land grant once held by her grandfather.[55]

In December 1872, Ruiz de Burton won her case in the U.S. Supreme Court and took the first major step toward being recognized as the owner of Rancho Jamul. Squatters, led by William N. Robinson, a onetime

California state representative, challenged the decision. Robinson claimed to have lived continuously on a 160-acre tract on the Rancho Jamul since July 1868.[56] The court denied his appeal, and in 1876, the United States recognized the Burtons' claim to the Rancho Jamul. The confirmation did not, however, dissuade the most stubborn squatters, who remained a formidable presence on the ranch until 1879 and compelled Ruiz de Burton to file still further suits against them.[57] Meanwhile, Ruiz de Burton's American creditors sued her to recoup their loans, and the courts ordered a forced sale of the ranch to cover the debts. It was in this context of perpetual litigation and impending dispossession that Ruiz de Burton wrote her antimonopolist novel, *The Squatter and the Don*.

The novel revolves around the relationship between squatters and a fictional Californio ranchero, Don Mariano Alamar, who is purportedly based on Ruiz de Burton's friend Vallejo. As the novel opens, Alamar's grant to a ranch near San Diego is under federal review. Believing that the courts will invalidate the grant and that the ranch will become public land, squatters descend, like sharks drawn to the scent of blood. Inspired by her experience on the Rancho Jamul, Ruiz de Burton created a stable of villainous squatters—sneaky, opportunistic, and cruel. They gleefully dispossess the landowners by violence and intimidation. They set up farms on Alamar's land and shoot his cattle, his only source of income, when the animals trample their crops. Taking one incident directly from her life in the adobe house on the Rancho Jamul, Ruiz de Burton described squatters removing all of the furniture from Alamar's friend's house to force his eviction (336–37).[58] Alamar devotes his dwindling financial resources to fighting the squatters in court, bribing them not to kill his cattle, and paying taxes on the land they occupy and the improvements they make.

Ruiz de Burton noted that among the squatters, there were also legitimate homesteaders, whom she portrayed through the character of William Darrell. Ruiz de Burton drew Darrell as a true cultivator and producer endowed with natural rights of ownership. Debating the principles of squatting and Mexican land grants with his wife, Darrell declares, "We aren't squatters. We are '*settlers*.' We take up land that belongs to us, American citizens, by paying the government price for it" (56–57). Perhaps Ruiz de Burton saw herself in the same way, as a "settler" and not a "squatter." By the time she wrote *The Squatter and the Don*, she, too, had done her share of squatting and homesteading. As would-be landowners in nineteenth-century California often did, she pursued multiple land-acquisition strategies, sometimes on the same tract of land, to protect her investments in a climate of uncertain property rights. After losing much of her San Diego property to her creditors, she acquired a "homestead" and the right to live in the adobe house on the Rancho Jamul by virtue of her long-term occupancy and use, and she attempted to extend the boundaries of one of her land claims in Ensenada by the same means.[59] Darrell's story reflected the squatter's precarious existence, a circumstance all too familiar to Ruiz de Burton. As long as property rights remained insecure in California, landowners risked eviction without compensation from claims they had worked for years. Alamar, Darrell's counterpoint in the novel, articulates their shared predicament: "I don't blame the squatters; they are at times like ourselves, victims of a wrong legislation, which unintentionally cuts both ways. . . . We are all sufferers, all victims of a defective legislation and subverted moral principles" (77). The novel added complexity to the customarily perceived dichotomy between squatter and land grantee. Legitimate homesteaders and Californio landowners alike were heirs to the Jeffersonian agrarian tradition. Their common enemy was the power that propagated "defective legislation and subverted moral principles": the railroad corporation.

In the novel, Alamar and other local landowners—Anglo and Californio, squatter and don—anticipate that Congress will approve a transcontinental railroad route from Texas to San Diego (the real-life Texas and Pacific Railway route). They sink their fortunes into real estate speculation and pin their hopes on the expectation that land values will soar with a San Diego railroad terminus. Landowners surrender the fate of their investments to the railroad: "All sat down to wait for the railroad to bring population and prosperity" (122). The novel reflected Ruiz de Burton's own experience with railroad speculation in San Diego. Although the Civil War had killed the Burtons' early hopes for a transcontinental railroad terminus in San Diego, Ruiz de Burton paid close attention to efforts to revive the project in the 1870s. To Vallejo, she wrote: "I have much interest in the good fortune of the Southern Pacific RR, or better said, the 'Memphis & El Paso RR'. . . . It will go right by the corner of the house at Jamul and, if carried out as planned, will make the ranch very valuable."[60] When Tom Scott, president of the Pennsylvania Railroad, became president of the Texas and Pacific and began scrutinizing San Diego as a potential terminus, Ruiz de Burton's expectant enthusiasm practically leaps off the pages of her letters. Not only would the railroad raise the value of her land—which she did not yet at that time possess free and clear—but she also imagined it would attract new residents to San Diego and create demand for the water, cement, and other goods that Rancho Jamul might provide.[61] But those dreams came to naught.

In the novel, as in real life, Charles Crocker, Mark Hopkins, Collis Huntington, and Leland Stanford, the so-called Big Four millionaire capitalists at the helm of the Texas and Pacific's rival, use their financial prowess to stifle plans for the San Diego terminus: "The monopoly triumphed, bringing poverty and distress where peace might have been!" (298).[62] *The Squatter and the Don* conveys the helplessness of ordinary individuals against the overwhelming power of corporate monopoly:

> How insidiously these monopolists began their work of accumulation. . . . They came before the Government at Washington, and before the people of California, as suppliant petitioners, humbly begging for aid to construct a railroad. The aid was granted most liberally, and as soon as they accumulated sufficient capital to feel rich . . . they became insolent, flinging defiance, as if daring the law to touch them, and truly, the law thus far has been powerless with them. (365–66)

In a letter to George Davidson, a surveyor, engineer, and professor helping Ruiz de Burton assess the potential water supply on the Rancho Jamul, Ruiz de Burton expressed the fervent wish that Stanford "would take a fancy to make a pet of San Diego, but he won't and so we must suffer if the pitying angels don't help us.[63] By the end of the novel, Ruiz de Burton's character Alamar acknowledges that his enemies are not Darrell and the squatters but the railroad corporations: "The work of ruining me begun by the squatters will be finished by the millionaires" (288).

Couched in melodrama, rife with outraged hyperbole and exclamation points, Ruiz de Burton's reform novel wore a veneer of radicalism over what was in fact a cautious, conservative call for regulation. There is throughout the novel a note of ambivalence toward the railroad that would become characteristic of her era. Her characters long for and need the railroad, but the corporation and its dealings deny them access. Cut off from the railroad and, by extension, national markets, San Diego landowners suffer financial devastation, and their plight reflects the consequences of an economy ruled by corporate monopoly. Ultimately, the solution Ruiz de Burton advocated was not land reform but political economic reform. She scolds the railroads for not paying their taxes and beseeches the federal government to regulate freights and fares (366).

She makes no calls for land limits or new legislation, as traditional anti–
land monopolists might have done in her place. Rather, she concludes
the novel with a strange invocation of the incident at Mussel Slough. In
its final pages, *The Squatter and the Don* recounts the injustices perpetrated by the Southern Pacific against the "poor farmers" of Mussel Slough,
but the tragedy of their story, as told by Ruiz de Burton, is shockingly
banal: poor government oversight killed the squatters in the Battle of Mussel Slough (371–72). Ruiz de Burton did not seek a radical transformation
of the relationship between producers and the land. She simply believed
that the government, representing the people, needed to rein in the power
of private corporate monopolies: "Our representatives in Congress, and in
the State Legislature, knowing full well the will of the people, ought to
legislate accordingly. If they do not, then we . . . must wait and pray for a
Redeemer who will emancipate the white slaves of California" (372). The
core problem for Ruiz de Burton was not the land question—who should
have the right to own land and how much of it—but whether government
should permit large corporations to impinge upon the enjoyment of land
rights and enlargement of land values within a community. Her brand of
regulatory antimonopolism would come to characterize antitrust policies in the Progressive Era. It would also marginalize the land question.

## Conclusion

In the late nineteenth century, stories about squatters provided a set of images, characters, and circumstances that writers used to make sense of
California in the Gilded Age. Squatter stories explored the social consequences of American conquest, the consolidation of land ownership, the
emergence of the industrial economy, and the growing political power
of railroad corporations. The questions posed by California writers about
squatters were not just questions about their state but questions about the
nation as a whole. Royce claimed that "our national character" was "dis-
played in that land" (*California*, 3). But California was not just a simple
reflection of national trends; it was a reflection magnified and intensified
by the speed of settlement in the Gold Rush years, the coexistence of di-
verse peoples, and the abundance of wealth and opportunity California's
natural resources promised to provide. For Royce, Ruiz de Burton, and
others, California offered vivid and urgent lessons for an industrializing
and diversifying nation. The state showed the best and worst outcomes
of mechanization and consolidation, the possibilities of interethnic and
interclass strife and compromise.

Writers applied different valences to squatters to justify or simply to explain different versions of American society and economy, but whether the writers portrayed squatters as victims or villains, the pulse of anti–land monopolism beat throughout these stories. In the late nineteenth century, landownership continued to represent opportunity, equality, and independence for many Americans, but land rights seemed all the more insecure under the new conditions of industrial capitalism and laws designed with the interests of large corporations in mind. California writers agreed that protecting property rights was crucial to building and maintaining democracy in the newly incorporated territories of the Far West.

Yet, stories about squatters also reflected the changing significance of the land question. The moral dimension remained, but its emphasis was shifting. Writers like Royce and Ruiz de Burton asked who should own land, but how much of it seemed to matter less and less. Their squatter stories reflected a new ambivalence toward monopoly that would play out in California politics and railroad reform.

## Tramps and Millionaires:
## Anti–Land Monopolism and Railroad Reform

I t may seem at first strange to speak of a beneficent principle in connection with monopolies," wrote Henry Carter Adams, "for we are
accustomed to associate them with all that is odious, grasping, and
tyrannous."[1] Nonetheless, it was the beneficence of monopoly that most
interested Adams, a professor of political economy at the University of
Michigan. In 1887 he set out to rehabilitate the image of monopoly in the
public mind. His research on the railroad and telegraph industries had led
him to some startling conclusions about monopoly as a form of industrial
organization, conclusions that would help transform antimonopolist politics and relegate the land question to the sidelines of industrial reform.
The opposition to land monopoly, as a defining tenet of antimonopolism, had long implied that free competition was both good and necessary for the economic and moral health of the nation. In the 1880s,
Adams and his fellow economists began to note that the new monopolies of the Gilded Age did not seem to abide by the same rules. Their research on capital-intensive industries like the railroad and the telegraph
led them to believe that free competition was, in fact, detrimental to the
new Gilded Age industries, whose high fixed costs made them operate
most efficiently under large-scale, consolidated ownership. Economists
began to call such industries "natural monopolies."[2]

The new economic scholarship complemented changing attitudes
toward Gilded Age monopolies among politicians and reformers in the
last two decades of the nineteenth century. At a time of increasing ambivalence toward monopolies, most especially the railroad, the theory of
"natural monopolies" offered a new framework with which to think about
the perils and possibilities of consolidated ownership. It introduced
shades of gray where the older logic of anti–land monopolism only offered black and white. Answering the land question forced reformers to
choose between monopoly and tyranny or antimonopoly and democracy.

The theory of "natural monopoly" took away that choice. It made consolidated ownership a matter of efficiency, dictated by immutable laws of technology and economics. Yet the perceived immutability of "natural monopolies" could not make them benign. Even as they learned to live with monopoly, antimonopolist reformers began to look for ways to make its efficiencies serve the public good. Although calls to reserve public lands for bona fide settlers continued to make boilerplate appearances in party platforms in the 1890s, antimonopolists no longer relied on the language and logic of land monopoly to articulate their concerns about railroad or other industrial monopolies. Instead of calls to break up or prevent monopoly, they substituted two reform strategies: regulation and nationalization. By the end of the nineteenth century, antimonopolist reform became defined not by free competition or independent freeholding, but by the attempt to maximize the benefits and minimize the costs of consolidation.

The transformation of antimonopolist politics can be understood only in the context of railroad reform. California, a state that grew up with the construction of the first transcontinental railroads, became the center of some of the most significant controversies in railroad reform. In the last two decades of the nineteenth century, California antimonopolists led state and national campaigns to limit the powers of private railroad companies, chief among them the Southern Pacific. Railroad corporations were unlike any corporation before them, most significantly in the demands they made on the government. Corporations had always been dependent on the state for their charters, but companies like the Southern Pacific forged new, closer, and more corrupt relationships with Gilded Age politicians. As the historian Richard White has argued, corporations like the Southern Pacific functioned only by virtue of the generosity of the national, state, and local governments and the scheming of their managers. Railroad corporations also had the ability to do unprecedented damage to economies, societies, and the environment. Reckless railroad speculation contributed to, if not caused, the most severe financial depressions of the Gilded Age. And that is to say nothing of the devastating effects on Indian populations and the environmental transformation inflicted wheresoever the railroad laid its tracks.[3]

Yet what concerned California's antimonopolists most was not the fate of the Plains Indian or the bison. The state's anti-railroad movement was initially based on the opposition to land monopoly. Large railroad land grants had, since their inception in the 1850s, aroused concerns about land monopolies, but, by the end of the century, a discomfited ambivalence had settled over California reformers. Private companies like the Southern Pacific turned capital into the mass network of railways, fuel, bodies, and trains that helped connect western producers to national and international markets. In an 1895 article for the *Overland Monthly*, California Democrat John Powell Irish outlined what the Southern Pacific had done for the state of California: "Wherever it touched transportation it cheapened and quickened it. Wherever it touched land its value rose."[4] Like it or not, the railroad corporation had become integral to California's agricultural and manufacturing sectors. It had, as Henry George predicted in 1868, brought people, investment, and productivity to the Golden State. To Irish, that was cause to celebrate, not excoriate the railroad corporation: "The Californian who is not a railroad man, and who does not wish to see a track laid in the service of each 30-mile strip of our dazzlingly rich soil, should take his pack-mule and go into the wilderness."[5] The praise for the railroads and their effects on land values and development was not misplaced, but it did threaten to mask the costs of their construction. California antimonopolists continued to fear, just as George had, that the benefits of modernity would not accrue to the masses, but rather to the few corporate executives. Unlike George, however, they ultimately could not find the answers they needed by asking the land question. In the 1880s and 1890s, Californians began to seek out new approaches to comprehend and control monopoly.

## Railroads as Land Monopolists

In many ways, railroad corporations acted like classical monopolies, and, up until the 1880s, the land question seemed well suited to articulate concerns about them. Railroad monopolies, by controlling major distribution channels, impeded free competition among producers, and they received special government privileges, most visibly in the form of subsidies for railroad construction. Government subsidies came from federal, state, and local governments and could assume different forms, but the land grant was the most controversial among them and the primary reason that the public associated railroad corporations with land monopoly. The U.S. Congress began extending gifts of land along with the right-of-way to railroad builders in 1850.[6] Just as Congress designed preemption and homesteading laws to expedite settlement of the western states and territories, so it intended the railroad land grants to connect far-flung producers and markets. By the 1930s, the total area granted by the federal and state governments to the railroads amounted to more than 179 million acres. Transcontinental railroads received approximately three-quarters of the federal land grants, and the remaining quarter went to regional railroads.[7] The land grants, political influence, and a flurry of corporate mergers aroused concerns that railroad executives wielded too much power. Images of the "Octopus," representing the railroad corporation as an insidious, grasping beast, with its many tentacles extended into government, industry, and agriculture, began to appear in cartoons, novels, and political stump speeches.[8]

The special enemy of the California antimonopolist was the Central Pacific Railroad and its parent, the Southern Pacific Railroad Company. Although the Central Pacific would, in some circles, become an icon for monopolistic power, the railroad engineer Theodore Judah and a group of Sacramento investors formed the company in 1860 to break up a monopoly held by the Sacramento Valley Railroad, which controlled transport between California and Nevada.[9] In 1861, the businessmen later known as the "Big Four," Charles Crocker, Mark Hopkins, Collis P. Huntington, and Leland Stanford, joined the Central Pacific, buying stock to fund its incorporation. Shortly thereafter, the board of directors made Stanford, Huntington, and Hopkins the company's president, vice president, and treasurer, respectively. Beginning in 1862, the federal government provided public-land grants to the Central Pacific for the completion of a transcontinental line. Stanford, who became governor of California in that same year, used his office to lavish favors on his company. He pushed for the issuance of state bonds to fund railroad construction, facilitated local communities' purchase of company stock, and blocked rival appeals for government aid.[10] Meanwhile, the company began to consolidate ownership of smaller regional railroads throughout California, Oregon, and the Southwest.[11] Drawing capital from an international pool of investors to supplement government subsidies, the Central Pacific Railroad Company was among the largest firms of its time.

The combination of vast land grants and political influence made it easy for early railroad reformers to link the older, agrarian danger of land monopoly and the newer, industrial danger of railroad monopoly. Henry George made the connection explicit in his 1871 pamphlet, *Our Land and Land Policy*. George accused the federal government of misappropriating public lands through the generous land grants extended to railroad corporations: "Since the day when Esau sold his birthright for a mess of pottage we may search history in vain for any parallel to such concessions." He lamented that the "25,600 acres of land for the building of one mile of railroad" would have been "land enough for 256 good-sized American farms."[12] Rather than proliferating opportunities for small freeholding,

the government had, in George's eyes, squandered a public good to construct a private railroad empire. George did not acknowledge the fact that
railroad corporations, to guarantee that there would be customers for their
services, sold much of their land to settlers.[13] To do so would have dis-
torted the picture George wanted to paint: a picture of a corrupt political
economy in service of the corporation and not the individual.

George had the ear of the Democratic governor Henry Haight. In
1871, when Haight sought reelection, he focused his campaign on the
issue of subsidies. Subsidizing railroad construction with public funds
and land, according to Haight, represented a form of unfair taxation. Like
George, Haight invoked anti–land monopolist rhetoric to make the social costs of railroad subsidies clear. He asked "whether the homestead
and property—large and small—acquired by industry and enterprise shall
be enjoyed by its owner . . . or whether it shall be in whole or in part
wrested from its owner to fill the coffers of those who for their own profit
choose to embark in railway construction and who have already at public cost accumulated colossal fortunes." Haight described subsidies as a
"monstrous system of taxing out of existence farmers and small property holders" and "violations of natural rights." The invocation of natural
rights and the references to small freeholders recalled an older language
of Jeffersonian agrarianism. For Haight, the campaign against railroad subsidies served the agrarian republican ideal of self-governance: "We are on
the eve of a great struggle in 1872. It is not manifest that on one side will
be the manufacturing, railway, and banking corporations contending for
power and exclusive privileges and on the other side the people contending for equal rights and especially for the right of governing themselves."[14] Publicly declaring his intention to run for reelection, Haight
reasserted his opposition to the "profligate grants of the public domain
to corporations, regardless of the rights of settlers," and this declaration
became integral to the California Democrat's platform.[15] Yet Haight was
not resolute in his opposition to the railroad corporations. Privately,
he wrote to a friend, "I am far from cherishing hostility to corporations
within their proper sphere." Corporations, after all, "execute works of
great public utility and ought to be fostered by all legislative methods."[16]
He wondered if the state could reap the benefits of corporate capitalism
without sacrificing individual freedoms. The railroad was foundational to
industrial development, but surely, there had to be some limits to the
corporation's power. His ambivalence led him to vacillate in campaign
speeches: "Not that we desire to deny corporations anything which a liberal policy would fairly suggest, but we do desire to see that governments,

state and federal, [are] administered for the benefit of the whole people and not for the benefit of a privileged few."[17]

That ambivalence may have lost Haight the election to Republican legislator Newton Booth. Booth was a rather late arrival to anti-railroad politics. As a state senator in the 1860s, he established himself as a "friend" to the Central Pacific. He lobbied against bills that reduced government subsidies or restricted the company's freedoms.[18] But, by the time he became the Republican candidate for governor in 1871, he had seemingly undergone a change of heart. As a contender for the Republican nomination, Booth circulated a public letter declaring his anti-railroad stance in no uncertain terms: "To avoid misapprehension, I am opposed to granting subsidies to railroads by the state, counties, cities, or towns of California."[19] His campaign centered on public regulation of private monopolies. Accepting the nomination, he asked his audience, "Shall this government be and remain a mighty agency of civilization, the protector of all, or shall it be run as a close corporation to enrich the few?"[20] Like Haight, he employed an agrarian vocabulary when he called for an end to the railroad subsidies that he had once championed in the state legislature: "For us this question of subsidy and anti-subsidy has a far broader significance than any partial application would assign to it. It means... whatever a man has, whether it be broad acres or a narrow home, whatever he has acquired by his industry and enterprise, is his."[21] Invoking similar language, California Republicans adopted a platform that stated its opposition to subsidies and its support of reserving public lands for actual settlers: "The concentration of the landed property of the country in the possession and ownership of a few, to the exclusion of the many, is in contravention of the theory of American government, subversive of the rights, liberties, and happiness of the masses of the people, and, if permitted, would inevitably terminate in the speedy establishment of an aristocracy upon the ruins of our free institutions."[22] Since the 1840s, the opposition to monopoly had alternated between the party platforms of Democrats and Republicans, but the 1871 election foretold of antimonopolism's broadening appeal among voters; both major parties claimed the reform ideology as their own.

## The Nature of Monopolies

New scholarship on the American political economy accompanied the rising popularity of antimonopolist politics. In the 1880s, American economists, trained in Germany, returned to the United States to rethink competition and challenge the laissez-faire model of classical economics.[23]

Arthur T. Hadley, a Yale University professor, led the vanguard. In 1884, he argued that industries requiring large, "permanent" investments of capital tended toward "combinations." The high fixed costs associated with railroad construction and operation meant that the marginal productivity of railroads increased with the level of output and its costs decreased. Competition forced railroads to slash rates simply to cover their fixed costs, which left them holding substantial variable costs, compelled them to operate at a loss, and eventually, drove them into bankruptcy. Therefore, in such industries, the classical economic dogma equating efficiency with free competition simply did not work. Hadley stopped short of calling railroads inevitable or "natural" monopolies, but he created an opening for other economists to think differently about how Gilded Age industries should be organized, encouraged, and governed to benefit the masses.[24]

The scholars that followed in Hadley's wake tended to promote federal regulation as a check on private monopolies.[25] Henry Carter Adams explained the necessity in *Relation of the State to Industrial Action.* This short book was published by the newly formed American Economic Association in 1887, the same year as the passage of the Interstate Commerce Act, which established a federal commission to regulate monopoly and restraint of trade among growing interstate business networks—particularly railroads—where the existing state laws had no jurisdiction.[26] Adams was a statistician for the commission. Drawing on his research on railroads, Adams concurred with Hadley that free competition made large, capital-intensive industries less efficient. Adams argued that not only did such industries "inevitably" grow into monopolies, but that there were also "benefits" to that form of industrial organization for the American public. Industries like the railroads and the telegraph sparked the boom years of the Gilded Age economy, and their failures—the result of corruption and inefficiencies, according to Adams—triggered the busts. Yet Adams was not so naive as to believe that the benefits of monopoly would accrue to all members of society. For industries that were "by nature" monopolies, he believed that regulation by a democratically elected government would eliminate corruption and protect public interest: "It should be the purpose of all laws, touching matters of business, to maintain the beneficent results of competitive action while guarding society from the evil consequences of unrestrained competition."[27]

Adams's peer, the Johns Hopkins professor Richard T. Ely, advocated a more radical approach to guarding society from the "evils" of monopoly. Labor unrest and the economic disparities of the Gilded Age deeply troubled Ely, and he infused his research with a moral imperative to achieve a more equitable distribution of wealth.[28] He had read and appreciated George's *Progress and Poverty*, but his vision for antimonopolist reform extended beyond the tax on land values.[29] Picking up where Hadley and Adams left off, Ely agreed that the railroads and the telegraph constituted "natural" monopolies, and thus, they were best operated by a single owner, but he went one step further. Ely determined that that single owner should be the federal government, answerable to the people, not a private corporation, answerable to no one but its shareholders.[30] Ownership by a democratically elected government, Ely reasoned, would ensure that the efficiencies of monopoly accrued to the public. He encouraged his readers to imagine how things might look if railways had been nationalized: "How differently would the wealth of the United States today be distributed!"[31] Yet, like George, Ely was careful to differentiate his vision from that of the socialists. Public ownership only made sense in industries that were most efficiently organized as monopolies. In all other cases, Ely remained a faithful adherent to free competition and laissez-faire. He believed in preserving private property as much as he believed in protections for labor, and he hoped that nationalizing natural monopolies might accomplish both ends.[32]

Thus, from Adams to Ely, the new political economists arrayed themselves on a reform spectrum from regulation to nationalization. Naturalizing monopoly may have stripped some of its opprobrium, but it did not release government from its obligation to protect citizens from concentrated power. The desire for a moral economy persisted even among those scholars who saw technological and economic imperatives as rational, neutral, and unchanging.[33] By the end of the 1880s, that thinking had spread beyond academic circles into the ranks of California's antimonopolist politicians and reformers.[34] In the 1880s and 1890s, public control of private monopolies became the rallying cry of California antimonopolists, but the forms and methods remained in question. To what extent would the government control private corporations? What laws and institutions would guide such interventions? And could a government with unprecedented and expanded powers uphold the freedoms nineteenth-century Americans cherished and expected?

## *Regulation vs. Nationalization*

Early experiments in railroad regulation centered on elected commissions, which were tasked with protecting farmers and merchants from exploitative transportation rates. In the absence of government oversight, private railroad companies could seemingly set and change their rates at will, and the shippers, merchants, and farmers who depended on rail service suffered for it. In 1874, the San Francisco Chamber of Commerce, representing the city's shippers, organized a committee to urge the state legislature to appoint a railroad commission, as other states had. This commission would fix maximum freights and fares. Members of the California State Grange, the state's branch of the national farmers' association, seconded the Chamber of Commerce's demand, and the state legislature responded by appointing a regulatory commission in 1878.[35] The commission succeeded only in giving railroad critics a new target. Throughout the 1880s and 1890s, California reformers and politicians wrangled over the commission's composition, competence, and corruptibility. Although the commission remained the government's primary lever of power, a new generation of antimonopolists began to seek alternative methods to wrangle the Octopus.[36]

The call for regulation defined the political career of Stephen Mallory White (fig. 11). Just as James McClatchy and Charles Robinson had witnessed and participated in the changing meanings of squatters' rights in the 1850s, so, too, did White experience and help shape the landscape of antimonopolism in the last two decades of the nineteenth century. White believed that the federal government had the moral obligation to protect producers in an industrial society, and, to that end, he advocated regulation to prevent the exploitation of farmers, merchants, and shippers and to diminish the railroad corporations' influence over politicians. One of his biographers, Edith Dobie, speculated that White's antimonopolism was the result of his youth spent on a farm in Santa Cruz, where he "probably heard the grievances of the farmers and the corruption of party politics discussed at length."[37] White never commented on the matter. Although White did indeed grow up on a farm, it was hardly of the yeoman variety. White's parents had come to California during the Gold Rush and used their earnings from a lucrative mercantile business in San Francisco to buy a large tract of land in Santa Cruz. They hired tenants and laborers to work the land.[38] Yet antimonopolism, even if it was not the squatter's anti–land monopolism, still ran in White's blood. His father, William White, was a prominent Democrat in the 1860s, but he switched allegiances to the Workingmen's Party in the 1870s. As a member of the Workingmen's Party, he fought government corruption, Chinese immigration, and railroad monopolies, and he unsuccessfully ran for governor on the party's ticket in 1879.[39]

Stephen White made his first foray into politics in the 1870s as an upstart lawyer in Los Angeles. Shortly after becoming part of the Democratic

Party, he defected from it. He joined a group of Democrats who splintered from the party in 1873 to unite with anti-railroad Republicans and California State Grange members in the People's Independent Party. Dedicated to "railroad and legislative reform," their party platform was essentially a list of farmers' grievances. The new party resolved to "wage no war against railroads or other modes of transportation . . . only so far as their treatment of the farming interest is manifestly unjust and oppressive. So far as they are governed by honesty and fair dealing, our aims and interests are identical."[40] The Independents recognized how modern agriculture depended on railroads to access markets. The party did not, therefore, oppose railroads, but rather railroad monopoly, which threatened to "cripple and crush out the vitality of this great paramount industry of the country, then we may be compelled to beat our plowshares into swords and our pruning hooks into spears, and go after the common enemy."[41] The Independents had a short, but highly successful lifespan. They won a majority in the state legislature and a U.S. Senate seat for their candidate, Newton Booth, who had defeated Haight on an anti-railroad ticket in 1871.[42] When the Independents dissolved in 1877, White returned to the Democrats and began working his way up through the party hierarchy.[43] In the same year, the party fractured again when a faction of urban workers followed White's father and Denis Kearney to form the Workingmen's Party.[44] By 1880, the Independent Party was a distant memory, the energy behind the Workingmen's Party had dissipated, and the Democrats began to rebuild around railroad reform. A coalition of antimonopolists led by Stephen White, the newspaper editor William Randolph Hearst, and the San Francisco party boss Christopher A. Buckley assumed leadership of local chapters and dominated the party.[45] There were dissenters, who favored a more laissez-faire approach to guarantee freedom of competition and whom White labeled "Railroad Democrats," but they comprised a minority and did not threaten the renewed party cohesion.

In California, antimonopolism became synonymous with railroad reform, and its popularity among voters meant that state elections pitted one strident anti-railroad candidate against another. In the 1882 election, the Democrats nominated George Stoneman, a winegrower, who had famously lowered rates while he was the railroad commissioner. White thought favorably of Stoneman and saw him as an appropriate representative for the antimonopolist cause. Stoneman promised to lower freight rates and fares, compel railroads to pay taxes, and end the "exactions and injustice" perpetrated by the railroad corporations. Despite the new focus

FIGURE 11.  U.S. Senator Stephen Mallory White. Courtesy of the U.S. Senate
Historical Office.

on railroad monopoly, antimonopolist politics in this period still relied on an old agrarian language. The California Democratic platform resolved that "all railroad land grants, forfeited by reason of the non-fulfillment of the contracts, should be immediately revoked by the government, and that hereafter the domain should be reserved exclusively as homes for actual settlers."[46] The Republican platform similarly denounced the railroad in agrarian language.[47] The Republicans advocated lower freight rates and fares, increased regulation, tax enforcement, and an end to subsidies: "We declare that railroad companies . . . must be kept subordinate to the interests of the people, and within governmental control. The people should be protected by law from any abuse or unjust exactions."[48] The party put forth a "railroad reform" candidate, Morris Estee, a state legislator who helped establish the railroad commission. In 1882, Stoneman and the Democrats swept the state elections, taking the governorship, all congressional seats, a majority in the legislature, and the three positions on the railroad commission. Calling for a higher tax rate for the Southern Pacific Railroad, White won the election for Los Angeles attorney general by a significant margin.[49]

Despite the enthusiasm for antimonopolism during the campaign, actual reform proved elusive for Stoneman's administration. The newly elected railroad commissioners were disappointingly cautious and conservative. Fearful of crippling the transportation industry, the commission took a hands-off approach to railroad rate schedules.[50] Stoneman, meanwhile, gave himself a thankless task: forcing the railroad corporations to pay taxes owed under the terms of the new state constitution, which had been ratified in 1879. Lawyers for the Central Pacific and Southern Pacific companies claimed that the tax, which applied only to mortgages held by corporations and not those held by individuals, violated the Fourteenth Amendment of the U.S. Constitution, and they challenged the California tax scheme in the federal courts. In the fall of 1882, U.S. Supreme Court Justice Stephen J. Field presided over the precedent-setting case, *County of San Mateo v. Southern Pacific Railroad Company.*

Field was one of White's so-called Railroad Democrats. A forty-niner and lawyer-turned-jurist, Field's affiliation with the California Democratic Party began early, with a failed effort to win the party's nomination for state legislature in 1851. Although he eventually ran and won in that year as an Independent in Yuba County, north of Sacramento, he continued to court favor with the Democrats like a besotted suitor. It may have seemed an odd coupling for a lawyer who hobnobbed with elite landowners and treated preemption rights with open contempt. In fact, it had been Field's antagonistic relationship with Yuba County squatters that scuttled his original bid for the Democratic nomination in 1851.[51] Yet Field doggedly pursued the alliance with the Democrats for two reasons, one expedient and the other ideological. First, Field had grand aspirations to become a U.S. senator, and, in the 1850s, he could not do so without the support of the state's dominant party. Although he never achieved that goal, he parlayed a failed bid for the senatorship in 1855 into the party's nomination for California supreme court justice in 1857.[52] Secondly, Field's political and juridical worldview connected him, not to White's regulatory antimonopolists, but to an older breed of Jacksonian Democrats, who feared overweening state power.[53] White's antimonopolism and Field's laissez-faire doctrine were two branches of the same Jacksonian family tree, joined by their belief in freedom of competition and contract but diverging on their understanding of how the federal government should best protect those freedoms. As a California supreme court justice, Field championed private property rights, applying liberal interpretations of the California Land Act of 1851 to favor Mexican land grantees and discount counterclaims.[54] Noting that the United States had promised to protect Mexican property holders under the Treaty of Guadalupe Hidalgo, Field was unmoved by arguments that the grants constituted land monopolies and should be dismantled by the government. "It was not for the Supreme Court of California to question the wisdom or policy of Mexico in making grants of such large portions of her domain," he wrote in his memoirs.[55] Field's decisions in cases involving Mexican land grants revealed his determination to protect individuals entering into contracts from interference by the state. In 1863, Field ascended to the U.S. Supreme Court, where he argued for a narrow range of state powers over private monopolies. His famous dissenting opinions in the 1873 Slaughterhouse cases and the 1877 *Munn v. Illinois* decision outlined his belief that government intervention—such as price or rate regulation—was permissible only when monopolies were "dedicated by their owner to public purposes."[56] By the 1880s, when he heard testimony in *County of San Mateo v. Southern Pacific Railroad Company*, he had come to disparage antimonopolist interventions as "agrarian and communistic." Whereas White embraced government regulation, Field feared that it diminished individual liberties and violated private firms' constitutional rights to enter freely into contracts. Not surprisingly, then, Field dismissed the California tax scheme as "palpable and gross" discrimination against the railroad.[57]

Despite their success in the courts, railroad executives felt obliged to maintain positive public relations and to extend an olive branch to state and county governments by paying some portion of the taxes. What ensued was a flurry of offers and counteroffers. Stoneman estimated that the Central Pacific and Southern Pacific owed $2,730,303.09 in taxes and penalties. Ultimately, the railroad companies offered to pay the taxes but not the penalties. After initial reluctance, California Attorney General Edward C. Marshall, a Democrat, accepted the compromise in the spring of 1884 because it maintained the state's right to tax the railroad companies. Marshall hoped it would appease antimonopolist Democrats in his party by maintaining the supremacy of the state over the corporation. Privately, perhaps, Marshall already sensed what he would later admit openly: the state would never compel the railroads to pay the full amount, and the ongoing effort to force them to do so would bankrupt the state. Not only was litigation costly, but the Southern Pacific was also the biggest taxpayer in the state, even with the adjustment. California needed the revenues its taxes provided.[58]

Marshall's decision reflected the divisions within the Democratic Party. Not all members were equally committed to antimonopolist reform. White was furious with Marshall's capitulation, and, in a letter to Stoneman, he called Marshall an "ass" and a "knave."[59] But as Los Angeles County's attorney general, White had limited ability to protest the compromise. He advised the County Board of Supervisors to refuse an adjusted settlement.[60] Stoneman also refused to compromise and issued an injunction, which Marshall ignored. In 1884, the year that the Southern Pacific Railroad Company absorbed the Central Pacific, railroad executives began issuing payments for far less than Stoneman and other state officials believed they owed. Stoneman called the compromise "humiliating," and, in response, the Democrat-led state legislature embarked on a frenzy of anti-railroad measures with thirty-two bills in the senate and sixty-three in the assembly. New restrictions on railroad rates and operations passed by large margins in the assembly, where antimonopolist Democrats predominated, but they were stymied in the senate, where thirteen conservative Democrats united with the Republican minority to defeat the bills, which they feared would damage the California economy.[61]

Sensing that the Democrats were in danger of fragmenting as they had in the 1870s, White rallied fellow antimonopolists William D. English and Delphin M. Delmas to put down the Railroad Democrats. In June 1884, at the party's state convention in Stockton, the antimonopolists wrested control of key leadership positions and thwarted Field's aspirations to the presidential nomination. They also successfully expelled Marshall and the thirteen conservative state senators from the party.[62]

Writing to Stoneman in the weeks after the convention, White declared, "The Dem[ocratic] party is now clearly the anti-monopoly party of Cal[ifornia]. Of this there is no question."[63]

An economic boom in the mid-1880s and the construction of a new rail line by the Atchison, Topeka, and Santa Fe Railroad Company in Southern California in 1885 temporarily quieted the anti-railroad fervor as a rate war between the new railroad and the Southern Pacific lowered the cost of freights and fares and ushered in a wave of new immigration and tourism that boosted the state economy.[64] Meanwhile, national legislation reflected widespread acceptance of antimonopolist principles. In 1887, Congress passed the Interstate Commerce Act, and White's call for regulation seemed to have been answered at the federal level.[65] Three years later, Congress passed the Sherman Antitrust Act, the most sweeping and influential piece of nineteenth-century antimonopoly legislation. It mandated federal protections against "unlawful restraints" on trade and commerce, and several states followed up with their own antitrust laws, patterned on the Sherman Act.[66] White and his fellow antimonopolists settled into a period of self-satisfied inactivity.

With California antimonopolist politics in a semi-dormant state and the legislature in recess, White and his law partner, John D. Bicknell, began to work as defense attorneys for the Southern Pacific in right-of-way and personal-injury suits. White and Bicknell were among the leading lawyers in Southern California, and with Bicknell's expertise in Mexican land grant adjudication, it came as no surprise that the Southern Pacific enlisted their services. White's tenure with the Southern Pacific between 1887 and 1889 might seem to recast his antimonopolism as mere political opportunism, but it was in fact consistent with the nature of his reform ideals: he never claimed to oppose land monopoly. Anti–land monopolist concerns about railroad companies appropriating land from "true cultivators" were insignificant to White. He did not offer sympathy or generosity in his dealings with landholders who impeded the railroads' right-of-way. When property owners balked at the railroad's offer to purchase their land, White sued them in court.[67] White recognized that California producers needed the railroad and that the railroad needed land. He was of a generation of antimonopolists who aimed to regulate, not eliminate, private monopolies. Nevertheless, with an eye to public scrutiny, White was careful to sever all ties with the railroad company when he returned to the legislature in January 1889.[68]

California's quiescent period of anti-railroad sentiment did not last long. Speculation in the boom times fueled a recession in 1890 and a widespread financial panic in 1893, which resuscitated antimonopolist politics and renewed White's fervor for the cause. But the political landscape had changed, and antimonopolist Democrats like White found themselves competing for voters with a new political party that swept out of the Midwest and across the country: the Populists, or the People's Party. The emergence of the People's Party reflected a larger shift in antimonopolist reform. By the late 1880s, a fault line had developed between two dominant interpretations of antimonopolism. On one side were antimonopolists like Stephen Mallory White, who aimed to preserve capitalism and private property in some measure. For White, antimonopoly was the key to maintaining free competition and individual liberties. White distinguished himself from postbellum laissez-faire liberals by advocating limits to concentrated wealth and power through targeted government intervention. On the other side of the fault line was a growing movement of radical agrarians, schooled as members of the Farmers' Alliance and then the Populist Party.[69] The more radical antimonopolists called for not only government regulation but also government ownership of natural monopolies in the hopes that restricting competition there would free it elsewhere.[70] At their national convention in Omaha in 1892, the Populist Party articulated the terms of their statist antimonopolism: "We believe that the power of government—in other words, of the people—should be expanded . . . as rapidly and as far as the good sense of an intelligent people and the teachings of experience shall justify, to the end that oppression, injustice, and poverty shall eventually cease in the land."[71] Their call for government ownership of natural monopolies grew out of their belief that small, independent farmers could not compete with large-scale industrial corporations in the late nineteenth century.[72] "The Populists," historian Charles Postel writes, "wanted active government to ensure fair access to the benefits of modernity."[73] In Omaha, the Populists advanced a three-part antimonopolist platform that targeted bank, railroad, and land monopolies. They aimed to restore power and independence to the "plain people," the producing classes, and to put down private monopolies: "The fruits of the toil of millions are boldly stolen to build up colossal fortunes for a few. . . . From the same prolific womb of governmental injustice we breed the two great classes—tramps and millionaires."[74]

Thomas Vincent Cator became White's chief political rival among the California Populists. Cator's career charted a different path for the late nineteenth-century antimonopolist. Whereas White was, despite a brief flirtation with the People's Independent Party, a staunch Democrat,

Cator was a political dilettante. In the course of a decade, he unsuccessfully ran for office as an Anti-Monopolist, a Republican, a Democrat, a Prohibitionist, a Nationalist, a Know-Nothing, and finally, in 1893, as a Populist. A native of New York and a longtime resident of New Jersey, his career in antimonopolism began in 1881 when he became a member of the National Anti-Monopoly League and participated in the group efforts to bring about the Interstate Commerce Act of 1887. In 1889, after a long illness, he moved to San Francisco. There, he encountered the Nationalist movement, which was inspired by Edward Bellamy's reform novel, *Looking Backward, 2000–1887*. Published in 1888, *Looking Backward* described the United States in the year 2000 as a Christian socialist utopia. More than half a million copies of the novel sold in subsequent years, and it inspired a wave of enthusiasm for socialist reform.[75] Nationalist clubs began to crop up in Boston in 1888, and the movement spread from there. The club in San Francisco boasted two hundred members, including Cator.[76]

In 1890, Cator made his public speaking debut in California at a Fourth of July celebration at the Metropolitan Temple in San Francisco. Rambling and rife with platitudes, his speech lamented the "increasing impoverishment of producers." He did not advance or elaborate the antimonopolist logic as much as he reiterated well-rehearsed themes. Cator urged his audience to recognize that "in the midst of unlimited natural and national wealth, the masses are in poverty and largely ignorant.... those who produce most have least. Those who produce nothing frequently have superabundance."[77] He parroted the old producerist remedies: "Labor should be entitled to what it produces. No one should be required to give a portion of his labor to another, for one's labor is his life, and to take a portion of one's lifetime is to reduce him to slavery."[78] His review would not have been complete without mention of land reform. As he concluded his speech, Cator noted, "We are by nature creatures of the soil, as well as of light. Ere we came into being the earth was created for us. Without access to it, we cannot blossom or fructify.... The common fountain for production, wealth, and enjoyment must be the possession, the right of all."[79] The speech, which was published as a pamphlet under the title *Millionaires or Morals: Which Shall Rule?*, introduced Cator to the public as an unflinching antimonopolist.

In the fall, the American Party (also known as the Know-Nothing Party), a nativist, anti-Catholic organization, nominated Cator as its candidate for Congress, and he ran on typical antimonopolist principles. His campaign materials highlighted his record as a member of the

Anti-Monopoly League, called him a friend to the workingman, and promised he would uphold Chinese exclusion. Like so many California politicians before him, Cator condemned the railroads: "The greed, the rapacity of [the Southern Pacific] knows no bounds."[80] But the land question was notably absent from his rhetoric. He did not use anti–land monopolism as a means of making sense of the railroad corporation's crimes against the republic. He did not need to. The problem with the railroad was not that it appropriated land that small producers might have put to better use. The problem was that exorbitant freight rates hamstrung producers and shippers. Cator claimed that government ownership of the railroads was the only way to guarantee lower rates and, by extension, the prosperity and independence of the American people.[81] The underlying logic was that independence stemmed from untrammeled access to markets. Cator implicitly severed the tie between independence and landholding.

When infighting among the California Nationalists brought about the party's downfall in 1890, and the members split between the Socialist Labor Party and the emergent Populist Party, Cator went with the Populists. In the People's Party, he found a forum for his radical reform ideals. The People's Party in California followed the broad strokes of the national party. The state's real estate boom of the mid-1880s led to overproduction and a decline in farm product prices. In 1890, a group of farmers gathered in San Jose to organize the state Farmers' Alliance to pressure Democrats and Republicans to break up land and transportation monopolies.[82] When bipartisanship failed to protect producers' rights, the members of the alliance began to agitate for a third party. In 1892, the Farmers' Alliance joined forces with various independent labor organizations to form an antimonopolist coalition of farmers and industrial workers. Echoing the national Populist platform, California's People's Party affirmed its commitment to currency reform, reservation of public lands for actual settlers, and government ownership of natural monopolies, including the railroad, telegraph, and telephone.[83] The People's Party nominated candidates for public office. Cator, who worked the alliance lecture circuit, received the nomination for presidential elector and became part of the California delegation to the first national convention of Populists in Omaha.[84]

In the lead-up to the 1892 elections, Cator toured California, espousing his reform philosophy. "The time is ripe! The hour has come!" he declared. "The necessity is urgent for Government Ownerships of Railroads and Telegraphs."[85] Regulation, he claimed, had proven ineffective, and consolidation had continued unabated, but there was no turning back to a preindustrial, agrarian economy: "The railway has become the great highway of nations. The producer must have railroads, more and more of them, of the greatest efficiency and operated at the least proper cost."[86] Cator did not advocate for the government to break up railroad monopolies. Rather, he advocated replacing private monopolies with public ones: "Corporations which own railroads and seek the largest possible dividends cannot be trustees for the people. They simply seek their own profit. How then can the public control them without owning them? ... It is not Government ownership of railroads, but *private ownership*, which will destroy the Republic."[87] Cator believed that the government, as the trustee for the people, would quiet labor unrest, guarantee producers low transportation costs, and end political corruption.

In California, as in the nation, Democrats watched and worried as their farm and labor constituencies joined the Populists. Reports circulated in antimonopolist newspapers like San Francisco's *Examiner* that White's former employment with the Southern Pacific made him a "railroad man," which forced him to go on the defensive.[88] Cator's call for nationalizing railroads compelled White to drift uncomfortably from his staunch defense of regulation: "If it be true that we cannot regulate these corporations by means of a commission, there is but one way to deal with them and that is we must run railroads ourselves."[89] Yet White quickly backtracked on what seemed like a radical departure from regulatory antimonopolism: "I do not mean that we shall confiscate property if we cannot settle the matter through present channels but we must provide for transportation which will not absorb the profits of agriculture and the results of the efforts of toil."[90] White envisioned nationalizing the railroads as a last resort.

Despite his concerns about nationalization schemes, White recognized the political advantages of fusing with the Populists to support one another's candidates over Republican opponents for the legislature and county offices. Cator was initially open to the idea of forging such an agreement with the Democrats. In 1891, he had exchanged a few letters with White on their shared interest in election reform, but he grew resolutely independent during the election year.[91] While White managed to develop a strong relationship with other Populists, including the Farmers' Alliance president, Marion Cannon, Cator refused to endorse the Democrats in his district.[92] In the 1892 elections, the Populists won significant victories. Although their gubernatorial candidate did not fare as well as the party would have liked, the Populists secured eight seats in the state assembly, and Cannon took a congressional seat.

With mounting trepidation, White observed Cator's ascent up the leadership ranks of the People's Party. Their rivalry came to a head with the election of the U.S. senator. White had long dreamt of serving in the Senate, and with the support of nearly all the Democrats of Southern California and most of the San Francisco delegation, he had every reason to expect that the office would be his. All he needed was the support of the eight newly elected Populists in the assembly. But rumors began to circulate that Cator, too, was making a bid for the senatorship.[93] White urged Cannon to rein in Cator: "I have no doubt that I can carry the Democratic caucus; but I wish you could get the Peoples party men in line so that they would have a definite policy on this subject. Cator is trying to control them, and my idea is that the best course that can be adopted is to have you go around and see the individual members and also be present at Sacramento when they are there."[94] Other prominent Democrats and even some Populists circulated letters, pressuring the eight People's Party assemblymen to support White over Cator, but largely to no avail. In the January vote, only one Populist, White's good friend from Los Angeles, Thomas J. Kerns, broke with his party to vote for White. Fortunately for White, one vote was enough. He scraped by with a narrow victory.[95]

## Taming the Octopus

In 1893, the year White went to Washington, D.C., to begin his term in the Senate, the nation's economy stumbled and fell to its knees. The exuberance of federally subsidized expansion in the agricultural and industrial sectors had precipitated the boom years of the 1880s, but it also encouraged overproduction, over-leveraging, and irresponsible speculation. Mechanized agriculture increased output of staple crops but then yielded market glut, not profits. Overseas markets provided little outlet for surplus American goods as financial panics swept through importing countries, like France and England, between 1889 and 1895.[96] The onset of an agricultural depression was just one of the crises confronting the nation in 1893. The giddy extension of railroad lines in the post–Civil War era had lowered transportation costs as it heightened competition among companies already beleaguered by indebtedness. Slashing rates to lure customers from rival lines, railroad companies like the Northern Pacific, the Atchison, and the Union Pacific could not cover their fixed operating expenses. With revenues and security prices plummeting and sources of foreign capital all but dried up, many railroad companies declared bankruptcy and went into receivership.[97] Failure in the railroad-building industry rippled out to its suppliers of iron and steel.[98] Foreclosures, bankruptcies, and credit defaults destroyed the liquidity of America's banks, and its government, shackled to the gold standard, could not expand the money supply to combat deflation.[99] The United States had experienced periods of economic contraction before, but the recession following the Panic of 1893 was its longest and deepest until the Great Depression of the 1930s.

The Panic of 1893 renewed antimonopolist fervor as railroad corporations took much of the blame for the financial meltdown. In California, public hostility toward the Southern Pacific—remarkably solvent during the depression—intensified. Railroad executives found themselves unable to exert the political influence they had once had in California, threatening the Octopus with extinction. Historians seeking to demonstrate this fact typically cite the examples of the American Railway Union strike of 1894 and the Los Angeles Free Harbor controversy of 1896. Pitting antimonopolists against railroad executives, these events suggested the strength of anti-railroad sentiment, and, in the case of the Free Harbor controversy, its power to effect change.[100] The fight to secure federal funding for a harbor in San Pedro was well timed for White, who needed to win back his antimonopolist credentials after being maligned as a railroad man during the elections. The real estate boom of the mid-1880s had transformed Los Angeles into a major population center of some fifty thousand residents with a bustling tourism industry and a gateway to trans-Pacific commerce. Unlike San Francisco, however, the Los Angeles coastline did not boast a natural harbor, and the city needed federal funding to develop one. The small existing harbor at San Pedro seemed like a good candidate for such a project. In the 1880s, the Los Angeles Chamber of Commerce began lobbying Congress for an appropriation to expand the breakwater and to deepen the harbor to accommodate larger ships. Initially, the Southern Pacific backed the plan. It had acquired most of the land around the small seaport and had built a rail line in 1888. But the company's construction plans ground to a halt when its president, Collis Huntington, alighted on another plan in 1890. As the site for Los Angeles's deep-water port, Huntington favored Santa Monica. The natural geography of the harbor at Santa Monica was such that the Southern Pacific, which had already acquired much of the land and the right-of-way, could exclude potential rivals and monopolize access. Huntington began a vigorous lobbying campaign to get Congress to appropriate funds for Santa Monica.[101] Supporters of the harbor at San Pedro—in particular, the owners of Southern Pacific's rival, the Los Angeles Terminal Railway

Company—refused to back down. The San Pedro faction organized a Free Harbor League, the name implying that their side opposed monopoly and supported free competition. A fight ensued, with each side commissioning its own engineering reports and expert testimony extolling the virtues of the harbor of its choice.[102]

As a new senator, White became involved with the issue. With energetic rhetoric, he brought the "Free Harbor Fight" to the Senate floor. In 1896, White urged Congress to appoint an independent board of experts before determining whether one harbor site was better suited to development than the other: "If the advocates of Santa Monica believe that they have the meritorious side, then let them face a commission chosen upon impartial lines. . . . Until some fair, competent, and disinterested man, appointed according to law, has determined that this appropriation is justifiable, I shall continue to oppose it and to raise my voice against it, even though I stand alone."[103] The committee adopted his proposal, and the board submitted its report in March 1897. The report recognized San Pedro as the superior location for a deep-water port.[104] When construction began in San Pedro in April 1899, White, by then no longer a senator, was present to give a celebratory address in which he described the harbor as a symbol of freedom over tyranny, of civilization over barbarity. "The harbor construction," he said, "paid for by the people for their benefit and for their advancement, is a product of free institutions."[105] White claimed the harbor as a victory for antimonopolists, and his association with the Free Harbor Fight restored his reputation as a railroad reformer. In 1896, Telfair Creighton, the president of the Herald Publishing Company in Los Angeles, sent a telegram to White in Washington, D.C.: "Your fight for San Pedro has made you by far the most popular man in California."[106]

During White's time in the Senate, regulatory antimonopolism eclipsed other expressions of antimonopolist reform, including Populism. In the 1896 elections, Democrats and Populists pursued strategies of fusion, but the Populists' continued calls for nationalizing railroads and other "natural" monopolies threatened to undermine the alliance. White, newly elected as a U.S. senator, wrote to Cannon in a private letter: "I am going to make a few suggestions in regard to your populist platform. You undertake to accomplish too much at once." White cautioned Cannon against seeking reforms that were too radical: "You offer so many changes that business men are afraid to risk the result, untried. Cut it down; abbreviate considerably."[107] He outlined an agenda for Cannon that included only conservative currency and banking reform and judicious support of new railroad construction. To the matter of nationalizing rail-roads, White urged Cannon to reconsider his position: "The buying up of all the railroads in the country will not gain you a vote, except with the producers and their vote you have mainly."[108] White also worried that government ownership of natural monopolies would not address the problems of industrial capitalism. Public monopolies, he reasoned, would have the same ability as private ones to enjoy unfair political privilege, sti-fle competition, and discourage new investments.

As for White's onetime rival, time had dulled Thomas Cator's com-mitment to railroad nationalization, and he began to focus on currency reform as the primary means of ameliorating conditions for farmers. He also continued to aspire to a U.S. senate seat, but he had learned an im-portant lesson from his failed attempt in 1892: he would need broader legislative support, and thus his resistance to fusion between Populists and Democrats faded. In an 1896 letter to E. M. Wardall, the state chair-man of California's People's Party, Cator described fusion as a "wise, far-reaching step." The Democrats, he wrote, "have placed themselves in a position where every honest silver man should support them."[109] In 1896, he stumped for the Democratic presidential candidate, William Jennings Bryan, and allied himself with former rival Stephen White in support of bimetallism.[110] In one letter, White joked, "There seems to be an idea upon the part of some of your friends that I can get you to do pretty near anything."[111] But in California, as in the nation at large, fusion failed to de-liver the results the Democrats and pro-silver Populists had hoped for. In-stead, fusion divided the Populists. Losing members to the right and the left, the Populists were unable to secure a base in the legislature.[112] Over-all, California antimonopolists fared very poorly in the 1896 election. The Republicans had a better-financed campaign, and they aggressively de-nounced Bryan as a "Jacobin" and bimetallism as an invitation to anar-chy.[113] These tactics enabled the Republican candidate, William McKinley, to secure eight out of nine electoral votes in California, and the Repub-licans also won a majority of the open seats in the state legislature. The results were deeply disappointing to Cator, as they were to White, who had high hopes for the fusion strategy and believed that the free-silver cause was a just one.[114]

## Too Big to Fail?

In the wake of the 1896 elections, antimonopolist politicians channeled their railroad reform efforts through the debate on repayment of the Pacific railroad debt. As the historian Maury Klein explains, the issue became "a symbol for public indignation against the devious machinations of businessmen and the overweening power of corporations."[115] It also reflected the entrenchment of White's regulatory antimonopolism and the disappearance of the land question from industrial reform. Without the land question, antimonopolist politics aimed for far less ambitious reform. In California, controversy swirled around the Central Pacific and its parent company, the Southern Pacific. Beginning in 1865, the Central Pacific had borrowed approximately $28 million in bonds from the federal government. When the Southern Pacific assumed a ninety-nine-year lease of the Central Pacific in 1884, it also took over the railroad's debt plus interest, which amounted to approximately $78 million by the mid-1890s. The bonds fell due between 1895 and 1899, but Collis Huntington let it be known that the Southern Pacific was cash poor and unable to pay. The Panic of 1893 and subsequent economic depression had severely diminished the company's revenues and reserves, and raising millions of dollars in a depressed market was impossible. Huntington proposed that the repayment be delayed from fifty to one hundred years and that the interest be slashed to a mere 0.5 percent.[116] Generally, Congress favored extending the terms of the bonds and lowering the interest rates to make repayment possible. If the railroad truly could not pay, the alternatives were canceling the debt, which would surely incite public outrage, or foreclosure, which might force Congress to assume the many burdens of the railroad's management and upkeep. Refunding the debt seemed like the most reasonable option, and a senate committee outlined a scheme in the Reilly Bill of 1894. The bill proposed to refund the debt through 3 percent bonds that matured in fifty-year terms.[117]

Californians cried foul. Outraged editorials peppered California newspapers, and the San Francisco *Examiner*, known for its antimonopolist political leanings, gathered nearly two hundred thousand signatures on a petition opposing the leniency that the Reilly Bill offered to the railroad company. In San Francisco, Mayor Adolph Sutro, who came to office on an anti–Southern Pacific platform, led a rally at the city's Metropolitan Hall to oppose the passage of the bill and to compel the railroad to pay its debts. The state legislature responded to the public uproar and, in January 1895, unanimously voted to condemn any congressional compromise with the Southern Pacific.[118] Stalwartly statist antimonopolists pressed for more drastic measures: foreclosure and nationalization. In 1894 Populist congressman Marion Cannon protested the Reilly Bill in an impassioned speech before the committee on railways and canals: "Our answer to these 'multimillionaire paupers' should be 'Pay your debts or retire from the business.'" The railroads, he insisted, were "public highways," intended for the free use of producers. He urged his fellow committee members not to extend the terms of the loan. Rather, as Thomas Cator might have done at an earlier time, Cannon called for nationalizing the railroads: "The Central Pacific, in the hands of the Government, with all the branch lines in California under its control is a magnificent property, and in a few years will be able to command such a price on the market that the debt would be secured. The government could then sell or lease the road, should it find ownership embarrassing."[119]

The government was not so convinced. The Central Pacific, with its clamoring investors, depreciating assets, and labor troubles, did not seem like such a "magnificent property." The Democrats' official stance on the Pacific railroad debt was seemingly firm but safely vague. In 1896, the national party platform declared that "no discrimination should be indulged in the Government of the United States in favor of any of its debtors."[120] For White, recovering the loaned funds and maintaining private ownership of the railroad were the primary goals. Believing nationalization was too radical, he never seriously entertained the idea of foreclosure, but he still balked at plans that afforded the railroads up to fifty years to repay the bonds. Some compromise had to be found.[121]

For the first part of White's term in the Senate, the Reilly Bill remained mired in committees and never reached the Senate floor, where White could have made a public declaration against it. Instead, White got his chance to speak out after the 1896 elections, when the Republicans used their new majority in the House of Representatives to introduce the Powers Bill. The Powers Bill favored the Southern Pacific with even lower interest rates and a lengthier extension on repayment, and it provoked a flurry of public protest, which compelled Congress to withdraw it and appoint a special commission to start anew.[122] The committee on Pacific railroad debt attached a new proposal, similarly favorable to the company, to a general deficiency bill, which passed in the House in 1896 and went before the Senate in 1898.[123] Angry Democrats in California clamored for White to stand up against the new scheme. An editorial printed in the *Los Angeles Times* exhorted Congress to grant the company no special privileges: "The Pacific railroad debts should be treated in all essential respects like private debts secured by mortgage." Foreclosing on the debts and nationalizing the railroad "would be far better than a weak and pusillanimous abdication of [the government's] rights in favor of the men who have already robbed it to the extent of millions of dollars."[124] White remained as cautious as ever. Initially, he opposed the commission's proposal. He feared that it would enable Huntington to target his lobbying efforts to just a handful of individuals and, thereby, more easily achieve his goals, but, speaking before the Senate, White declared his intent to support a modified amendment rather than rejecting it outright: "While I do not approve of any deferring of payment at all, I have deemed it best to perfect the amendment or to get it as near perfect as practicable."[125] White successfully pressed for a ten-year, not fifty-year, extension on the debt repayment and prohibiting the commission from settling for anything less than the full amount. In 1899, the general deficiency bill passed, and ultimately, the railroad company did pay back what it owed within the ten-year time frame. White patted himself on the back for a job well done. The bill avoided what he had feared most: a "give-away" to the railroad company.

White touted his amendment as representing "very radical" and "vital" change, but it did not seem so to his Californian constituents who had dreamt of the foreclosure and nationalization of the railroad.[126] White's changes were clearly designed to regulate the industrial economy without overhauling it. Not only did the compromise with the Southern Pacific enable the federal government to recoup the money it had loaned to the company, but it also affirmed that private railroad corporations were necessary and desirable. Private corporations assumed the risks, liabilities, and responsibilities that the national government was reluctant to take on.[127] For a country with deeply embedded values of economic independence and possessive individualism, rejecting nationalization upheld the supremacy of private enterprise, even in an age where the close relationship between the railroad and the government—through loans and other privileges as well as through regulation—threatened to collapse the meaningful divides between the public and private sectors.

Perhaps most importantly, the controversy and ultimate decision to refund the Pacific railroad debt reflected the dominant mode of anti-monopolism at the end of the nineteenth century. Antimonopolist reformers had learned to live with monopolies and to value them. Breaking up monopolies was no longer an imperative, as it had been for the California squatters of days gone by and as it had been for Henry George and Terence Powderly. The purpose of the state was no longer to eliminate monopolies but to harness their power. Refunding the debt was, like government subsidies and special privileges or regulations and restrictions, a means to make monopoly work for the squatter's republic.

## Conclusion

In the last decades of the nineteenth century, Stephen Mallory White's brand of regulatory antimonopolism became dominant in California and the nation. His was the antimonopolism that sought regulation and oversight rather than radical reform of industrial, corporate capitalism. It was the antimonopolism that resisted change to private property arrangements and instead sought to make corporations more benevolent, to maximize their benefits to society, and to minimize their costs. It was the antimonopolism that accepted and even embraced corporate monopoly and its efficiencies. It was the antimonopolism that sought a peaceful coexistence with monopoly. Regulatory antimonopolism guided federal policies toward trusts and monopolies into the early twentieth century, and more broadly, it became the antimonopolism that characterized Progressive reform.[128]

That Stephen White's more conservative brand of antimonopolism won out over the more radical calls for nationalization reflected the optimism of the age. Naive, perhaps, but not disingenuous, White believed that government could tame the Octopus and make it perform for the people. Firmly lodged at the center of the regulatory state was the notion that big business was a permanent fixture in the American economic landscape, and good governance sought compromise and reconciliation between its needs and those of the public good. The opposition to land monopoly, its promise to break up concentrated wealth and empower producers, had receded from the center of antimonopolist politics and taken with it some moral clarity.

OUTCASTS IN HEAVEN ITSELF

L ate nineteenth-century Americans asked the land question to make sense of their changing world. They recalled the land disputes of the Gold Rush era and examined corporate land grabs in the Gilded Age as a way of thinking about whom they had been, whom they were, and whom they would become as the country seemed to shift from the agrarian to the industrial. Antimonopolists used the land question to measure how far they had deviated from the democratic ideals of the squatter's republic. They also used the language of anti–land monopolism to construct a language of anti-industrialism. In this way, telling stories about land monopoly provided a moral blueprint for their present. It drew the lines between those who upheld the American republic and those who betrayed it, those who abided by a higher law of natural rights and those who defied it.

The opposition to land monopoly was one expression of antimonopolism, a reform ideology that encompassed a range of ideals from the classically liberal shades of Henry George's single tax to the more radical, statist reforms of the Populists and the conservative, regulatory approach championed by Stephen Mallory White. The common thread that tied nineteenth-century American antimonopolists together was the desire to protect free competition among small proprietors and producers in an era characterized by increasing consolidation and large-scale industrialization. While antimonopolism endured into the twentieth century, the sweeping transformation of American society, the great social and economic leveling among small producers and proprietors that nineteenth-century anti–land monopolists had envisioned, never did come to pass. By the end of the century, the land question became a marginal part of industrial reform.

The fate of the land question in America would have been a grave disappointment to George. Like so many others of his generation, he ardently believed in anti–land monopolism's redemptive capacities for agriculture and industry, for laborers and capitalists. In 1889, the year before a stroke ended his public-speaking career, George addressed an audience in Scotland regarding the connections between land monopoly and industrial labor reform. He told them a story of a man who went to heaven. The first thing the man did upon arrival was to search out a quiet place to take a nap. Spotting a particularly appealing stretch of grass beneath the shade of a tree, he ambled toward it. "A fine-looking old gentleman angel," identified as the "warden" of heaven, stopped the man in his tracks and cautioned, "The angel who owns that knoll does not like to encourage trespassing. Some centuries ago . . . we introduced the system of private property in the soil of heaven. So we divided the land up. It is all private property now." The man quickly gathered that the privatization of the celestial plane had favored the wealthy angels over the common, but the warden encouraged him, "If you go to work, and are saving, you can easily earn enough in a couple of centuries to buy yourself a nice piece. You get a pair of wings free as you come in, and you will have no difficulty in hypothecating them for a few days' board until you find work. But I would advise you to be quick about it, as our population is constantly increasing, and there is a great surplus of labor. Tramp angels are, in fact, becoming quite a nuisance." Having pawned their wings, these downtrodden angels wandered "the streets of New Jerusalem" as "outcasts in heaven itself."[1] For George, poverty in the United States was as absurd and unjust as land monopolies in heaven. With its abundance of land and natural resources, and its energetic, healthy population, the country should have been like a heaven on earth, particularly for the producers whose labor transformed and improved on nature's bounty. Instead, land laws favored monopolists, speculators, and landlords while trampling all over agrarian republican ideals. Producers were "outcasts" in the society their work had built. They were forced to surrender their independence just as the angels had surrendered their wings. When private monopolies ruled the republic, there would be no grassy knoll on which to rest, no reward for a lifetime of labor.

## The Land Question in Progressive Era California

Even as it retreated to the margins of industrial reform, the opposition to land monopoly remained central to rural reform throughout the first decades of the twentieth century. The land question owed its survival in the Progressive Era to the persistent and close connections between agriculture and issues of race and immigration in California. Antimonopolist land reformers still aspired to protect opportunities for independent, white cultivators and to provide an alternative career track for disaffected, under-employed urban laborers. Their interests intersected with California's efforts to restrict the rights of Japanese immigrants. In 1917, California land reformers led by Elwood Mead, a civil engineer and irrigation specialist, secured the passage of the Land Settlement Act. The legislation supported family farms by offering low-interest loans and encouraging close settlement to foster community and cooperation among farmers. By these means, the Land Settlement Act set about ensuring the survival and success of family farms in California and, by extension, the agrarian republican ideals that once underpinned American democracy. The initiative adopted and combined the variants of anti–land monopolism that had developed in the late nineteenth century: George's racist attitudes toward nonwhite freeholders and the Populists' statist antimonopolism. In many ways, the Land Settlement Act was the coda to California's history of anti–land monopolism. Its short and unsuccessful tenure reflected the diminishment of the land question as a tool for broad social reform.

The Land Settlement Act was based on the premise that small, independent farms formed the social and economic foundation of American democracy; therefore, the state should strive to preserve them. The future of small farms worried California legislators in the Progressive Era. The modern farm required more capital and expertise than the average American family had at its disposal. Farm technology and irrigation, particularly in the naturally arid parts of California, were essential to competing against large-scale agribusiness. Small farms could stagger under the costs and fall into indebtedness, farm failure, and foreclosure. By creating a state bureaucracy to extend services that were previously only provided by independent banks and land companies, the Land Settlement Act replaced private monopolies with state monopolies.[2] The legislation was part of a regional trend in state-sponsored rural reform initiatives; by 1930, five state legislatures—Arizona, California, South Dakota, Minnesota, and Washington—organized colonies, and eleven—Arizona, Colorado, Idaho, Minnesota, Montana, North Dakota, Oklahoma, South Dakota, Utah, Wisconsin, and Wyoming—established farm loan programs.[3] It was no coincidence that these legislatures represented some of the largest public-land states. Colonies and farm loan programs attempted to correct the shortcomings of the Homestead Act of 1862.[4] In the late nineteenth and early twentieth centuries, a severe economic depression gripped the country from 1893 until 1897 and exacerbated the already-chronic problem of underemployment in the cities.[5] The effects of the depression were apparent in national studies showing rising rates of farm tenancy and outmigration from rural to urban areas, which created a so-called landless proletariat. Concerns about the changing demographics of rural America reflected pervasive anxieties about European socialism and anarchism spreading among workers in the United States. In 1917, the Bolshevik Revolution in Russia further spurred fears of radical uprisings among the growing numbers of American poor.[6]

Initially, Mead portrayed the anti–land monopolist Land Settlement Act as a conservative force to counteract radicalism in the United States. Reflecting on the legislation's origins, Mead said, "We were beginning to feel, as yet vaguely and uncertainly, that no country founded on land monopoly or menaced by it could be truly free."[7] California's Land Settlement Act promised to fulfill the promise of the Homestead Act and to halt the spread of radicalism by providing an outlet for the restive unemployed and giving land to the "landless." Reports published by the board administering the Land Settlement Act called it "a homestead law modified to suit the present day conditions. It lowers the wall against ownership which high land prices [are] raising. It helps people who aspire to be farmers, but who, under ordinary conditions, could not make the attempt."[8] Another report suggested the political economic urgency of the Land Settlement Act:

> We are only just beginning to realize that our future is likely to be determined primarily by the relation of the people to the land. The chaos of Russia has grown out of land hunger; no one fears for the safety of France where nearly half of the people are landowners.... We have yet to learn what the older countries of the world already know—that keeping people on the land in the years to come must be one of the main endeavors of civilized nations. People cannot be kept on the land where non-resident ownership and tenantry prevail. Nothing short of ownership of the land one toils over will suffice to overcome the lure of the city.[9]

The act's promotional literature identified farmers as the bulwark against radical movements: "No such dangers confront government from the unrest of the farmer... He is both laborer and capitalist."[10] An article reprinted in one pamphlet stated, "A prosperous farmer on his land does not turn berserker or run amuck."[11] The act, in short, promised to uphold

American democracy and property rights by supporting their line of defense—agrarian freeholders.

Prior to coming to California, Mead devoted his career to promoting state-sponsored irrigation projects in the American West. In 1899, after stepping down as state engineer for Wyoming, he became the director of irrigation investigations for the U.S. Department of Agriculture. There, he joined a growing number of policy makers and engineers who believed that the supply of nonirrigated, cultivable public land was diminishing, and that large-scale irrigation projects were necessary to transform the West into land suitable for farming. Mead supported a decentralized approach to organizing irrigation works in which the federal government would cede some portion of its land to the arid states. The states would fund and oversee irrigation projects that promised an increased population and tax base, or they could dispose of the land to private investors. This "home rule" approach, Mead felt, would lead to greater productivity and prosperity in the irrigated lands and a more democratized distribution of irrigation's economic benefits.[12] Unfortunately, Mead was out of step with the dominant trend in reclamation policy in Washington, D.C., where officials favored federal management of large reservoirs and dam construction to irrigate as much land as possible. Maintaining federal control of arid lands eliminated the problems of apportioning interstate rivers and made it possible for predominantly nonarid states like Oregon to benefit from irrigation schemes.[13] In 1902, officials favoring federalized irrigation pushed the National Reclamation Act through Congress, which was the nail in the coffin for Mead's career in the department. The act gave the federal government control over the development of arid lands by creating a fund to finance large irrigation projects.[14] After 1902, Frederick Haynes Newell, the head of the newly formed Reclamation Service, attempted to have Mead discharged from his position with the Department of Agriculture. Mead managed to hold on to the job for a time, but he began to look for other opportunities to make his land-reform vision a reality.[15]

In 1907, Mead escaped from Washington, D.C., and the unpleasantness with Newell, to accept an invitation from the Australian government to design a dense settlement and irrigation plan for the state of Victoria. Whereas he had opposed federal reclamation in the United States, Mead helped the Australian government nationalize Victoria's water resources and establish a bureaucracy to oversee irrigation and water-rights policy.[16] It was in Australia that Mead began to dabble with state monopoly programs. Mead believed that a state monopoly there would better protect small farmers' access to water than private monopoly would. Under Mead's advisement, the Australian government began a program of state-administered land colonies. According to Mead, a "preliminary study showed that the success of a settler largely depends on two things: First obtaining a living income from his farm within a year; and second, getting the whole of his land into cultivation and production inside of two years."[17] To that end, the Australian government purchased land and prepared it for farmers by subdividing it into ten- and fifteen-acre lots and then seeding it with alfalfa so that cows and other grazing animals might eat.[18] In each district, the government appointed a "farm instructor or adviser" to supervise the colonies. "It was his business to drive continually through the district observing the habits and methods of the beginners, to correct their mistakes when seen, and where they refused to adopt proper methods or showed lack of industry and persistence, it was his duty to notify the authorities in charge."[19] The government also extended cheap credit to its farmers to finance the purchase of land and any improvements.[20] "The way Australian states and commonwealth ... use the national credit for purposes of social advancement astonishes the stranger," Mead wrote. "The per capita indebtedness is far in advance of that of other English-speaking nations; still their credit remains good. The reason lies in the soundness of the view that investments made for social benefits when they are associated with material resources can never become insecure."[21] Success in Victoria led to consulting engagements for Mead in other states, and the number of irrigated farms soared during his eight years in Australia.[22]

When Mead returned to the United States in 1915, he felt assured that state colonies were the "solution to the land question." By seeking to marshal the power of the state to benefit the independent farmer, Mead's land-reform agenda echoed the Populists' political agenda. "This system of land settlement," Mead wrote in 1916 in a letter to the *New Republic*, "would perpetuate all the opportunities of the Homestead law and introduce a reform in rural life."[23] Only public monopolies, with the common interest at heart, could mount a sufficient challenge to private land monopolies. Mead envisioned a new era of state monopolies overseeing large public works and providing the financial resources to underwrite the land tenure of small freeholders.

In 1916, Mead came to California to direct an investigation into rural conditions.[24] Sponsored by the state's Commission on Colonization and Rural Credits, the investigation was a response to a perceived crisis in California's agricultural sector in the early twentieth century. Signs of the crisis were not where one might expect to find them. Between 1900 and 1910, rates of farm tenancy remained fairly constant. In 1900, 76.9 percent of farms were operated by owners and managers and 23.1 percent by tenants. In 1910, the percentage of farms operated by owners and managers increased to 79.4 percent and tenants decreased to 20.6 percent.[25] In the same years, the median farm size did grow from between 50 and 99 acres to between 100 and 175 acres, but because more land was brought into agricultural production, the total number of small farms also grew. The number of farms between 20 and 49 acres grew by 57.2 percent, while the number of farms between 3 and 9 acres rose by 74.2 percent, the greatest relative and absolute gains for farms of any size.[26]

What concerned the commission was not tenancy or farm size so much as farmland values, which had more than doubled between 1900 and 1910. In 1900, farmland (without improvements) had been valued at $630 million. In 1910, it was valued at $1.3 billion.[27] The additional land brought into production did not explain the difference. The average value per acre of farmland increased proportionally, from $21.87 in 1900 to $47.16 in 1910. The commission's report claimed that high land values were the result of speculation and land monopoly. The commissioners feared that higher land values would mean fewer small farms, and fewer small farms would spell disaster for California's democracy. Mead's investigation found that private colonization schemes, which were popular between 1900 and 1915, had contributed to the escalation of land prices. The colonies accounted for much of the group settlement of suburban Southern California as well as parts of Central and Northern California. They were organized by private real estate developers who bought large tracts of land and subdivided them for sale to individual farmers. The colonies attracted settlers because they promised to create a community of closely settled farms and alleviate the isolation of the homestead. Many private colonies offered cost sharing for irrigation projects that would have been too expensive for any single farmer to undertake.[28] In reality, the private colonies did not encourage the settlement of farming freeholders. The report claimed that developers exacted such a high commission from their land sales and offered so little in contributions to irrigation projects, that settlers paid as much as 100 percent in excess of the land's value. Small landowners could not afford to buy into colonies, which led to a concentration of landownership among those few settlers who could.

The Land Settlement Act was the culmination of the commission's investigation. Through state colonies, the act aspired to achieve the same ends envisioned by Jeffersonian agrarians, single taxers, and Populists. "There are many things in country life that need to be eliminated, and some that ought to be created," Mead wrote. "Among those that ought to be abolished are land monopoly and farm tenantry. Among those that need to be created is a sentiment which distinguishes between home owning and land owning that will make men buy farms, not as speculation, not to sell again as soon as there is an increase in price, but to buy farms as a place to live, to follow a vocation, to rear families, and to create homes for their children and their children's children."[29] Mead stated his land-reform logic in the framework of agrarian freeholding: "Now we are beginning to believe vaguely and uncertainly that the men who cultivate the soil ought to own it."[30] However, he went on, "the people who would like to own farms are finding it too difficult. They are accepting tenantry or are moving to the cities." The Land Settlement Act restricted its benefits to small landholders, who were defined as anyone who held land valued at no more than $15,000. To discourage concentrated land-ownership, the Land Settlement Act stipulated that settlers receive "no more than one farm allotment" in the colony, and it prohibited them from selling, mortgaging, subleasing, or otherwise transferring title to the allotment for a period of five years.[31] The law also broke up land monopolies by stipulating the government purchase of land from large landholders.[32] "With the object of promoting closer settlement, assisting deserving and well qualified persons to acquire small improved farms," the Land Settlement Act provided state-sponsored, low-interest loans for small farmers to cover start-up costs and irrigation, an essential element of the infrastructure in California's arid climate.[33]

In the 1910s, the survival of the small farmer was not the California legislature's only concern. The Land Settlement Act emerged from the same social and political context as California's Alien Land Laws of 1913 and 1920, which denied the right to own land to immigrants who were ineligible for citizenship. The Alien Land Laws were part of a wider campaign against Japanese immigrants in California between 1900 and 1924, and they were a response to the growth in the numbers of Japanese farm owners and tenant farmers.[34] The Japanese population in California had increased from 10,151 in 1900 to 41,356 in 1910, which made them the largest nonwhite minority group in the state. The majority of immigrants had worked in agriculture in Japan and sought out similar employment once in the United States.[35]

Like the Alien Land Laws, the Land Settlement Act aimed to whiten California agriculture by endowing white farmers with government-subsidized advantages over their Japanese competitors. The commission had observed a disturbing tendency among California farmers to hire tenants, and since the Japanese would agree to contract for terms most favorable to farm owners, the commission found that three-quarters of the tenant farmers were Japanese.[36] The landowners' preference for Japanese tenants drove white farm labor—"the young, virile, and ambitious"—into the cities. "We want to keep the red blood on the farm," Mead declared.[37] Thus, the inherent racism of George's late nineteenth-century anti–land monopolism endured in the Land Settlement Act's restrictions on eligibility.[38] Only a "citizen of the United States, or any person who has intention of becoming a citizen of the United States" could apply for a farm. Japanese and other Asian immigrants, who were ineligible for naturalization, were excluded from participating in the state colonies. Mead justified their exclusion thus: "The American rural population is being displaced by an alien peasantry drawn in many sections from the Orient, or from those portions of Europe where the conditions of living are hardest." If tenantry, and particularly foreign tenantry, remained the prevailing condition of rural life, "anything resembling an American democracy is impossible."[39] Mead considered the Land Settlement Act to be a crucial part of the state's campaign against alien—and in particular, Japanese—land tenure, which lent a sense of urgency to his endeavor. He declared, "The more [state land colonies] there are, the more certain it is that rural California will in the next half century remain the frontier of the white man's world."[40] The displacement of white families from the farm began with land leases to "oriental" tenants:

> The owners of great landed properties derived their income mainly from rentals. As the demand for land grew, the rent rose through the competition of tenants. The one who would pay the most money or give the largest share of the crop got the land. In these competitions, oriental farmers or other aliens who could pay high prices because they have a low standard of living secured control of a larger and larger percentage of the best farming land.[41]

Mead unfavorably compared the character of the "alien" renter to the Anglo-American settler: "As citizens and as builders of rural society, these aliens were in sorry contrast to the State's first settlers, who were the finest type of American citizen this nation has produced." He neatly overlooked the gold hunger of the mid-nineteenth-century migrants and the lawlessness of the Gold Rush era to claim that "the California pioneer had been a citizen first, a money maker second. He was generous and public spirited to a fault. In contrast, the alien renter had no interest in rural welfare. He had a racial aloofness and he farmed the land to get all he could out of it in the period of his lease.[42]

In this assessment, Mead repeated an argument that George had made in his 1871 pamphlet *Our Land and Land Policy*.[43] The land monopolists of California combined with the "alien renter" to create a crisis in rural life that was both environmental and social. The environmental problem stemmed from the tenants' custom of farming quick-growth, high-yield crops that leeched the soil and ruined it for future cultivation. The related social problem came from their transience. Without attachments to one plot of land, they did not care to cultivate the earth or the community. "This kind of tenant cultivation had been robbing the soil of the stored up fertility of centuries," Mead wrote. "The kind of agriculture practiced by the tenants would end in rural poverty."[44] As had been the case with George, Mead offered no evidence to back his assertion that Asian farmers practiced unsustainable farming, but he promised that the Land Settlement Act would solve the presumed problem: "Making farm workers land owners and their families a respected part of a social life of a settlement is drawing American workers back to the land. It shows that the exodus of American farm labor to cities is not because they object to hard work, but because they object to competition with Orientals and backward people and to the kind of life unplanned development imposes on their wives and children."[45] Like George's anti–land monopolism and the Alien Land Laws, the Land Settlement Act aimed to protect white manhood and womanhood from unnatural competition with "Orientals and backward people," who did not conform to white, middle-class racial and gender norms.

Although Mead shared a vocabulary of agrarian and antimonopolist ideals, he reached for a degree of government intervention that neither Thomas Jefferson nor even Henry George had imagined possible or desirable. The Land Settlement Act copied Mead's Australian plan with only minor tweaking of the financing agreement between settlers and the state.[46] Under the Land Settlement Act, Mead and a board of agricultural engineers set up two "demonstrations" of state colonies: the first in 1918 and the second in 1920.[47] In the administration of the colonies, Mead's statist antimonopolism blended with Progressive Era ideals of scientific expertise and bureaucratic efficiency. As was characteristic of

Progressive Era reformers, Mead believed that the expertise of the board would guarantee the success of the colonies. The Land Settlement Act stipulated that "the purchaser shall cultivate the land in a manner to be approved by the board and shall keep in good order and repair all buildings, fences, and other permanent improvements situated on his allotment."[48] The board hired a farmstead engineer to advise settlers on a range of matters from the layout of farm buildings, orchards, and gardens to the aesthetics and upkeep of the homestead.[49] "The oversight of the superintendent," one promotional pamphlet boasted, "is a stimulant to those who might otherwise become negligent and shiftless."[50] In the 1920 progress report, Mead claimed, "Each settler farms his land as he sees fit but he farms it better than in an unplanned development because he has the great advantage of being in close contact with the state experts of the Agricultural College and having in his midst the superintendent employed by the Board."[51]

Mead and his board of experts designed the colonies to be models of efficient agricultural production. In addition to funding the purchase of farm technology and the construction of irrigation works, Mead expected the colonies' cooperative associations to achieve economies of scale typical of large-scale agribusiness but normally elusive to small freeholders on isolated farms: "The man who markets as an individual, as the isolated settler has to, is at great disadvantage. . . . The benefits of cooperation and group marketing have . . . lessened costs of things bought, of increased prices of things sold, and in the saving of time and labor."[52] The board required colonists to participate in marketing cooperatives for fruits and vegetables, which amortized the costs of bringing produce to consumers. Colonists also agreed to raise one breed of livestock so that the sires might be shared across farms for fertilization.[53] Given the early twentieth-century connotations of "cooperation" with socialism and unionism, Mead was careful in his 1920 report to state explicitly that "while cooperation is encouraged, these communities are in no sense socialistic enterprises. Each settler pays his own way. Every dollar that the state advances is returned to the state with interest. Every individual farmer or farm laborer pays for his own land and owns it as an individual exactly as he would if he bought it privately."[54] The Land Settlement Act created a system of cooperative capitalism that was antimonopolist, not socialist. Cooperation on the colonies emphasized competitiveness. The cooperative associations echoed George's vision of a "cooperation of equals" and the Populists' farmers' associations in which independent producers worked together to achieve the same scale efficiencies in production as in monopoly.[55]

The first state colony, located in Durham, a town in Butte County, near Chico, encompassed 6,239 acres (fig. 12). Using the original appropriation of $260,000, the committee bought the bulk of the land, approximately 3,500 acres, from Stanford University and then purchased adjoining lots from individual landowners. In total, the land cost $500,000, exceeding the state appropriation by almost 100 percent. To cover the difference, the first settlers at Durham took out additional loans from the Federal Land Bank, a government-backed lender that specialized in agricultural credits. Taking out additional loans was an inauspicious beginning for the financial integrity of Mead's progress.[56] But the land was fertile, well watered, and well located near major transportation routes, including a state highway, the Northern Electric Railway, and the Southern Pacific Railway, which boded well for future success. Mead subdivided the land into 110 farms ranging in size from eight to one hundred acres. Almost immediately, the board was overwhelmed by applications to purchase the farms from the state.[57] To screen potential colonists, the board relied on a lengthy application to determine the applicant's "fitness and qualifications to hold the land." The questions on the form covered the topics of citizenship, marital and family status, and records of personal assets. Applicants had to have at least $1,500 to demonstrate that they were financially sound and unlikely to default on a loan.[58] In 1918, between January 1 and June 1, the committee reviewed applications and met with potential settlers. When two or more settlers applied for the same subdivision, the committee interviewed each one to determine who was "most deserving or best qualified." A report from Durham claimed that "Considerably more than half of the settlers were tenant farmers, and they would still be renters if they had been compelled to buy under ordinary commercial conditions," which indicated that the Land Settlement Act had successfully reduced land tenancy.[59]

The subdivisions in Durham also included two-acre blocks for farm laborers who could secure a state-sponsored mortgage for a twenty-dollar down payment on the land. In the Australia plan, Mead had considered the farm laborer allotments to be the most significant contribution to democratized land reform: "This gave [farm] laborers a home for their families, enough land to keep a cow and some poultry and grow their fruits and vegetables. It tied them to the soil and has changed their nomadic character. No feature of this system has proved of greater economic or social value than the two-acre farm laborer's block."[60] In reviewing farm laborer applications for Durham colony, "the board faced a harder task when it came to deciding between the applicants. . . . There was some

FIGURE 12. Elwood Mead (in glasses), as Chairman of the Land Settlement Board, conferring with visiting professors at the Durham State Land Settlement in 1920; BANC PIC 1966.034. Courtesy of the Bancroft Library, University of California, Berkeley.

doubt as to the use a single man would have for such an area. It was believed that these homes would be worth far more to the married worker who had a family than to unmarried men, unless it was to enable them to marry. Other things being equal, applicants with families were chosen."[61] Mead intended these small tracts to permit farm laborers to garden, which would supplement their wages and provide some fraction of their food supply. Mead offered prizes for the best gardens and hoped that the laborers would eventually accumulate enough capital to buy larger allotments.[62] A *Collier's* article later reported that Mead's plan for the social advancement of farm laborers enabled at least two such families to move into the "farm-owner class" through intensive cultivation of their two-acre tracts.[63]

Durham was to be a community for American family farms, a real-life expression of the agrarian dream infused with a new level of state control. The board turned away "a number of applicants for [the farm laborers' allotments] who were not farm workers and did not intend to work on farms for wages" but who were drawn to Durham because they "liked the easy payments and the prospect of securing at small cost a comfortable home in a progressive neighborhood."[64] For farm families, life in the Durham colony encouraged "independence, ambition, [and] self-respect, the things that develop character," personal attributes that were unattainable where "the farm laborer's family . . . had as a rule to live in town. The head of the family was away from home and children."[65] As Mead described it, Durham would be a space in which many elements of the old Jeffersonian agrarian vision remained. In Durham, the patriarchal family labored on the land, and in cultivating personal independence and virtue, the family perpetuated American democratic ideals.

At first, the experiment in Durham seemed to work. As of 1920, all of the settlers were current on their payments to the state, and farm revenues were high, although perhaps artificially so, due to increased demand for American crops in European nations recovering from World War I.[66] The signs of success at Durham led the California state legislature to appropriate an additional $1 million for the establishment of a second colony in Delhi, a town in Merced County. The board purchased 8,400 acres, mostly from a single landowner, for nearly $800,000. The land in Delhi was sandier than Durham and required more extensive irrigation and leveling, both of which raised the cost per acre. At least one board member voiced his concern that the price of the land exceeded its value. But the board went ahead with the purchase. Its members were confident that irrigation would solve any fertility problems.[67]

Although the goal of the Land Settlement Act was to create self-sustaining colonies, the reality was that the farms could only become financially viable in the long term. The cultivation of new orchards and crops and the raising of livestock took time, and the colonies needed the state to keep the money flowing. To secure public support and the funds that came with it, Mead emphasized the Land Settlement Act's contribution to the anti-Japanese movement. In 1920, as California passed its second Alien Land Law, Mead lobbied for more money for the state colonies and called them "the antidote to the Japanese racial aggression."[68] Mead contributed to a report by the State Board of Control called *California and the Oriental*. He outlined the Land Settlement Act's contribution to California's solution of the Japanese "problem." Mead insisted that "the State Land Settlement Act, if sufficiently extended, will settle the problem of intelligent, dependable American labor on the farm. It is the most direct and effective way of mitigating, if not ending the menace of alien land ownership and of creating communities that do not amalgamate, and of subjecting this state to the menace of racial antagonisms." Mead offered Delhi as an example of the solution in practice: "The 8,000 acres of land bought by the Land Settlement Board in Merced County would have been purchased for Japanese settlers if the Board had not bought it."[69] This statement may or may not have been true. The numbers of Japanese in the county were growing. The population of Japanese residents in Merced had more than quadrupled between 1910 and 1920, from 99 to 424, but the Japanese remained a tiny fraction of the county's total population, which numbered 14,412 in 1910 and 24,602 in 1920.[70] Nonetheless, Mead portrayed the state colonies as an essential part of staving off the Japanese "invasion" of California:

> If the Board does buy it [a tract of an additional 1,200 acres owned by the Japanese in Merced County], it means a permanent democratic American community, farm workers and farm owners living in their own homes, meeting together in the cooperative associations. The sons of the farm laborer today will be the farm owners of the next decade and California will have the rural life as patriotic and stable as that of France. The trouble today is that our progress along this line is too slow. Not enough money is being furnished.[71]

Despite Mead's attempt to weave together appeals to anti-Japanese racism and agrarian sentiment, he failed to recapture the legislature's enthusiasm for the state colonies.

In the 1920s, state support trickled off. It dwindled for two main reasons. First, the Alien Land Law of 1913 had proven ineffective at eliminating Japanese landowners, which diminished nativists' endorsement of land reform as an anti-immigration measure.[72] Even as the California legislature passed a second Alien Land Law in 1920 to address the shortcomings of the first Alien Land Law, anti-Japanese groups had already set their sights on a bigger prize: national immigration restriction. They focused their energies on that and abandoned the issue of alien land ownership.[73] Secondly, Mead had exaggerated the success of the colony at Durham to secure funding for Delhi, and he failed to report the challenges faced by both colonies. Thus, California legislators did not realize the necessity of further appropriations for Mead's experiment. The apparent progress in Durham between 1918 and 1920 obscured the fact that farms were not yet profitable, and many colonists had drawn down their savings to make loan payments.[74] Durham fared better than Delhi, where, as predicted, the sandy soil exacerbated the challenges of farming. In the first two years, Delhi colonists sustained themselves with wages paid by the state for the construction of a massive underground irrigation system, but state funds for the project dwindled, and the colonists abandoned the work in 1922. The poor soil conditions at Delhi were compounded by the onset of a national agricultural depression in the post–World War I period. Demand for farm allotments dropped, and 40 percent of the acreage remained unsold. Mead and the board lowered their standards and approved applicants with less capital and less experience in farming. Mead's biographer, James Kluger, argues that, as a result, the colonists at Delhi borrowed money in amounts exceeding their ability to repay.[75]

With public support running dry and postwar price deflation setting in, the colonists looked for private funding from corporations, a decision that Mead opposed. His plan had been to use state monopoly to create opportunities for small landholders and perpetuate democratic institutions. Depending on private land companies and agribusiness ran counter to that agenda. By way of compromise, the Delhi colonists took out a loan from the Federal Land Bank. The colonists at Durham also suffered from the economic downturn in the agricultural sector, and along with their counterparts in Delhi, they spiraled into receivership.[76]

In 1923, Mead effectively gave up and skipped town. He stepped down as chairman of the board and left the country to oversee irrigation projects in Australia and Palestine. He formally tendered his resignation from the board in 1924.[77] Four years and $2.5 million later, California followed Mead's lead. The state phased out its involvement with the colonies, a decision that resulted in extensive litigation, and it closed the book on Mead's land-reform "demonstrations."[78]

The Durham and Delhi failures did not, however, signal the demise of the land question for rural reformers.[79] During the Great Depression, the federal government sponsored hundreds of colonies across the United States through the rural resettlement program, which was eventually reorganized as the New Deal's Farm Security Administration (FSA). The program relocated farmers from submarginal land, and these resettlement farms shared some similarities with California's state land colonies. The federal government extended low-interest loans to farmers and organized producers' cooperatives. In addition, the government built and furnished homes, leveled and cleared the land, and even arranged social activities for the community. From the program's inception in 1935 to its termination in 1943, the resettlements experienced varying levels of success, but they still represented the persistence of the antimonopolist agrarian ideal into the twentieth century.[80] Yet there were critical differences between the federal resettlement program and earlier attempts to protect small freeholders. Whereas the anti–land monopolist movements of the nineteenth century sought to correct industrial problems by restoring land rights to producers, the New Deal initiative did not attempt to transform wage laborers into farmers. American policy makers believed that overproduction in the agricultural sector had contributed to the Great Depression. Rural resettlement did not seek to multiply the number of farms or farmers. It aimed to improve rural conditions for small farmers, to make them more productive and prosperous, and, perhaps most importantly, to discourage them from seeking alternative employment in oversaturated manufacturing labor markets. In the context of the Great Depression, anti–land monopolism was deployed to stanch the flow of farm failures, not to effect sweeping and systemic change in the American political economy.[81] After Mead's botched experiment in California, no state program matched the scope or ambition of Henry George, the Knights of Labor, and the Populists' antimonopolism.

## New Questions for a New Age

The Gilded Age, along with the Great Depression, has become something of a touchstone for early twenty-first-century America. Journalists, economists, and the occasional historian have grown fond of heralding the advent of "the Second Gilded Age." In doing so, they have made the nineteenth century's Gilded Age a representation of our past sins and a possible road to our redemption. The problems that the era's antimonopolists wrestled with have not disappeared in the present day. For the first time since the 1920s, income inequalities between the very rich and everyone else resemble the disparities of the Gilded Age. The great fortunes of the old Gilded Age were built on large-scale industry—manufacturing, railroads, coal, and steel—whereas the new Gilded Age fortunes were forged in a deindustrialized landscape and hewn of stock options, IPOs, private equity, and hedge fund deals. Nonetheless, the Second Gilded Age was similarly facilitated by cheap credit and the largesse of the federal government toward big business.[82] A protracted economic recession and a sluggish recovery resurrected concerns not only about the vitality of the American political economy but also about its morality. Strains of xenophobia reminiscent of the first Gilded Age appeared in new, extremist attempts to police the United States's border with Mexico and deny protections to undocumented immigrants while public controversy regarding unemployment benefits recalled late nineteenth-century concerns about "tramps." Amid news of stimulus packages and government bailouts, financial reform and its discontents, we continue, as late nineteenth-century antimonopolists did before us, to ponder the obligations of government to regulate the very rich, to reduce great incomes through taxation, and to create opportunities for a more equitable distribution of the vast wealth that the United States produces.

The question of who should own the land and how much of it is not a question we ask ourselves very much anymore, but we remain troubled by a host of related questions that we continue to pose about social mobility and opportunity, corporate greed and political privilege, and the impacts of immigration and globalization on the economy. Underlying these questions is a deep concern that not all of the deserving have or will share in the social and material progress of our time. We are still, as they were then, searching for ways to make sense of and to improve on our political economy and society. And we are still, as they were then, very far from any resolution.

What lessons the first Gilded Age can offer to our Second Gilded Age remains to be seen, but if the history of the land question can offer any direction, it is this: history is as much a record of what came to be as it is a record of what might have been. The history of the land question suggests that the range of possibilities imagined by past generations was more broad, inventive, and ambitious than it may seem to us today. For Gilded Age reformers, antimonopolism was neither a stepping stone toward socialism nor a veiled form of liberal capitalism. Rather, it represented a distinct approach to organizing the American political economy, an approach that restored the rights of producers by deploying the power of the state to harness large-scale industries. Antimonopolists perceived modern capitalism and merger mania as well as cronyism and corruption as choices, not inevitabilities. With choice came the power to make changes, to envision better outcomes, to vanquish inequity, to live better with one another on the land. Gilded Age reformers believed they had the power to make those choices and those changes. So should we.

# NOTES

## INTRODUCTION

1   *A Squatter's Republic* builds on land-reform scholarship by Benjamin Horace
    Hibbard, Roy M. Robbins, Vernon Rosco Carstensen, and, most notably, Paul
    Wallace Gates and Donald J. Pisani, who studied American public-land policy
    as it evolved in the nineteenth and early twentieth centuries. With the ex-
    ception of Gates's and Pisani's scholarship, much of this work made Wash-
    ington, D.C.—or, more precisely, the U.S. Senate floor—the epicenter of
    debates over western land distribution, as historians relied on government
    records and congressmen's personal papers to explain how and why the fed-
    eral government disposed of public land. The historians largely empathized
    with the small freeholder and portrayed the history of federal land policy as
    the United States's missed opportunity for a more egalitarian distribution of
    public lands and wealth. Gates, perhaps the most prolific of the public-land
    historians, has considered land policy and its consequences at the state, re-
    gional, and national levels, and he often highlights tensions between state
    governments and federal interests. Following in Gates's footsteps, Pisani has
    enriched the study of public-land policy by emphasizing California's unique
    environmental circumstances and the ways in which they shaped natural re-
    source laws. See especially Benjamin Horace Hibbard, *A History of the Public
    Land Policies* (New York: P. Smith, 1939); Paul Wallace Gates, *Fifty Million
    Acres: Conflicts over Kansas Land Policy, 1854–1890* (Ithaca, N.Y.: Cornell
    University Press, 1954); *The Public Lands: Studies in the History of the Public
    Domain*, ed. Vernon Rosco Carstensen (Madison: University of Wisconsin
    Press, 1963); Paul Wallace Gates, "An Overview of American Land Policy,"
    *Agricultural History* 50, no. 1 (1976): 213–29; Roy M. Robbins, *Our Landed
    Heritage: The Public Domain, 1776–1970*, 2nd ed. (Lincoln: University of
    Nebraska Press, 1976); Paul Wallace Gates, *Land and Law in California:
    Essays on Land Policies*, Henry A. Wallace Series on Agricultural History
    and Rural Studies (Ames: Iowa State University Press, 1991); and Donald J.
    Pisani, *Water, Land, and Law in the West: The Limits of Public Policy, 1850–
    1920*, Development of Western Resources (Lawrence: University Press of
    Kansas, 1996).

2    For more on the economic history of Gold Rush–era California, see Gerald D. Nash, *State Government and Economic Development: A History of Administrative Policies in California, 1849–1933* (Berkeley: Institute of Governmental Studies, University of California, 1964); and *A Golden State: Mining and Economic Development in Gold Rush California*, ed. James J. Rawls, Richard J. Orsi, and Marlene Smith-Baranzini (Berkeley: University of California Press, 1999). Numerous cultural and social histories of the California Gold Rush deal expressly with the expectations prospectors brought with them; see especially Gates, *Land and Law in California*; Albert L. Hurtado, *Indian Survival on the California Frontier* (New Haven, Conn.: Yale University Press, 1988); Susan Lee Johnson, *Roaring Camp: The Social World of the California Gold Rush* (New York: W. W. Norton, 2000); Malcolm J. Rohrbough, *Days of Gold: The California Gold Rush and the American Nation* (Berkeley: University of California Press, 1997); and David Vaught, *After the Gold Rush: Tarnished Dreams in the Sacramento Valley* (Baltimore, Md.: Johns Hopkins University Press, 2007).

3    William Deverell, *Railroad Crossing: Californians and the Railroad, 1850–1910* (Berkeley: University of California Press, 1994), 35, 38–39; Leonard Pitt, *The Decline of the Californios: A Social History of the Spanish-Speaking Californians, 1846–1890* (Berkeley: University of California Press, 1966), 247–48; and R. Hal Williams, *The Democratic Party and California Politics, 1880–1896* (Stanford, Calif.: Stanford University Press, 1973), 15.

4    Abbott Kinney and Helen Hunt Jackson, *Report on the Conditions and Needs of Mission Indians* (Washington, D.C.: Office of Indian Affairs, 1883), 3; C. C. Painter, *A Visit to the Mission Indians of Southern California, and Other Western Tribes* (Philadelphia: Press of Grant and Faires, 1886), 13–14.

5    Henry George, "What the Railroad Will Bring Us," *Overland Monthly* 1, no. 4 (1868): 302.

6    American common law inherited its definition of *monopoly* from the British. In sixteenth-century England, the courts defined *monopoly* in terms of production and distribution. Private enterprises constituted monopolies when they dominated, controlled, and manipulated a good, market, or industry in a way that restrained competitors. In the seventeenth and eighteenth centuries, the term *monopoly* expanded to include "royal patents," the exclusive rights of distribution granted to courtiers by the crown. The public repudiated royal patents as unfair privileges. See Hans Birger Thorelli, *The Federal Antitrust Policy: Origination of an American Tradition* (Baltimore, Md.: Johns Hopkins University Press, 1954), 14, 25–26.

7    Sean Wilentz, Mark A. Lause, and Reeve Huston have devoted attention to the alliance between the National Reform Association, a short-lived organization of New York City agrarians, and the "anti-rent" movement, a group of tenant farmers combating an oppressive leasehold system in upstate New York. Jamie L. Bronstein adds a transatlantic perspective to the history of antebellum working-class land reform. The stories that Wilentz, Lause, Huston, and Bronstein tell culminate in the failure of the Anti-Rent Wars, the collapse of the National Reform Association in the 1850s, and the passage of

the Homestead Act, which granted free land to settlers, in 1862. See Jamie L. Bronstein, *Land Reform and Working-Class Experience in Britain and the United States, 1800–1862* (Stanford, Calif.: Stanford University Press, 1999); Reeve Huston, *Land and Freedom: Rural Society, Popular Protest, and Party Politics in Antebellum New York* (New York: Oxford University Press, 2000); Mark A. Lause, *Young America: Land, Labor, and the Republican Community* (Urbana: University of Illinois Press, 2005); and Sean Wilentz, *Chants Democratic: New York City and the Rise of the American Working Class, 1788–1850* (New York: Oxford University Press, 1984).

8    The roots of this mischaracterization lie in labor history's traditional preoccupation with the question of why socialism did not take root in the United States as it did in Europe. The capitalist-versus-socialist/liberal-versus-radical debate has animated the work on nineteenth-century labor reform of John Patrick Diggins, Eric Foner, T. J. Jackson Lears, Seymour Martin Lipset, Roger Smith, and Sean Wilentz. In a quest for resolution, much of the scholarship has too readily drawn a line between a labor movement attracted by European socialism and the more conservative "bread-and-butter" reform agendas that would eventually dominate the trade unions while dealing only cursorily with workers' movements, like anti–land monopolism, that did not conform to one or the other. Even Gerald N. Grob, whose book *Workers and Utopia* approached the political ideologies of the American working class with great nuance, classified antimonopolist land reform as an entirely backward-looking movement and not a workable means of reorganizing the American industrial economy. Grob argued that the "reform unionism" of the Knights of Labor sought to eradicate wage work and create a society wholly composed of self-employed, middle-class producers—a mission doomed to failure. According to Grob, liberal capitalism was a permanent condition of the American economy, a fact workers had to face. Trade unions created a set of achievable goals—shorter workdays, better working conditions—that aimed to improve the wage system without revolutionizing it; see Grob, *Workers and Utopia: A Study of Ideological Conflict in the American Labor Movement, 1865–1900* (Evanston, Ill.: Northwestern University Press, 1961), 168. This practicality and limited ambition permitted trade unions like the American Federation of Labor to survive, whereas reform unions like the Knights of Labor perished. Grob argued that American labor unions, "functioning in a materialistic, acquisitive, and abundant environment" (vii), were destined to submit to the modern capitalist order. More recently, questions about economic democracy and industrialization have been at the center of American labor historiography. Antimonopolist reform does play a part in this literature, but as with earlier scholarship, it typically serves as a foil to or an extension of liberalism or socialism rather than its own coherent ideology. For example, Nancy Cohen, who focuses on political economists in the wake of the Civil War, argues that antimonopolist regulation was a liberal scheme to promote the interests of big business at the expense of workers; see Cohen, *The Reconstruction of American Liberalism, 1865–1914* (Chapel Hill: University of North Carolina Press, 2002). In hindsight, it may have seemed that antimonopolism reflected the diminishing rights of individual citizens and the

ascension of overweening corporate power, but it certainly was not what nineteenth-century Americans like Henry George, Terence Powderly, and other reform unionists and agrarians believed. As *A Squatter's Republic* relates, Gilded Age antimonopolists perceived regulation as protection for American citizens and as fulfillment of American democracy. Rosanne Currarino endeavors to move away from a declensionist narrative of economic democracy in an era of industrialization and consolidation; see Currarino, *The Labor Question in America: Economic Democracy in the Gilded Age* (Urbana: University of Illinois Press, 2011). She explores the ways in which Gilded Age unionists came to embrace consumerist citizenship over proprietary producerism, an ideology based on the principle that producers (farmers and artisans, for example) were naturally entitled to the fruits of their labor, a key tenet of antimonopolism. *A Squatter's Republic* means to complement her work by exploring the roots of proprietary producerism in anti–land monopolist movements.

9    Recent crises in the American economy have inspired historians to reconsider the Gilded Age broadly and, for a few, antimonopolism more specifically. Researching and writing in the dreary aftermath of the heedlessly exuberant 1990s, one cannot help but look for paths not taken in the history of the American political economy. Three recent monographs endeavor to restore antimonopolism to the center of Gilded Age political and economic reform. Charles Postel's *Populist Vision* (Oxford: Oxford University Press, 2007) focuses on the modernity of the Populists' antimonopolism and argues, through the group's business and reform ideals, that its members were anything but backward-looking, anti-industrial farmers. Antimonopolism also plays a central role in *Network Nation: Inventing American Telecommunications* (Cambridge, Mass.: Harvard University Press, 2010), Richard R. John's superb study of American telecommunications from the telegraph to the telephone. John shows how, in an unexpected, ironic way, the laws and institutions inspired by antimonopolism accelerated and facilitated the rise of private monopolies and modernized America. *Railroaded: The Transcontinentals and the Making of Modern America* (New York: W. W. Norton, 2011), Richard White's landmark work on the transcontinental railroads, paints antimonopolist reformers as the most significant and vocal critics of railroad corruption, incompetency, and profligacy. Antimonopolists were not Luddites, according to White; they were republican idealists looking to direct the energy of the transcontinental toward egalitarian ends. White also notes the racialized logic of Gilded Age antimonopolists; their vision of egalitarianism was confined to the white race. See Postel, *The Populist Vision*, 4; John, *Network Nation*, 8; and White, *Railroaded*, xxxiv, 493.

10    Two recent monographs explore the history of the Southern Pacific Railroad Company with more depth, detail, and insight than I can accomplish here. See Richard J. Orsi, *Sunset Limited: The Southern Pacific Railroad and the Development of the American West, 1850–1930* (Berkeley: University of California Press, 2005); and White, *Railroaded*.

11    The anti–land monopolist impulse to break up concentrated land ownership and endow small cultivators with land rights is older than antiquity. References

to periodic land redistribution to promote income equality appear in the Old Testament and in accounts of ancient China. In the second century BCE, Roman politician Tiberius Gracchus established a *lex agraria* that mandated limits on the size of landholdings to diminish the power of large landholders and landlords. He confiscated excess land and gave it to peasants in an attempt to instate a class of small landholders, who would then support him. Ultimately, both Tiberius and his brother and successor, Gaius, were murdered and their reforms reversed by the understandably displeased large landholders and landlords. See Russell King, *Land Reform: A World Survey* (Boulder, Colo.: Westview Press, 1977), 28, 31–32.

12    Bronstein, *Land Reform and Working-Class Experience*; Malcolm Chase, *"The People's Farm": English Radical Agrarianism, 1775–1840* (Oxford and New York: Clarendon Press and Oxford University Press, 1988); and Elizabeth Fox-Genovese, *The Origins of Physiocracy: Economic Revolution and Social Order in Eighteenth-Century France* (Ithaca, N.Y.: Cornell University Press, 1976).

13    Thomas Jefferson, *Notes on the State of Virginia*, ed. Frank Shuffelton (New York: Penguin, 1999), 170.

14    Ibid., 171.

15    Chester E. Eisinger, "The Freehold Concept in Eighteenth-Century American Letters," *William and Mary Quarterly* 4 (1947): 44–45; and Henry Nash Smith, *Virgin Land: The American West as Symbol and Myth* (Cambridge, Mass.: Harvard University Press, 1950), 125, 128–29.

16    Eisinger, "The Freehold Concept," 44–45; and Jefferson, *Notes on the State of Virginia*, ed. Shuffelton, 170–71.

17    The label "Jacksonian Democrat" refers to members of the political party led by Presidents Andrew Jackson and Martin Van Buren in the 1830s and 1840s. Jacksonian Democrats championed egalitarianism among white men, limited federal powers, and antimonopolism. For more on Andrew Jackson, his cohort of Democrats, and their campaign against the Second Bank of the United States, see Harry L. Watson, *Liberty and Power: The Politics of Jacksonian America* (New York: Hill and Wang, 1990), 132–71.

18    Alexander Saxton, *The Rise and Fall of the White Republic: Class Politics and Mass Culture in Nineteenth-Century America* (London and New York: Verso, 1990), 143–44.

19    Quoted in Hibbard, *A History of the Public Land Policies*, 142–43.

20    Pisani, *Water, Land, and Law in the West*, 51–52.

21    See Hibbard, *A History of the Public Land Policies*, 168; Robbins, *Our Landed Heritage*, 91; and Robert P. Swierenga, *Pioneers and Profits: Land Speculation on the Iowa Frontier* (Ames: Iowa State University Press, 1968), 4–6. In California in the 1850s and early 1860s, reports of "squatter" conflicts suggested the commingled nature of land-acquisition methods. In 1859, Tyler Curtis attempted to eject forty-eight squatters from his Bodega Ranch, north of Petaluma. Curtis contended that all of the squatters were trespassing, but the local newspapers reported that at least some of them were in fact tenants,

renting parcels from Curtis's wife. Similarly, on the Rancho Yerba Buena in Santa Clara County, legitimate squatters lived side by side with families who had purchased deeds to their land or were renting from Antonio Chabolla, the original grantee. See "Land Troubles in Santa Clara," *Sacramento Daily Union*, April 30, 1861, 2.

22   Wilentz, *Chants Democratic*, 342.

23   For an in-depth account of the anti-rent movement in New York, see Huston, *Land and Freedom*.

24   The Free Soil Party absorbed the remnants of the National Reform Association's membership. In his book on the association, Mark Lause identifies a handful of the elderly National Reformers who spread the news of Henry George's land-reform philosophies among northeastern labor organizations in the early 1880s. Lause, *Young America*, 118, 131–32.

25   As a study of California land-reform movements, this book renews an old debate about how to characterize squatters. In the 1880s, Hubert Howe Bancroft and Josiah Royce portrayed mid-nineteenth-century California squatters as land thieves and opportunists, and in the twentieth century, historians of California continued to cite their work as received wisdom. See Bancroft, *California Inter Pocula* (San Francisco: History Company, 1888), 397–98; and Josiah Royce, *California: A Study of American Character: From the Conquest in 1846 to the Second Vigilance Committee in San Francisco* (Berkeley, Calif.: Heyday Books, 2002), 376. W. W. Robinson's encyclopedic tome *Land in California* reiterated Bancroft's and Royce's negative portrayals of squatters by calling them "locusts" and "trespassers"; see *Land in California: The Story of Mission Lands, Ranchos, Squatters, Mining Claims, Railroad Grants, Land Scrip, Homesteads* (Berkeley: University of California Press, 1948), 106, 126. In 1966, Leonard Pitt similarly equated squatters with aggressors as he described the relationship between Mexican landowners and white American migrants in *The Decline of the Californios*: "The gringos came out of the mines and entered into combat with the Californios for control over the ranchos" (82). In the 1960s, Paul Wallace Gates became the first historian to challenge the Bancroft/Royce portrayal and defend California squatters. In doing so, Gates perhaps took his counter-narrative too far. Where Bancroft and Royce cast squatters as the villains of California history, Gates recast them as heroes, labeling them "frontier democrats" for their dedication to the ideal of small freeholds. Gates's villains were the speculators, the Mexican land grantees, and the politicians who failed to protect "bona fide" settlers from land monopolists. Like Benjamin Horace Hibbard and Roy M. Robbins, Gates dealt with squatters in the aggregate, which made it easier to ascribe "heroic" motives to them as a group but obscured the complexity of the squatters' experience as individuals. It was this complexity that allowed squatters to become antimonopolists and to shape the political culture not only of California but also of their nation. More recently, Mark A. Eifler has published a community study of Sacramento during the Gold Rush, *Gold Rush Capitalists: Greed and Growth in Sacramento* (Albuquerque: University of New Mexico Press, 2002). Eifler argues that a downturn in the local economy

in the winter of 1849–50 heightened tensions between two sets of Sacramento residents: on one side, failed miners squatting on city lots and, on the other, speculators and merchants trying to enforce order in a chaotic, expanding frontier town. By 1851, Eifler suggests, the squatters had given up their demands for free land and acquiesced to participating in the land market, but that was not the case (24). Scholarship by Paul Wallace Gates and Donald Pisani has shown that squatters continued to fight for recognition of their land rights after 1851, and that their issues dominated local and state politics throughout the 1850s and into the 1860s. See Gates, *Land and Law in California*; and Donald J. Pisani, "Squatter Law in California, 1850–1858," *Western Historical Quarterly* 25, no. 3 (1994): 277–310. This book similarly shows that the quest for squatters' rights persisted beyond the Gold Rush days, and more importantly, that squatters' anti–land monopolism, their vision for the American republic, provided a language and a logic for reformers confronting the new challenges in the Gilded Age.

## CHAPTER ONE

1   Samuel W. Brown to his wife, August 14, 1850, Sacramento, California Historical Society.

2   In a chapter entitled "Land Troubles," Albert L. Hurtado details the arrangements that Sutter and his son made to sell portions of the Mexican land grants to speculators. See Hurtado, *John Sutter: A Life on the North American Frontier* (Norman: University of Oklahoma Press, 2006).

3   Gates, *Land and Law in California*, 4, 6.

4   For examples, see chap. 2 of Hurtado, *Indian Survival*.

5   Ibid., 55, 97; George Harwood Phillips, *Vineyards and Vaqueros: Indian Labor and the Economic Expansion of Los Angeles, 1771–1877* (Norman, Okla.: Arthur H. Clark, 2010), 17–18; Stephen W. Silliman, *Lost Laborers in Colonial California: Native Americans and the Archaeology of Rancho Petaluma* (Tucson: University of Arizona Press, 2004).

6   Phillips, *Vineyards and Vaqueros*, 163–65; Silliman, *Lost Laborers*, 20–21.

7   Phillips, *Vineyards and Vaqueros*, 176–77.

8   J. N. Bowman, "Index of the Spanish-Mexican Private Land Grant Records and Cases of California," 1958, Bancroft Library, University of California, Berkeley (hereafter, Bancroft Library).

9   Hurtado, *Indian Survival*, 7, 12, 72; Robinson, *Land in California*, 29–30. The Mexican government secularized the mission lands between 1834 and 1836 and distributed the holdings among private grants. The Roman Catholic Church, therefore, maintained a claim to only a small area where descendants of Indian congregants resided and worked at farming or husbandry. Sherburne Cook has estimated that the total Indian population of California in 1850 was about one hundred thousand; it plummeted to 50 percent by 1855. See Cook, *The Population of the California Indians, 1769–1970* (Berkeley: University of California Press, 1976), 42–44, 48–49.

10    Hurtado, *Indian Survival*, 129–32.

11    George Harwood Phillips, *Indians and Indian Agents: The Origins of the Reservation System in California, 1849–1852* (Norman: University of Oklahoma Press, 1997), 11–12.

12    Hurtado, *Indian Survival*, 147.

13    Treaty of Guadalupe Hidalgo, February 2, 1848, 9 Stat. 922, T. S. 207, and Protocol of Querétaro, May 26, 1848. A manuscript of the treaty is reproduced on the Library of Congress website, http://www.loc.gov/rr/hispanic/ghtreaty (accessed March 11, 2013). Article 8 of the treaty states: "Mexicans now established in territories previously belonging to Mexico, and which remain for the future within the limits of the United States, as defined by the present treaty, shall be free to continue where they now reside, or to remove at any time to the Mexican Republic, retaining the property which they possess in the said territories, or disposing thereof, and removing the proceeds wherever they please, without their being subjected, on this account, to any contribution, tax or charge whatever."

14    Robinson, *Land in California*, 92.

15    Gates, *Land and Law in California*, 6.

16    Ibid., 229–30; Robinson, *Land in California*, 203; White, *Railroaded*, 24.

17    Gates, *Land and Law in California*, 20; Robinson, *Land in California*, 208.

18    Gates, *Land and Law in California*, 233.

19    Examples of these announcements are too numerous to cite here. Just about any California newspaper published in the decades after statehood contained notices of public auctions, estate sales, and other transfers of property. See ibid., 126.

20    Robinson, *Land in California*, 207–8.

21    Ibid., 214.

22    John Hill McKune, *Minority Report of the Hon. J. H. McKune of the Judiciary Committee, to Which Was Referred Assembly Bill to Repeal the Act for the Protection of Actual Settlers, and to Quiet Land Titles in this State, Submitted April 25th, 1857, in the Assembly of the State of California* (Sacramento, Calif.: James Anthony & Co., 1857), California State Library; "To the Miners and Settlers of California," *Daily Bee*, July 13, 1857.

23    Economic historians have conducted extensive research to quantify the effects of such criteria on land values in the United States in the 1850s, with mixed results. For examples of recent scholarship summarizing the ongoing debate, see Michael R. Haines and Robert A. Margo, "Railroads and Local Economic Development: The United States in the 1850s" (working paper 12381, National Bureau of Economic Research, July 2006), 4–6.

24    Israel Shipman Pelton Lord, *At the Extremity of Civilization: A Meticulously Descriptive Diary of an Illinois Physician's Journey in 1849 Along the Oregon Trail to the Goldmines and Cholera of California, Thence in Two Years to Return by Boat Via Panama*, ed. Necia Dixon Liles (Jefferson, N.C.: McFarland & Co., 1995), 171.

25    Alonzo Delano, *Alonzo Delano's California Correspondence: Being Letters Hitherto Uncollected from the Ottawa (Illinois)* Free Trader *and the New Orleans* True Delta, *1849–1952*, ed. Irving McKee (Sacramento, Calif.: Sacramento Book Collectors Club, 1952), 48.

26    Henry Haight to Fletcher Matthews Haight, July 17, 1850, San Francisco, box 1, file 151, Henry Haight Papers, Huntington Library, San Marino, California (hereafter, Huntington Library).

27    Lord, *At the Extremity of Civilization*, 171.

28    The protection of Mexican citizens' property rights was not unique to the Treaty of Guadalupe Hidalgo. Since the Jay Treaty of 1794, the United States had promised to uphold the property rights of individuals in annexed foreign territories. See Gates, *Land and Law in California*, 186; and Maria E. Montoya, *Translating Property: The Maxwell Land Grant and the Conflict over Land in the American West, 1840–1900* (Berkeley: University of California Press, 2002), 173–75.

29    William Henry Ellison, *A Self-Governing Dominion: California, 1849–1860*, Chronicles of California (Berkeley: University of California Press, 1950), 103–4; Robinson, *Land in California*, 97–98.

30    Ellison, *A Self-Governing Dominion*, 104; Robinson, *Land in California*, 92–95.

31    Gates, *Land and Law in California*, 6–7. The position may have seemed out of character for the senator, who had championed squatters' rights since the 1820s, but Benton had also used his time in the Senate to uphold the interests of large landholders. According to the historian Stephen Aron, Benton "aligned himself with the interests of [St. Louis's] elite" (French merchants and Spanish land grantees), and he "urged the federal government to be generous in validating still unconfirmed old land claims" in Missouri. There was not necessarily a contradiction between Benton's dealings with the foreign landholders and his support for preemption rights. By liberalizing public-land policy, Benton did not aim to eradicate the rights of private landholders in the West by promoting squatters' rights on public land. He may have simply accepted that some land in the new territories was private and, therefore, would not be open to squatters. See Aron, *American Confluence: The Missouri Frontier from Borderland to Border State* (Bloomington: Indiana University Press, 2006), 193.

32    Gates, *Land and Law in California*, 4.

33    Ibid., 157, 305.

34    Robinson, *Land in California*, 63–64. According to Robinson, Anglo-American and European ranchers, who had purchased or married into possession of the land along the Sacramento and San Joaquin Rivers, comprised the majority of the population in Sacramento and the surrounding Central Valley.

35    Samuel C. Upham, *Notes of a Voyage to California Via Cape Horn, Together with Scenes in El Dorado, in the Years of 1849–'50. With an Appendix Containing Reminiscences ... Together with the Articles of Association and Roll of Members of "The Associated Pioneers of the Territorial Days of California"* (Philadelphia: the author, 1878), 307.

36    Ibid., 307–8. Emphasis is Upham's.

37    Ibid., 308.

38    Pisani, *Water, Land, and Law in the West*, 67.

39    Upham, *Notes of a Voyage to California*, 307.

40    Lord, *At the Extremity of Civilization*, 192.

41    William Prince to Charlotte Prince, October 21, 1849, Sacramento, William Prince Papers, Bancroft Library.

42    John Plumbe, *A Faithful Translation of the Papers Respecting the Grant Made by Governor Alvarado to John A. Sutter*, trans. William E. P. Hartnell, with an introduction by Neal Harlow (Sacramento, Calif.: Sacramento Book Collectors Club, 1942), 6–7; Hurtado, *John Sutter*, 93, 145.

43    Plumbe, *A Faithful Translation*, 11.

44    *History of Sacramento County, California*, ed. George F. Wright (Oakland, Calif.: Thompson & West, 1880), 50.

45    William Prince to Charlotte Prince, October 21, 1849.

46    Pisani, "Squatter Law in California, 1850–1858," 280–81.

47    *Placer Times*, May 5, 1849; quoted in Winfield J. Davis, *An Illustrated History of Sacramento County, California. Containing a History of Sacramento County from the Earliest Period of Its Occupancy to the Present Time* (Chicago: Lewis Publishing, 1890), 23.

48    U.S. Bureau of the Census, Population Census, Sacramento County, 1850, 359; http://www.ancestry.com.

49    Sacramento City Settlers' Association, *Sacramento City Settlers' Association*, broadside, December 15, 1849 (Sacramento, 1850), fZ209.C25 E13 no.154, Bancroft Library.

50    *History of Sacramento County*, ed. Wright, 50.

51    Sara Tappan Doolittle to Mrs. Stone, January 9, 1851, Belchertown, Mass., Charles Robinson Collection, Kenneth Spencer Research Library, University of Kansas (hereafter, Spencer Library).

52    J. H. McKune to Mary L. Robinson, November 9, 1895, Sacramento, box 2, Charles Robinson Collection, Spencer Library.

53    Sacramento City Directories, 1851–57, Center for Sacramento History. It is not possible to determine the number of Settlers' Association members. If a roster once existed, no record of it remains. Most likely, membership fluctuated with the arrival and departure of failed miners. As with other western boom towns in the nineteenth century, the population of Sacramento was highly transient.

54    Huston, *Land and Freedom*, 107.

55    Wilentz, *Chants Democratic*, 337–40.

56    In an undated composite photograph of the Land Reform Association, as the National Reform Association was sometimes later called, James McClatchy stands behind George Henry Evans. See Eleanor McClatchy Collection, Center for Sacramento History.

57  Greeley later described McClatchy as a "zealous reformer on either side of the continent." Horace Greeley to C. Cole, n.d., box 15, Eleanor McClatchy Collection, Center for Sacramento History.

58  James McClatchy, "A Texas Route to California," *New York Daily Tribune* Supplement, July 2, 1849, box CD1, Eleanor McClatchy Collection, Center for Sacramento History; Davis, *An Illustrated History*, 34–35.

59  This analysis is from a sample of 177 entries in the Preemption Claims Index. See Sacramento County Preemption Claims Index, 1852–54, Center for Sacramento History; Sacramento County Tax Assessor's Record, 1852 and 1854, Center for Sacramento History.

60  Sacramento County Preemption Claims Index, 1852–54, Center for Sacramento History; Sacramento County Tax Assessor's Record, 1852 and 1854, Center for Sacramento History.

61  Although nineteenth-century Americans often condemned speculation as antidemocratic, in reality, it was common practice in all public-land states. Squatters habitually occupied more land than they intended to use and sold the excess at a profit to raise funds for improving their homesteads. This pattern among California squatters conforms to the patterns of land acquisition Robert Swierenga has observed in nineteenth-century Iowa. See Swierenga, *Pioneers and Profits*, 15.

62  Sacramento City Settlers' Association, *Notice to Immigrants!!* broadsheet, June 14, 1850 (Sacramento; reprint, New York: Argus Books, 1977), Beinecke Library, Yale University (hereafter, Beinecke Library), BrSides Zc72 850nob.

63  James McClatchy, deposition in United States v. Sutter, 319 (N.D. Calif. 1861), 126.

64  U.S. Bureau of the Census, Population Census, Sacramento County, 1850, 146, 149; Sacramento County Tax Assessor's Records, 1853, Center for Sacramento History.

65  Sacramento City Directories, 1851–57, Center for Sacramento History; Sacramento County Tax Assessor's Records, 1851 and 1853, Center for Sacramento History; Sacramento City Recorder Preemption Claims Register, 1852–54, Center for Sacramento History; U.S. Bureau of the Census, Population Census, Sacramento County, 3rd Ward, 1860, 184.

66  Brannan also owned land in partnership with other Sacramento speculators valued at $3,000.

67  Sacramento County Preemption Claims Index, 1852–54, Center for Sacramento History; Sacramento County Tax Assessor's Record, 1852 and 1854, Center for Sacramento History.

68  Robbins, *Our Landed Heritage*, 9.

69  Sacramento Common Council Meeting minutes, December 15, 1849, and January 10, 1850, Center for Sacramento History. See also Eifler, *Gold Rush Capitalists*, 83–84.

70  Lord, *At the Extremity of Civilization*, 206.

71    William Prince to Charlotte Prince, January 7, 1850, Sacramento, William Prince Papers, Bancroft Library.

72    *History of Sacramento County*, ed. Wright, 51.

73    Sacramento Common Council Meeting minutes, March 4, 1850, Center for Sacramento History.

74    Samuel Brannan, *Scoundrel's Tale: The Samuel Brannan Papers*, ed. Will Bagley (Logan: Utah State University Press, 1999), 308–9.

75    *History of Sacramento County*, ed. Wright, 51; Brannan, *Scoundrel's Tale*, 310.

76    Charles Robinson, *The Kansas Conflict* (Lawrence, Kans.: Journal Publishing Company, 1898), 40.

77    Samuel W. Brown to his wife, August 14, 1850.

78    Plumbe, *A Faithful Translation*, 8–10.

79    Ibid., 11. Emphasis is Plumbe's.

80    Davis, *An Illustrated History*, 25.

81    Samuel W. Brown to his wife, August 14, 1850.

82    Sacramento City Settlers' Association, *Notice to Immigrants!!*

83    Upham, *Notes of a Voyage to California*, 335–36.

84    Davis, *An Illustrated History*, 26.

85    Upham, *Notes of a Voyage to California*, 335–36.

86    Ibid., 340–41. Emphasis is McClatchy's.

87    Reprinted in Davis, *An Illustrated History*, 25–26.

88    Robinson, *The Kansas Conflict*, 42.

89    Reprinted in Davis, *An Illustrated History*, 25–26.

90    Ibid.

91    Reprinted in Robinson, *The Kansas Conflict*, 47.

92    Ibid., 49.

93    Caulfield was a notorious brawler. He survived multiple bullet wounds, a vicious caning, and a nearly fatal stabbing only to be flattened by an evening train from Folsom while he was crossing 4th Street in Sacramento in 1888. By that point, he was well into his sixties, deaf, and unable to hear the warning whistle. See Davis, *An Illustrated History*, 34–35.

94    Ibid., 29; Robinson, *The Kansas Conflict*, 51; Upham, *Notes of a Voyage to California*, 341–42.

95    Upham, *Notes of a Voyage to California*, 343–45.

96    Samuel W. Brown to his wife, August 14, 1850.

97    J. H. McKune to Mary L. Robinson, November 9, 1895.

98    Upham, *Notes of a Voyage to California*, 343–45.

99    *History of Sacramento County*, ed. Wright, 55–56.

100   Davis, *An Illustrated History*, 33.

101   Samuel W. Brown to his wife, August 14, 1850.

102   Upham, *Notes of a Voyage to California*, 347–48.

103   "Allen the Squatter," *Alta California*, June 14, 1851, 2.

104   Davis, *An Illustrated History*, 34; Robinson, *The Kansas Conflict*, 56–57.

105   "Allen the Squatter," 2.

106   Henry Dalton to Governor [George Clement Perkins], June 6, 1882, DL1116, Henry Dalton Collection, Huntington Library; Abel Stearns to [Cave Johnson] Couts, July 6, 1855, CT2153, Cave Johnson Couts Papers, Huntington Library; "Large Restoration of Land at Pulgas Ranch," *Daily Bee*, July 13, 1861, p. 4, col. 1; "Land Troubles in San Joaquin," *Sacramento Daily Union*, June 2, 1862, p. 8, col. 3; "Excitement in Solano County," *Sacramento Daily Union*, December 18, 1862, p. 1, col. 7; "The Settlers in Sonoma County," *Sacramento Daily Union*, September 29, 1862, p. 8, col. 2; John Forster to [Cave Johnson] Couts, October 1864, CT850, Cave Johnson Couts Papers, Huntington Library; *Illustrated History of Sonoma County, California* (Chicago: Lewis Publishing, 1889), 131–38, 140–41. See also Tamara Venit Shelton, "A More Loyal, Union Loving People Can Nowhere Be Found: Squatters' Rights, Secession Anxiety, and the 1861 'Settlers' War' in San Jose," *Western Historical Quarterly* 41, no. 4 (2010): 473–94.

107   Frank Soulé, John H. Gihon, and James Nisbet, *The Annals of San Francisco* (New York, 1855; reprint, Berkeley, Calif.: Berkeley Hills Books, 1999), 467. Emphasis in original.

108   Ibid., 456–57.

109   "The Squatter Movement," *Alta California*, January 29, 1851, 2.

110   Soulé, Gihon, and Nisbet, *The Annals of San Francisco*, 365–66.

111   Ibid., 456–58, 540–42; "After the Battle," *Alta California*, October 11, 1867, 1; "The Squatter Riot," *Alta California*, October 12, 1867, 1.

112   *Illustrated History of Sonoma County*, 111–12.

113   Ibid., 129.

114   Vaught, *After the Gold Rush*, 52–53, 68.

115   *History of Alameda County, California* (Oakland, Calif.: M. W. Wood, 1883), 485.

116   Ibid., 488.

117   Ibid., 376.

## CHAPTER TWO

1   Charles Robinson to James McClatchy, May 29, 1856, box 15, Eleanor McClatchy Collection, Center for Sacramento History.

2   This chapter will not provide extensive detail of "Bleeding Kansas." For more on the social, cultural, and political history of Kansas in the pre–Civil War years, see Nicole Etcheson, *Bleeding Kansas: Contested Liberty in the Civil War Era* (Lawrence: University Press of Kansas, 2004); Gates, *Fifty Million Acres*; James Claude Malin, *John Brown and the Legend of Fifty-Six*, Memoirs

of the American Philosophical Society 17 (Philadelphia: American Philosophical Society, 1942); H. Craig Miner, *Seeding Civil War: Kansas in the National News, 1854–1858* (Lawrence: University Press of Kansas, 2008); Kristen Tegtmeier Oertel, *Bleeding Borders: Race, Gender, and Violence in Pre–Civil War Kansas* (Baton Rouge: Louisiana State University Press, 2009); Robert W. Richmond, *Kansas: A Land of Contrasts* (Saint Charles, Mo.: Forum Press, 1974); and William E. Unrau, *Indians of Kansas: The Euro-American Invasion and Conquest of Indian Kansas* (Topeka: Kansas State Historical Society, 1991).

3    John Hill McKune to Mary L. Robinson, November 9, 1895, Sacramento, Charles Robinson Collection, Spencer Library. McKune was a candidate for state senate in the same election. He also won.

4    "The Squatter Candidate," *Alta California*, October 12, 1850, 2; "Squatterism," *Alta California*, October 25, 1850, 2; and *History of Sacramento County*, ed. Wright, 56.

5    "Preemption in California," *Settlers and Miners Tribune*, November 28, 1850, 2.

6    Milton A. Latham, district attorney, Sacramento County, indictment for conspiracy, reprinted in "Indictment against the Squatter Leaders," *Alta California*, November 10, 1850, 2.

7    "Sutter's Grant," *Settlers and Miners Tribune*, November 14, 1850, 1.

8    "Two Weeks Later from California—Terrible Riot in Sacramento City," *Settlers and Miners Tribune*, November 14, 1850, 2.

9    "Opinion of the Press in the Eastern States on the Land Monopolists Riot in Sacramento," *Settlers and Miners Tribune*, November 14, 1850, 2–3; and "Opinion of the Press in the Eastern States on the Land Monopolists Riot in Sacramento," *Settlers and Miners Tribune*, November 21, 1850, 1.

10    "Indictment against the Squatter Leaders," 2.

11    Lord, *At the Extremity of Civilization*, 315–16.

12    "District Court of Solano County—November 15, 1850," *Settlers and Miners Tribune*, November 28, 1850, 2.

13    "From Our Benicia Correspondent," *Alta California*, November 12, 1850, 2; and "District Court of Solano County—November 15, 1850," 2.

14    Sara Tappan Doolittle to Phebe Stone, January 20, 1851, Belchertown, folder 1, Sara Tappan Doolittle Robinson Collection, Spencer Library.

15    *Journals of the Legislature of the State of California; at its Second Session: Held at the City of San Jose, Commencing on the Sixth Day of January, and Ending on the First Day of May, 1851* (San Jose, Calif.: Eugene Casserly, State Printer, 1851); and Don W. Wilson, *Governor Charles Robinson of Kansas* (Lawrence: University Press of Kansas, 1975), 9.

16    Quoted in Sara Tappan Doolittle to Phebe Stone, February 11, 1851, folder 1, Sara Tappan Doolittle Robinson Collection, Spencer Library.

17    Sara Tappan Doolittle to Phebe Stone, June [no day], 1851, folder 1, Sara Tappan Doolittle Robinson Collection, Spencer Library.

18    Sara Tappan Doolittle to Phebe Stone, November 15, 1851, folder 1, Sara Tappan Doolittle Robinson Collection, Spencer Library.

19    Gates, *Land and Law in California*, 160–62.

20    Mission and pueblo grants were considered separately.

21    Henry Halleck to Pablo de la Guerra, San Francisco, March 1, 1852, FAC667 (487), De la Guerra Family Collection, Huntington Library. Original held by the Santa Bárbara Mission Archive-Library.

22    Robinson, *Land in California*, 100.

23    Hoffman, *Reports of Land Cases.*

24    Gates, *Land and Law in California*, 35.

25    All private land case data is based on an analysis of Bowman, "Index of the Spanish-Mexican Private Land Grant Records and Cases of California." The total number does not include claims made by municipalities or by the Catholic Church; it does include claims for which no patent exists on record. Indian claimants were identified in the claim as "Indian." I use the term "Anglo" to denote claimants of non-Mexican and non-Indian descent, typically natives of Western Europe or the United States. To distinguish Anglo from Californio claimants, I first considered the surname. Where the surname was ambiguous or an Anglo claimant may have adopted a Spanish version of his original name (John Brown as Juan Moreno, for example), I cross-referenced the claimant with Hubert Howe Bancroft's *California Pioneer Register and Index* (Baltimore, Md.: Regional Publishing Company, 1964), which identifies the place of birth of people living in California before 1848. Paul Wallace Gates performed similar analysis of a less comprehensive log of 813 private land cases compiled by Judge Ogden Hoffman in 1862. Gates admits to the "incompleteness" of the Hoffman log in the third footnote of "The California Land Act of 1851," a chapter in his book *Land and Law in California*. Nonetheless, he arrived at a comparable breakdown of Anglo claimants—42 percent (see p. 41).

26    Successful claims only include claims for which patents exist on record. Unsuccessful claims only include claims for which records for discontinuance or rejection exist. The discrepancy between the total number and the sum of successful and unsuccessful claims represents cases for which records have been lost and the outcome of the case is consequently unrecorded in the Bowman index.

27    Leonard Pitt's history of Mexican ranching families in Southern California explains this finding. Southern California was spared the land rush that afflicted Northern California. It was distant from the major gold fields and, in many places, better suited for raising stock than for farming. Mexican grantees were therefore better able to retain their land, Pitt writes: "In general, then, notwithstanding debts, tax liens, extravagant expenses, subdivisions, and ownership changes, southern rancheros had less acute problems than their northern compadres. At the end of the first American decade they still held enough of their birthright to sustain the round of duties and pleasures that gave communal life its meaning" (*The Decline of the Californios*, 110).

28    Gates, *Land and Law in California*, 35.

29    Robinson, *Land in California*, 106. Data derived from Bowman, "Index of the Spanish-Mexican Private Land Grant Records and Cases of California."

Historians of California generally agree that protracted, expensive legal proceedings contributed to the economic decline of Californios, people of Mexican descent residing in California who stayed in the United States after the Mexican–American War. In *The Decline of the Californios*, Leonard Pitt argues: "If the Treaty of Guadalupe Hidalgo itself did not create the land-tenure trouble of 1853, the Land Law of 1851 was more culpable" (85). For Pitt, the land commission held Mexican grants to an unfair standard of scrutiny, a standard that made it nearly impossible for Mexican claimants to secure a patent to their land. On the other side of the debate, Paul Wallace Gates points to case studies that contradict Pitt's conclusion: "Studies of individual ranchos show that other factors, particularly the drought years, litigation over division of the ranchos among the many heirs, high living, taxes, and inability to compete with shrewder Yankee businessmen were more important" (*Land and Law in California*, 17). Karen B. Clay takes a more equivocal stance on the issue as she acknowledges the flaws of the Land Act but concludes that it was the best balance Congress could achieve among the interests of the federal government, squatters, and claimants; see Clay, "Property Rights and Institutions: Congress and the California Land Act of 1851," *Journal of Economic History* 59, no. 1 (1999): 124.

30   Gates, *Land and Law in California*, 28.

31   Pitt, *The Decline of the Californios*, 87.

32   Gates, *Land and Law in California*, 164–65.

33   The Know-Nothings were members of a short-lived political party united by nativism. They also called themselves the American Party.

34   "Settlers and Miners Meeting," *Settlers and Miners Tribune*, November 21, 1850, 2; and "The Coming Election," *Settlers and Miners Tribune*, November 28, 1850, 2.

35   Gates, *Land and Law in California*, 163–64.

36   The exact number of squatters is unknown, but state politicians believed that squatters constituted a large voting bloc in the state. Historian Donald Pisani notes: "By 1853, California squatters held the balance of power between the Democratic, Whig, and Know-Nothing parties" (*Water, Land, and Law in the West*, 72). An 1854 recession further swelled the ranks of potential squatters as it drove miners out of the mountains and into the valleys and cities. An article in the *Sacramento Daily Union* estimated that fifteen thousand miners left the mines to acquire land by preemption (Frank Blunt, "Mexican Grants— Settlers—Jumpers—the Causes that Depress Business, etc.," *Sacramento Daily Union*, February 11, 1854). I do not think there is a way to verify the accuracy of this number.

37   Gates, *Land and Law in California*, 164.

38   John Bigler, First Inaugural Address, Sacramento, January 8, 1852; transcription on the Governors' Gallery website, http://governors.library.ca.gov/addresses/03-bigler01.html (accessed March 15, 2013).

39   Henry Halleck to Pablo de la Guerra, San Francisco, July 24, 1853, FAC667 (487), De la Guerra Family Collection, Huntington Library.

40  Henry Halleck to Pablo de la Guerra, San Francisco, August 25, 1853, FAC667 (487), De la Guerra Family Collection, Huntington Library.

41  Henry Halleck to Pablo de la Guerra, San Francisco, January 29, 1852, FAC667 (487), De la Guerra Family Collection, Huntington Library. In his chapter "Pre–Henry George Land Warfare," Paul Wallace Gates details several squatter–claimant disputes stemming from the 1851 Land Act in Northern California (*Land and Law in California*, 185–208).

42  Gates, *Land and Law in California*, 74.

43  Ibid., 75–76.

44  Ellison, *A Self-Governing Dominion*, 116.

45  A. B. Nixon and I. W. Underwood, "To the Miners and Settlers of California," *Daily Bee*, July 13, 1857, 1.

46  Gates, *Land and Law in California*, 169–71; and Pisani, *Water, Land, and Law in the West*, 75–77.

47  McKune, *Minority Report*, 7.

48  "The Settlers Moving," *Daily Bee*, June 23, 1857, 2.

49  Southern slaveholders sought to extend slavery into the West to maintain a balance of power in Congress, where free and slave states vied for control. Free territories tended to become free states, and free states diluted the voting power of slave states in Congress. See Jonathan Halperin Earle, *Jacksonian Antislavery and the Politics of Free Soil, 1824–1854* (Chapel Hill: University of North Carolina Press, 2004); and Robbins, *Our Landed Heritage*, 171.

50  *Report of the Debates in the Convention of California, on the Formation of the State Constitution, in September and October, 1849* (Washington, D.C.: John T. Towers, 1850), 169–70. William Gwin, who was then only aspiring to the U.S. Senate, proposed to draw the state borders in a manner that would indirectly open up the southern- and western-most areas to slavery. He never stated that introducing slavery to the Far West was his intention. Rather, he argued that the far eastern boundary had been recognized by Mexico and, thus, was likely to be adopted by the United States. Antislavery delegates, including William Shannon and Morton McCarver, doubted Gwin's intent because they knew he held slaves back in his home state of Mississippi. They believed that his proposal to extend an eastern boundary to New Mexico Territory would create a state so large that Congress would be tempted to divide it in two: one free and one slave. Historians and biographers have debated Gwin's ambiguous attitudes toward slavery. Many scholars have concluded that Gwin was a "moderate," reluctantly pushed to embrace secession because of his party loyalties but not because of a genuine commitment to slavery. The evidence of Gwin's voting record between 1849 and 1861, however, supports historian Gerald Stanley's argument that Gwin's vote for a free California in 1848 did not reflect a "moderate" view on slavery. Gwin's initial vote to organize as free was likely a ploy to win voters among California's antislavery constituents. For the duration of his tenure as a senator thereafter, Gwin repeatedly supported expanding slavery, southern interests, and, eventually, secession. See Stanley, "Senator William Gwin: Moderate or Racist?,"

*California Historical Quarterly* 50, no. 3 (1971): 245–46. See also Ellison, *A Self-Governing Dominion*, 168–88.

51    *Assembly Journal*, 2 Sess., p. 798 (January 7, 1851) (statement of Peter Burnett). See also Stacey L. Smith, "Remaking Slavery in a Free State: Masters and Slaves in Gold Rush California," *Pacific Historical Review* 80, no. 1 (2011): 28–63.

52    *Report of the Debates in the Convention of California*, 48. Over the course of the decade, the black population remained small; in 1850, California's population of African-Americans was 962, less than 1 percent of the overall population, and by 1860, it had only increased to 4,086, just over 1 percent. See U.S. Census Office, *Report on the Population of the United States at the Eleventh Census: 1890*, pt. 1, "General Tables" (Washington, D.C.: Government Printing Office, 1895), 400–401.

53    *Report of the Debates in the Convention of California*, 46. The prohibition on monopoly was proposed by delegate Pacificus Ord, who asked that a constitutional provision be included that acknowledged that "perpetuities and monopolies are contrary to the genius of a republic, and shall not be allowed; nor shall any hereditary emoluments, privileges, or honors, ever be conferred in this State." Delegate Robert Semple added an explicit reference to state-chartered banks, asking that "no class of men should continue from generation to generation, to enjoy privileges given to them by the Legislature, which are not conferred under general law. The principle of monopolies includes banking privileges. The Legislature should have no power to grant charters or privileges to certain men to the exclusion of others." Semple believed that antimonopolism was "a question of great importance—the equal rights of mankind."

54    Etcheson, *Bleeding Kansas*, 27; and Abraham Lincoln and Stephen A. Douglas et al., *In the Name of the People: Speeches and Writings of Lincoln and Douglas in the Ohio Campaign of 1859*, ed. Harry V. Jaffa and Robert W. Johannsen (Columbus: Ohio State University Press, 1959), 39. Douglas did not anticipate the conflict that popular sovereignty would provoke in Kansas. He believed that slave labor was economically and environmentally incompatible with the western territories. In drafting the legislation for Kansas, he assumed that a majority of territorial residents would not vote to extend slavery. He was wrong.

55    Eric Foner, *Free Soil, Free Labor, Free Men: The Ideology of the Republican Party before the Civil War* (Oxford: Oxford University Press, 1995), 9–10.

56    Quoted in Winfield J. Davis, *History of Political Conventions in California, 1849–1892* (Sacramento: Publications of the California State Library, 1893), 61.

57    Quoted in ibid.

58    Although California Republicans opposed the expansion of slavery into the territories, they were not abolitionists. At the first Republican convention in Sacramento on April 30, 1856, the delegates refused to back an antislavery resolution over the protests of just a handful of abolitionists. They disavowed any repeal of slavery in any of the states where it existed. Instead, they declared that "we adopt as the cardinal principle of our organization the prohibition

of slavery in all the national territories." By opposing slavery's extension into the territories, California Republicans distinguished themselves from the Democrats and the Know-Nothings, who both upheld popular sovereignty but stopped short of demanding the more radical measure of abolition. See ibid., 60; and Foner, *Free Soil, Free Labor, Free Men*, 249.

59  Gerald Stanley, "Racism and the Early Republican Party: The 1856 Presidential Election in California," *Pacific Historical Review* 43, no. 2 (1974): 178–79.

60  "Republican Ratification Meeting," *Alta California*, July 20, 1856, 2.

61  Stanley, "Racism and the Early Republican Party," 182.

62  "Republican Ratification Meeting," 2.

63  Cornelius Cole, quoted in Stanley, "Racism and the Early Republican Party," 183.

64  Quoted in Catherine Coffin Phillips, *Cornelius Cole, California Pioneer and United States Senator: A Study in Personality and Achievements Bearing upon the Growth of a Commonwealth* (San Francisco: J. H. Nash, 1929), 88.

65  Robinson, *The Kansas Conflict*, 63. In the senate election, Frémont ran against Solomon Heydenfeldt, T. Butler King, J. B. Weller, J. W. Geary, and J. A. Collier. William Gwin, Frémont's fellow U.S. senator, was not up for re-election in 1851.

66  *Journals of the Legislature of the State of California*, 1162–65, 1188.

67  Robinson, *The Kansas Conflict*, 63.

68  Foner, *Free Soil, Free Labor, Free Men*, 198–99; and Stanley, "Racism and the Early Republican Party," 185–86. The election results were as follows: Democrats—96,695; Know-Nothings (aka Americans)—36,196; Republicans —20,695. Stanley's analysis of the ballots reveals that the Republicans captured the votes of anti-expansionist Democrats. However, conservative ex-Whig voters, in California and elsewhere, shied away from the new party.

69  "Squatter-ocracy," *Sacramento Daily Union*, September 5, 1851, 2; and obituary for James McClatchy, *Daily Bee*, October 26, 1883, 3.

70  "Yolo County Squatterism," *Sacramento Daily Union*, September 6, 1851, 2.

71  "Judge Ralston's Letter—The Settlers," *Daily Bee*, June 23, 1857, 2.

72  "The Present Position of Affairs," *Daily Bee*, July 8, 1857, 2.

73  *Daily Bee*, July 16, 1857, 2.

74  "The Present Position of Affairs," 2.

75  "The Settler Meeting," *Daily Bee*, July 20, 1857, 2.

76  "Settlers Convention," *Sacramento Daily Union*, August 5, 1857, 2.

77  "Republican State Convention," *Alta California*, May 1, 1856, 2; and Sacramento City Directory, 1854, Center for Sacramento History.

78  "Republican State Convention," 2.

79  Ibid.

80  "Republican Ratification Meeting," *Alta California*, July 21, 1856, 1.

81    "The Lecompton Constitution," *Daily Bee*, March 1, 1858, 2.

82    Etcheson, *Bleeding Kansas*, 28, 43. Etcheson understates the significance of slavery to the early immigrants in Kansas. She argues that the majority were first and foremost seeking wealth in land and either intended to keep the land for their own use or hold it for speculation. The same was true for anti-slavery immigrants. The passage of the Kansas-Nebraska Act in 1854, however, thrust Kansas and its immigrants into the center of the growing sectional crisis over slavery.

83    Report of the Special Committee Appointed to Investigate the Troubles in Kansas, 34th Cong., 1st Sess., 1856, Report 200, 953.

84    Ibid, 954–55.

85    Etcheson, *Bleeding Kansas*, 31. Etcheson argues that Missourians have been unfairly generalized as proslavery "border ruffians" because the majority actually went to Kansas as non-slaveholders. However, Missouri migrants played a foundational role in establishing anti-abolitionist squatters' associations. This connection made the label *Missourian* shorthand for identifying a squatter with an interest in expanding slavery.

86    Report of the Special Committee Appointed to Investigate the Troubles in Kansas, 950–51.

87    Wilson, *Governor Charles Robinson of Kansas*, 10.

88    Report of the Special Committee Appointed to Investigate the Troubles in Kansas, 878, 885.

89    Amos Lawrence to Charles Robinson, November 6, 1856, Charles Robinson Collection, Spencer Library; Charles Robinson to Joseph Lyman, November 21, 1856, Charles and Sara Robinson Papers, Kansas State Historical Society; and Joseph Lyman to the Kansas Land Trust trustees, March 13, 1860, Charles and Sara Robinson Papers, Kansas State Historical Society.

90    Robinson, *The Kansas Conflict*, 72.

91    Ibid., 70.

92    Frank W. Blackmar, *The Life of Charles Robinson: The First State Governor of Kansas* (Topeka, Kans.: Crane & Company, 1902), 111; and Etcheson, *Bleeding Kansas*, 36. Lawrence was a cotton merchant whose trade had inspired an utter abhorrence for the institution of slavery. Since stock sales never managed to cover the company's expenses, Lawrence paid the overdrafts and almost single-handedly rescued the endeavor from bankruptcy and failure.

93    Wilson, *Governor Charles Robinson of Kansas*, 11.

94    Report of the Special Committee Appointed to Investigate the Troubles in Kansas, 886–88. Between 1854 and 1855, the mission of the New England Emigrant Aid Company was unchanged. I could not find detailed demographic data on the two 1854 parties, but the composition of the third party is suggestive of the types of emigrants drawn by the company to Kansas.

95    Etcheson, *Bleeding Kansas*, 39.

96    Wilson, *Governor Charles Robinson of Kansas*, 57. This floating grant, based on a hurried and nebulous cession agreement between the Wyandotte Indians

and the federal government, would later become the source of extensive litigation between Robinson and other claimants.

97  John Baldwin to Charles Robinson, October 6, 1854, Charles and Sara Robinson Papers, Kansas State Historical Society. Sara Robinson identified Baldwin and his fellow squatters as "proslavery men, mostly from Missouri." Sara T. L. Robinson, *Kansas: Its Interior and Exterior Life*, 10th ed. (Lawrence, Kans.: Journal Publishing Company, 1899), 13.

98  Ibid.

99  Quitclaim records, 1855–59, box 1, folders 24–26, Charles Robinson Collection, Spencer Library.

100  Robinson, *The Kansas Conflict*, 80.

101  Ibid., 82–83.

102  Ibid., 85.

103  Etcheson, *Bleeding Kansas*, 74–75; and Robinson, *The Kansas Conflict*, 179.

104  Robinson, *The Kansas Conflict*, 236–38. If Robinson's detention in Lexington brought back memories of the Sacramento prison brig, they were made all the more vivid by an unexpected visit from R. H. McDonald, the Sacramento doctor who had removed the bullet from Robinson's back after the 1850 squatter riot. McDonald was in the area, heard of the famous prisoner, and went to see if it was indeed the same Charles Robinson. It was a remarkable but unhappy coincidence.

105  Tony R. Mullis, *Peacekeeping on the Plains: Army Operations in Bleeding Kansas* (Columbia: University of Missouri Press, 2004), 170.

106  There was some question as to whether the murdered settlers were in fact proslavery. The victims did not own slaves, but some among them were known to be affiliated with the proslavery cause. See Etcheson, *Bleeding Kansas*, 103–4.

107  Robinson, *The Kansas Conflict*, 323.

108  Etcheson, *Bleeding Kansas*, 43.

109  Charles Robinson to James McClatchy, June 28, 1857, box 15, Eleanor McClatchy Collection, Center for Sacramento History.

110  Ibid.

111  John C. Frémont to Charles Robinson, March 17, 1856, box 1, Charles Robinson Collection, Spencer Library.

112  Office of the Treasurer, Douglas and Shawnee Counties, 1860, Charles and Sara Robinson Papers, Kansas State Historical Society.

113  Charles Robinson, miscellaneous letters to Amos Lawrence, box 1, Charles Robinson Collection, Spencer Library.

114  Robinson, *The Kansas Conflict*, 121.

115  Amos Lawrence to Charles Robinson, May 16, 1857, box 1, Charles Robinson Collection, Spencer Library.

116  Gates, *Fifty Million Acres*, 78–79.

117    "The First Sale of Government Lands in California," *Daily Bee*, October 27, 1857, 2; and "Who May be Preemptors," *Daily Bee*, October 29, 1857, 2.

118    Gates, *Fifty Million Acres*, 83.

119    Ibid., 86–87.

120    Kirk Harold Porter and Donald Bruce Johnson, *National Party Platforms, 1840–1968* (Urbana: University of Illinois Press, 1970), 30–33.

121    Ibid. The Democrats split on the issue of slavery's extension into the territories. Stephen Douglas, ever optimistic that popular sovereignty would save the Democratic Party and the Union, led a faction against John Breckinridge, whose constituents argued that Congress had no right to interfere with slave property in any state or territory.

122    Foner, *Free Soil, Free Labor, Free Men*, 27–28; and Robbins, *Our Landed Heritage*, 171–74. Southern states also had relatively small acreage in public land and did not reap the benefits of revenues from sales of public lands in the West, which accrued to the western states and territories or went directly to federal coffers.

123    Robbins, *Our Landed Heritage*, 180. The bills were almost identical. In broad strokes, the House bill granted 160 acres of public lands free of cost to citizens or alien residents who declared their intention of becoming citizens. The Senate bill also granted 160 acres, but to citizens only and at a cost of twenty-five cents per acre. Both bills stipulated five-year residency and cultivation requirements.

124    Ibid., 180–81.

125    Ellison, *A Self-Governing Dominion*, 308–9.

126    Davis, *History of Political Conventions in California*, 121–24.

127    Ellison, *A Self-Governing Dominion*, 309; and Stanley, "Senator William Gwin: Moderate or Racist?," 251. The election results were as follows: Republicans (Lincoln)—38,733; Democrats (Douglas)—37,999; Democrats (Breckinridge)—33,969; Unionists—9,111.

128    Antonio Chabolla's name appears in the written record as Chaboya, Chavoya, Chavolia, and Chavaya.

129    Benjamin Franklin Gilbert, "The Confederate Minority in California," *California Historical Society Quarterly* 20 (1941): 154–55.

130    "It Is Crushed," *Daily Bee*, December 26, 1860, 2.

131    Benjamin Franklin Gilbert, "California and the Civil War: A Biographical Essay," *California Historical Society Quarterly* 40 (1961): 291; and Gilbert, "The Confederate Minority in California," 157–59.

132    Clarence C. Clendenen, "Dan Showalter—California Secessionist," *California Historical Society Quarterly* 40 (1961): 310–11.

133    Antonio Chabolla, Last Will and Testament, October 31, 1865, History San Jose; Anastasio Chabolla, Last Will and Testament, November 25, 1852, History San Jose.

134    Hoffman, *Reports of Land Cases*, 130–31.

135  Anastasio Chabolla, Last Will and Testament, November 25, 1852.

136  Bowman, "Index of the Spanish-Mexican Private Land Grant Records and Cases of California."

137  John M. Murphy, Certificate of Sheriff or Constable's Sale, Book B, July 13, 1861, Santa Clara County Recorder, History San Jose; Antonio Chabolla, Last Will and Testament, October 31, 1865; William Matthews, Deed, Book X, pp. 110–11, January 7, 1867, Santa Clara County Recorder, History San Jose; Patricia Loomis, "Scenery Change on Aborn Road," *San Jose News*, March 26, 1976, Signposts Scrapbook, San Jose Public Library; Loomis, "Fair Family Park Once the Old Bill Healy Place," *San Jose News*, August 20, 1976, Signposts Scrapbook, San Jose Public Library; and Loomis, "Property Fights along San Felipe Still Go On," *San Jose News*, March 10, 1978, Signposts Scrapbook, San Jose Public Library.

138  They were: John Aborn, Truman Andrews, Patterson Barnard, Chauncey C. Barbour, Thomas J. Baxter, James W. Bottsford, Thomas B. Farnsworth, Andrew Gehringer, Benjamin Kenny, William McClay, Jacob Newhouse, George Ostick, and William Raymond. See "Santa Clara Land Troubles," *Daily Bee*, April 20, 1861, 2; and Ancestry Library Edition, "1860 United States Federal Census, San Jose Township Schedule," http://www.ancestry.com (accessed April 11, 2013).

139  Antonio Chabolla, Deed, Book B, November 5, 1862, Santa Clara County Recorder, History San Jose.

140  John M. Murphy, Sheriff of Santa Clara County, Statement on the Writ of Restitution in the case of Antonio Chabolla v. William P. Raymond et al., Santa Clara County, April 13, 1861, Governors' Papers, folder 2, State Archive of California.

141  "Accounts of Eye Witnesses," *Daily Bee*, April 13, 1861, 4. Subsequent quotes in this paragraph come from the same source.

142  Ancestry Library Edition, "1860 United States Federal Census."

143  Alfred Doten, *The Journals of Alfred Doten, 1849–1903*, ed. Walter Van Tilburg Clark (Reno: University of Nevada Press, 1973), 597.

144  Ibid.

145  John Murphy to John Downey, April 15, 1861, Governors' Papers, folder 2, State Archive of California.

146  H. Brett Melendy and Benjamin F. Gilbert, *The Governors of California: Peter H. Burnett to Edmund G. Brown* (Georgetown, Calif.: Talisman Press, 1965), 101–2.

147  John Downey to William D. Raymond et al., April 18, 1861, Governors' Papers, folder 2, State Archive of California.

148  Although William Raymond is named as "William P. Raymond" in court documents, he appears as "William D. Raymond" in the census manuscript and in all correspondence with John Downey; Ancestry Library Edition, "1860 United States Federal Census."

149   William D. Raymond to John Downey, April 23, 1861, Governors' Papers, folder 2, State Archive of California.

150   W. G. Morris to John Downey, April 23, 1861, Governors' Papers, folder 2, State Archive of California.

151   Ibid.

152   Antonio Chabolla, propositions to William D. Raymond, William McClay, James M. Botherford [*sic*], and others, defendants, April 25, 1861, Governors' Papers, folder 2, State Archive of California.

153   "What South Carolina Could Do to Prevent the Reinforcement of Fort Sumter," *Alta California*, April 14, 1861, 1; "Civil War Probably Commenced," *Alta California*, April 22, 1861, 2; and "News of April 11th," *Alta California*, April 24, 1861, 1.

154   "The San Jose Settlers," *Daily Bee*, April 17, 1861, 2.

155   Quoted in "The Santa Clara Land Troubles," *Daily Bee*, April 20, 1861, 2.

156   Ibid.

157   Ibid.

158   *Daily Bee*, April 22, 1861, 2.

159   "The 'Chabolla' Tract near Santa Clara," *Alta California*, April 22, 1861, 1.

160   Quoted in "Settlers and Secession," *Daily Bee*, April 24, 1861, 22.

161   Ibid.

162   Letter from John Murphy to John Downey, May 2, 1861, Governors' Papers, folder 2, State Archive of California.

163   "The Santa Clara Imbroglio," *Daily Bee*, May 7, 1861, 2.

164   "Santa Clara Land Troubles," *Daily Bee*, May 2, 1861, 2.

165   Ibid.

166   "Land Troubles in Santa Clara," *Sacramento Daily Union*, April 30, 1861, 2. Subsequent quotes in this paragraph come from the same source.

167   William D. Raymond to John Downey, May 6, 1861, Governors' Papers, folder 2, State Archive of California. Subsequent quotes in this paragraph come from the same source.

168   Ibid. Subsequent quotes in this paragraph come from the same source.

169   Receipt from William Governeur Morris for services in Santa Clara County, May 7, 1861; William Matthews to John Downey, May 16, 1861; John Murphy to John Downey, May 24, 1861, Governors' Papers, folder 2, State Archive of California.

170   "Large Restoration of Land at Pulgas Ranch," *Daily Bee*, July 13, 1861, 4; "Land Troubles in San Joaquin," *Sacramento Daily Union*, June 2, 1862, 8; "Excitement in Solano County," *Sacramento Daily Union*, December 18, 1862, 17; and "The Settlers in Sonoma County," *Sacramento Daily Union*, September 29, 1862, 8.

171   Loomis, "Scenery Change on Aborn Road"; Eugene T. Sawyer, *History of Santa Clara County, California* (Los Angeles: Historic Record Company,

1922), 298; and Map of the Yerba Buena Rancho, [1900?], Hanging Maps Collection, Rod #1, San Jose Public Library.

172    Map of the Yerba Buena Rancho, [1900?], Hanging Maps Collection, Rod #1, San Jose Public Library.

173    Robbins, *Our Landed Heritage*, 207.

174    Passed in 1862, the act granted 160 acres to heads of household who were over the age of twenty-one, who were citizens or foreigners who had declared their intent to become citizens, and who had occupied the land and improved it for a period of five years. After those five years, homesteaders received title to the land for a nominal filing fee of $34 in Pacific coast states and $26 in all other states. The failures of the Homestead Act of 1862 have been well documented. For an overview, see Paul Wallace Gates, "The Homestead Law in an Incongruous Land System," in *The Public Lands*, ed. Carstensen, 317, 339.

175    Clarence Danhof, "Farm-Making Costs and the 'Safety Valve': 1850–1860," *Journal of Political Economy* 49, no. 3 (1941): 317–59; and William Deverell, "To Loosen the Safety Valve: Eastern Workers and Western Lands," *Western Historical Quarterly* 19, no. 3 (1988): 269–85.

176    The Pacific Railway Acts of 1862 and 1864 extended land grants to private railroad corporations building transcontinental railroads, which continued a practice that had begun in 1850 with a grant to the Illinois Central Railroad, a regional line. Congress intended the grants to subsidize railroad construction (with sales to individual settlers providing revenues with which railroad corporations could cover their costs) and to increase land values, especially on the alternating tracts retained as public land along the railway corridors. The government also used the grants to lower its own transportation costs by requiring railroads accepting land grants to carry troops and matériel free of charge or at reduced rates. See Albro Martin, *Railroads Triumphant: The Growth, Rejection, and Rebirth of a Vital American Force* (New York: Oxford University Press, 1992), 168; Lloyd J. Mercer, *Railroads and Land Grant Policy: A Study in Government Intervention* (New York: Academic Press, 1982), 3–6; and White, *Railroaded*, 24.

177    Wilson, *Governor Charles Robinson of Kansas*, 188.

178    Ibid., 114–15, 152.

179    Ibid., 162, 164–65. To promote readership, Robinson gave a free copy to any public library in the state that sent him a letter. After his death in 1894, Robinson's wife, Sara, continued the revisionist crusade by commissioning a biography by Frank Blackmar, dean of the graduate school at the University of Kansas. The biography failed to eclipse the memory of James Henry Lane and John Brown, so Sara recruited former free-state newspaper editor George W. Brown to write two other books on Robinson's behalf: *False Claims of Kansas Historians Truthfully Corrected* (Rockford, Ill.: the author, 1902) and *Reminiscences of Gov. R. J. Walker: With the True Story of the Rescue of Kansas from Slavery* (Rockford, Ill.: the author, 1902).

CHAPTER THREE

1    Charles K. McClatchy to Henry George Jr., Sacramento, April 8, 1899, box 15,
     Eleanor McClatchy Collection, Center for Sacramento History. Other biogra-
     phical accounts of George suggest that he and McClatchy met in Sacramento,
     and that George joined the printing office of the *Times* with assurances that
     he would move up into a reporting position, but neither George nor James
     McClatchy left a record to contradict Charles McClatchy's letter.

2    Henry George, journal entry, May 22, 1866, Henry George Papers, New York
     Public Library (hereafter, NYPL); and Henry George Jr., *The Life of Henry
     George* (Garden City, N.Y.: Doubleday, 1911), 173.

3    Henry George, *Progress and Poverty: An Inquiry into the Cause of Industrial
     Depressions and of Increase of Want with Increase of Wealth* (New York: Robert
     Schalkenbach Foundation, 1936).

4    For an account of apocryphal stories that it was McClatchy, not George, who
     authored *Progress and Poverty*, see *Sacramento County and Its Resources, a
     Souvenir of the Bee* (Sacramento: McClatchy and Company, 1895), Eleanor
     McClatchy Collection, Center for Sacramento History.

5    Sean Dennis Cashman, *America in the Gilded Age: From the Death of Lincoln
     to the Rise of Theodore Roosevelt*, 3rd ed. (New York: New York University
     Press, 1993), 24–25.

6    Henry George, "The American Republic: Its Dangers and Possibilities" (lecture,
     California Theatre, San Francisco, July 4, 1877), reprinted in George, *Our
     Land and Land Policy: Speeches, Lectures, and Miscellaneous Writings*,
     ed. Kenneth C. Wenzer (East Lansing: Michigan State University Press,
     1999), 119.

7    Years later, George's eldest son and biographer tactfully described the time-
     less adolescent dilemma: "Home life had much attractiveness for young
     George, yet he found it full of restrictions, for with all the heavy toil and hard
     discipline the preceding year and a quarter complete freedom of thought,
     and of actions, too, in the hours off duty. And now to come back to condi-
     tions where the most innocent of card-playing was regarded as an evil and
     riding in a public conveyance on Sunday as a desecration of the Lord's Day,
     made the energetic, masterful boy, or rather youth, for he was now in his
     eighteenth year, see new charms in the sea life" (*The Life of Henry George*,
     40–41).

8    Ibid., 41.

9    Henry George to Rebecca Curry, Philadelphia, June 1, 1857, Henry George
     Papers, NYPL.

10   Henry George to Ben Ely (unsent), Philadelphia, September 30, 1857, Henry
     George Papers, NYPL.

11   Henry George to Emma Curry, Philadelphia, June 29, 1857; and Henry George
     to Thomas B. Florence of the US Coast Surveying Steamer *Shubrick*, Phila-
     delphia, n.d., Henry George Papers, NYPL.

12    Henry George to Mrs. R. D. Curry, Philadelphia, May 29, 1858, Henry George Papers, NYPL.

13    "Justice the Object—Taxation the Means" (lecture, Metropolitan Hall, San Francisco, February 4, 1890), reprinted in George, *Our Land and Land Policy*, ed. Wenzer, 204.

14    Ibid.

15    George Jr., *The Life of Henry George*, 75–81.

16    Henry George, journal entry, December 26, 1864, Henry George Papers, NYPL.

17    Henry George, journal entry, February 17, 1865, Henry George Papers, NYPL.

18    Henry George, journal entries, June 7, 1868, April 30, 1876, and October 25, 1876, Henry George Papers, NYPL.

19    Henry George, journal entries, February 20 and 22, 1865, Henry George Papers, NYPL.

20    Quoted in George Jr., *The Life of Henry George*, 159.

21    Quoted in ibid.

22    George, "What the Railroad Will Bring Us," 301. Further citations of this work are given in the text.

23    Rohrbough, *Days of Gold*, 186.

24    Board of Supervisors, *San Francisco Municipal Reports for the Fiscal Year 1868–1869* (San Francisco: Cosmopolitan Printing, 1869), 554; and Charles A. Barker, *Henry George* (New York: Oxford University Press, 1955), 89–91.

25    Williams, *The Democratic Party and California Politics, 1880–1896*, 17; and Deverell, *Railroad Crossing*, 35.

26    Roger Daniels, *Asian America: Chinese and Japanese in the United States since 1850* (Seattle: University of Washington Press, 1988), 19–21.

27    Najia Aarim-Heriot, *Chinese Immigrants, African Americans, and Racial Anxiety in the United States, 1848–82* (Urbana: University of Illinois Press, 2003), 30–31; and Alexander Saxton, *The Indispensable Enemy: Labor and the Anti-Chinese Movement in California* (Berkeley: University of California Press, 1995), 5–6.

28    Saxton, *The Indispensable Enemy*, 7.

29    Henry George, journal entries, March 14, 15, and 22, 1867, and August 17, 1867, Henry George Papers, NYPL. After extensive searching through the *Daily Herald*, I was unable to find the article.

30    Saxton, *The Indispensable Enemy*, 72.

31    Henry George, "The Chinese in California," *New-York Tribune*, May 1, 1869, 2. Further citations of this work are given in the text.

32    Anti-Chinese agitation in California developed alongside a conceptualization of race that used cultural and physical traits as evidence of innate and un-changeable racial types. Nineteenth-century scientists and intellectuals di-vided humanity into three distinct groups—Caucasoid, Mongoloid, and Negroid—and made elaborate studies of the physiological and psychological

differences that supposedly defined them. The identification of a "Caucasoid" group had the effect of elevating Irish, Italian, and non-Anglo-Saxon whites into a common white race. This new racial order was particularly found in regions like the far western United States, where the presence of "Mongoloid" Asians made cultural and physical differences among whites seem less significant. See Matthew Frye Jacobson, *Whiteness of a Different Color: European Immigrants and the Alchemy of Race* (Cambridge, Mass.: Harvard University Press, 1998), 31, 46.

33    George's assessment of Chinese bachelor societies and their low standards of living are detailed in Nayan Shah, *Contagious Divides: Epidemics and Race in San Francisco's Chinatown*, American Crossroads 7 (Berkeley: University of California Press, 2001). Perceptions of "queer domesticity" among all-male Chinese households and violations of the "American standard of living" were widespread. Shah describes the ways in which these perceptions animated campaigns against Chinese workers and formed the justification for discriminatory ordinances targeting Chinatown businesses and residences in late nineteenth-century San Francisco.

34    John Russell Young, managing editor of the *New-York Tribune*, New York City, May 11, 1869, Henry George Papers, NYPL.

35    John Stuart Mill to Henry George, Avignon, France, October 23, 1869, published in the *Oakland Daily Transcript*, November 20, 1869, Henry George Papers, NYPL; and editorials on John Stuart Mill and Chinese immigration, typewritten copies, Henry George Papers, NYPL.

36    John Stuart Mill to Henry George.

37    George, editorials on Mill.

38    Saxton, *The Indispensable Enemy*, 80.

39    Ibid., 68, 90–91.

40    Ibid., 93.

41    Williams, *The Democratic Party and California Politics, 1880–1896*.

42    Nash, *State Government and Economic Development*, 134, 208.

43    Henry George, journal entries, March 3 and 26, 1871, Henry George Papers, NYPL.

44    George, *Our Land and Land Policy*, reprinted in George, *Our Land and Land Policy: Speeches, Lectures, and Miscellaneous Writings*, ed. Wenzer, 7–8. Further citations of the pamphlet are to this edition and are given in the text.

45    U.S. Census Office, *The Statistics of the Wealth and Industry of the United States . . . from the Original Returns of the Ninth Census* (Washington D.C.: Government Printing Office, 1872), 340–41.

46    Sucheng Chan's *This Bittersweet Soil: The Chinese in California Agriculture, 1860–1910* (Berkeley: University of California Press, 1986) disproves George's thesis that Chinese labor allowed land monopoly to proliferate in California by dispelling the myth that Chinese workers were demographically dominant or universally inexpensive and compliant. Moreover, farm laborers, Chinese and white, may have actively pursued tenantry as a landholding strategy. They

turned to tenantry as a means of working toward ownership, increasing the area of their farmland, rotating crops to avoid soil depletion, and diversifying their financial operations to protect against downturns. More recently, Orsi's book on the Southern Pacific Railroad, *Sunset Limited,* has demonstrated how railroad corporations sold land to facilitate the settlement of California by small freeholders.

47    For examples of railroad corporations' land sales to individual settlers, see Orsi, *Sunset Limited,* 78–82; and Richard Cleghorn Overton, *Burlington West: A Colonization History of the Burlington Railroad* (Cambridge, Mass.: Harvard University Press, 1941).

48    In the 1860s, Chinese tenants rented relatively small plots of agricultural land (usually under sixty acres), but in the 1870s, they began to rent and occupy larger lots, many over one hundred acres in size; see Sucheng Chan, *This Bittersweet Soil,* 158.

49    "Chinese Matters," *Daily Bee,* March 26, 1859, 2.

50    "What is to be done with the Chinese?" *Daily Bee,* November 3, 1859, 2.

51    Kenneth L. Kusmer, *Down and Out, On the Road: The Homeless in American History* (Oxford: Oxford University Press, 2002), 38.

52    Samuel Rezneck, "Distress, Relief, and Discontent in the United States during the Depression of 1873–78," *Journal of Political Economy* 8, no. 6 (1950): 494–512.

53    *Report of Special Committee on Resolutions of Mr. Barker of Nevada, Concerning Land Monopoly* (Sacramento, Calif.: T. A. Springer, State Printer, 1872).

54    *Reports of the Joint Committees on Swamps and Overflowed Lands and Land Monopoly: Presented at the Twentieth Session of the Legislature of California* (Sacramento, Calif.: G. H. Springer, State Printer, 1874), 28.

55    Henry George to Catherine Vallance George, San Francisco, November 13, 1876, Henry George Papers, NYPL.

56    The national Republican platform of 1876 included a statement affirming the party's "opposition to further grants of the public lands to corporations and monopolies, and a demand that the national domain be devoted to free homes for the people." The Democrats had no monopoly on antimonopolism. See Porter and Johnson, *National Party Platforms,* 54.

57    Henry George, speech made during the 1876 presidential election, San Francisco, n.d., Henry George Papers, NYPL, 14–15.

58    Ibid., 12.

59    Ibid., 75.

60    Ibid., 30.

61    Ibid., 72.

62    Henry George, "The American Republic: Its Dangers and Possibilities," reprinted in George, *Our Land and Land Policy,* 117–18.

63    Ibid., 119.

64　Henry George, *Why Work Is Scarce, Wages Low, and Labor Restless: A Lecture by Henry George, Delivered in the Metropolitan Temple, San Francisco, Cal., March 26, 1878* (San Francisco: The California Tax Reform League, 1885), 8.

65　If George made a public comment on the Chinese Exclusion Act of 1882 when it passed, it has been lost in the historical record. He did vocally support its subsequent renewal in 1892, according to the biography of George written by his son Henry George Jr., *The Life of Henry George*, 202–3.

66　Henry George, "The Kearney Agitation in California," *Popular Science Monthly* 17 (1880): 448.

67　Saxton, *The Indispensable Enemy*, 113–14.

68　George, "The Kearney Agitation in California," 443.

69　Alexander Saxton contends that Kearney's anti-Chinese movement was a thinly veiled attempt to gain "control of clubs which largely comprised the Democratic Party's city machinery"; see Saxton, *The Indispensable Enemy*, 119–20.

70　Edith Dobie, *The Political Career of Stephen Mallory White: A Study of Party Activities under the Convention System* (Stanford, Calif: Stanford University Press, 1927; reprint, New York: AMS Press, 1971), 28.

71　George, "The Kearney Agitation in California," 450.

72　Ibid., 445–46.

73　Although George rejected Kearney's brand of anti-Chinese politics, he maintained his view on the Chinese up to the final years of his life. On an international lecture tour in 1890, George sent reports of his travels back to the editors of *The Standard* for publication. Arriving in Honolulu in February, he was moved by the plight of the Native Hawaiians, dispossessed of their land and decimated by disease. He blamed the "heathen Chinee," who had spread so prodigiously across the island that "it seems now manifest destiny that the bulk of the population of these islands in the future will be Mongolian or a Mongolian admixture." Efforts at exclusion seemed futile to George, who surmised that "the Chinese are too firmly rooted for [exclusion] to succeed." In December 1890, George experienced a mild stroke, which forced him to withdraw from his career as a writer, although he continued to give lectures when his health permitted. Even as his public appearances dwindled, his support of Chinese exclusion continued unabated. Privately, George defended Congressman James Maguire's support for renewal of the Chinese Exclusion Act in 1893. The congressman from California, a devotee of George's single tax, received public censure by William Lloyd Garrison Jr., son of the famous antebellum abolitionist and president of the Chinese Defense League of Massachusetts. Garrison accused Maguire of violating the egalitarian principles of the single tax by supporting Chinese exclusion. However, in a letter to Garrison, George reaffirmed the centrality of anti-Chinese racism to his reform agenda and asked Garrison, "Is there no such thing as family, nation, race?" In his reply to George, Garrison expressed his shock and disappointment at George's bald-faced racism, but he would not have been so surprised, had he read the canon of George's work. For his part, George probably saw

Garrison, who had family ties to the Northern Pacific Railway, as an agent of monopoly and was not at all surprised that such a man would oppose the renewal of the Chinese Exclusion Act and welcome a new legion of cheap immigrant laborers. See Henry George, "Dispatch from Honolulu," *The Standard,* March 26, 1890, 2; and William Lloyd Garrison to Henry George, Boston, December 4, 1893, Henry George Papers, NYPL.

74    The notable exception is George's first biographer, his son Henry George Jr., who devoted a chapter to the topic of Chinese exclusion in his biography, *The Life of Henry George.* Some discussion of George's anti-Chinese activism within the context of land reform also appears in Ian Tyrrell's *True Gardens of the Gods: Californian–Australian Environmental Reform, 1860–1930* (Berkeley: University of California Press, 1999), but Tyrrell only refers to *Our Land and Land Policy,* and he does not suggest the extent to which Chinese exclusion helped George formulate his antimonopolist reform vision through the course of his career. In *The Indispensable Enemy,* Alexander Saxton analyzes George's 1869 *Tribune* article on the Chinese but within the context of anti-Chinese sentiment, not land reform.

75    Jacobson, *Whiteness of a Different Color,* 43–44.

CHAPTER FOUR

1    Reprinted in Terence Vincent Powderly, *Thirty Years of Labor, 1859–1889* (New York: A. M. Kelley, 1967), 173. This volume, originally published in 1889, four years before Powderly resigned from the position of grand master workman, contains reprints of many documents from the Knights of Labor and its predecessors (including the Industrial Brotherhood and the National Labor Union), as well as Powderly's lectures and letters. Powderly also interspersed commentary throughout and gave historical context for each of the reprinted texts.

2    Henry George to Terence Vincent Powderly, New York City, April 19, 1883, Terence V. Powderly Papers [microfilm], Stanford University Library.

3    Lee Benson, *Merchants, Farmers, & Railroads: Railroad Regulation and New York Politics, 1850–1887* (Cambridge, Mass.: Harvard University Press, 1955), 17, 150–51; Cashman, *America in the Gilded Age,* 358–59; William Cronon, *Nature's Metropolis: Chicago and the Great West* (New York: W. W. Norton, 1991), 137–42; and Sanford D. Gordon, "Attitudes Towards Trusts Prior to the Sherman Act," *Southern Economic Association* 30, no. 2 (1963): 158–59.

4    Other antimonopolist political parties included the Labor Reform (1872), Anti-Monopoly (1884), and United Labor (1888) Parties. For an extensive discussion of financial antimonopolism among Greenbackers and Populists, see Gretchen Ritter, *Goldbugs and Greenbacks: The Antimonopoly Tradition and the Politics of Finance in America* (Cambridge: Cambridge University Press, 1997).

5    Porter and Johnson, *National Party Platforms,* 43; and Ritter, *Goldbugs and Greenbacks,* 47.

6    See, for example, *Our Land and Land Policy* (1871), in which George defined land monopoly as "the tendency to the aggregation of land" and land monopolists as "a few individuals who hold thousands and hundreds of thousands of acres a piece." In this pamphlet, George called for the government to "break up present monopolization" and again emphasized the size of land monopolies. Reprinted in George, *Our Land and Land Policy*, ed. Wenzer, 24–25, 72.

7    George, *Progress and Poverty*, 217.

8    Ibid., 272.

9    Ibid., 386.

10   George Jr., *The Life of Henry George*, 324.

11   Ibid., 300.

12   John L. Thomas, *Alternative America: Henry George, Edward Bellamy, Henry Demarest Lloyd, and the Adversary Tradition* (Cambridge, Mass.: Belknap Press, 1983), 183.

13   Thomas N. Brown, *Irish-American Nationalism, 1870–1890* (Philadelphia: Lippincott, 1966), 102.

14   Ibid., 101–3.

15   Attributed to James McClatchy, August 13, 1879, box CD1, Eleanor McClatchy Collection, Center for Sacramento History.

16   Henry George to James McClatchy, New York, October 9, 1881, Henry George Papers, NYPL.

17   Henry George to Abram S. Hewitt, New York, October 1897, Henry George Papers, NYPL.

18   Henry George, "The Land Question," *Irish World*, May 1, 1880, 6.

19   "What Is the Matter?," *Irish World*, March 13, 1880, 4.

20   George, "The Land Question," 6.

21   Ibid.

22   Kusmer, *Down and Out, On the Road*, 47–48.

23   George, "The Land Question," 6.

24   Henry George to James McClatchy, New York, October 9, 1881.

25   James McClatchy to Henry George, Sacramento, March 14, 1883, Henry George Papers, NYPL.

26   James McClatchy obituary, *Daily Bee*, October 26, 1883, 3; and "Themis," *Daily Bee*, October 26, 1889, 1.

27   Brown, *Irish-American Nationalism*, 104, 106; "Resolutions of the New York Hotel Conference," March 11, 1880; Patrick Ford to Terence V. Powderly, March 25, 1881, New York; Patrick Ford to Terence V. Powderly, November 12, 1881, New York, Terence V. Powderly Papers [microfilm], Stanford University Library.

28   Terence Vincent Powderly, *The Path I Trod: The Autobiography of Terence V. Powderly*, ed. Harry J. Carman, Henry David, and Paul N. Guthrie (New York: Columbia University Press, 1940), 178–79, 182.

29   Powderly, *Thirty Years of Labor*, 3–4.

30   Ibid.

31   By the late nineteenth century, economists identified these industries as "natural monopolies"—industries whose high fixed costs made free competition less efficient than monopoly.

32   Reprinted in Powderly, *Thirty Years of Labor*, 3–4, 199.

33   Ibid., 173.

34   By the end of his life in 1924, Powderly embraced George's broader understanding of land use. In his memoirs, written between 1907 and 1921 and published posthumously, he wrote: "The owner of land cannot remove the acres from where their creator placed them at creation, he cannot take it with him when he dies. All he can get out of it is the use of it in what he digs from it and every being on earth whether he be tiller of the soil or delver in the mine, home, or factory must live off the land" (*The Path I Trod*, 228–29).

35   Powderly, *Thirty Years of Labor*, 178.

36   Ibid., 177–78.

37   Postel, *The Populist Vision*, 32–33, 209; and Powderly, *Thirty Years of Labor*, 176.

38   Harold H. Dunham, "Some Crucial Years of the General Land Office, 1875–1890," in *The Public Lands*, ed. Carstensen, 181–98.

39   Powderly, *Thirty Years of Labor*, 180.

40   See, for example, "Land and Labor," *Journal of United Labor* 3, no. 2 (June 1882): 250; "Landlordism," *Journal of United Labor* 6, no. 18 (January 25, 1886): 1182; and "The Land," *Journal of United Labor* 7, nos. 11–12 (October 10–25, 1886): 477.

41   Robert E. Weir, "A Fragile Alliance: Henry George and the Knights of Labor," *American Journal of Economics and Sociology* 56, no. 4 (1997): 423.

42   Ibid.

43   See, for example, *Journal of United Labor* 6, no. 7 (August 10, 1885): 1049.

44   George, *Progress and Poverty*, 327.

45   Ibid., 545.

46   George, "The Crime of Poverty" (lecture, Opera House, Burlington, Iowa, April 1, 1885), reprinted in George, *Our Land and Land Policy*, ed. Wenzer, 138–39.

47   George, *Progress and Poverty*, 456–57.

48   Ibid., 405. Emphasis in the original.

49   Ibid., 452–53.

50   This was a common criticism of the Homestead Act, which came under attack as early as 1868 and continued to be a subject of public debate through the 1880s. See Robbins, *Our Landed Heritage*, 273.

51   Reprinted in Powderly, *Thirty Years of Labor*, 172.

52   George, *Our Land and Land Policy*, 150.

53   Andrew Gyory, *Closing the Gate: Race, Politics, and the Chinese Exclusion Act* (Chapel Hill: University of North Carolina Press, 1998), 246–47; and Powderly, *Thirty Years of Labor*, 129. The Knights of Labor supported prohibitions on convict labor and the Foran Act of 1885, which excluded immigrants from entering the country under labor contracts, for the same reasons. Inexpensive contract labor swelled the ranks of workers competing for the same jobs.

54   The preamble to the constitution of the Knights of Labor is reprinted in Powderly, *Thirty Years of Labor*, 128–30.

55   Ibid., 219.

56   David A. Wolff, *Industrializing the Rockies: Growth, Competition, and Turmoil in the Coalfields of Colorado and Wyoming, 1868–1914* (Boulder: University of Colorado Press, 2003), 86.

57   "Memorial of Chinese Laborers, Resident at Rock Springs, Wyoming Territory, to the Chinese Consul at New York," reprinted in *"Chink!" A Documentary History of Anti-Chinese Prejudice in America*, ed. Cheng-Tsu Wu (New York: World Pub., 1972), 152–64. The testimony was signed by 559 Chinese residents of Rock Springs. There are conflicting reports as to how many Chinese miners were employed by the Union Pacific. The numbers were likely between three hundred and four hundred in Rock Springs and an additional one hundred to two hundred in Evanston. There may also have been Chinese residents of Rock Springs working in ancillary businesses who gave testimony, but it was not recorded because they were not on the Union Pacific payroll.

58   "The Wyoming Massacre," *New York Times*, September 6, 1885, 7; and "Memorial of Chinese Laborers."

59   Reprinted in W. W. Stone, "The Knights of Labor on the Chinese Situation," *Overland Monthly* 7, no. 39 (1886): 230.

60   Reprinted in ibid.

61   Ibid., 225.

62   Ibid.

63   Powderly to W. W. Stone, Scranton, Pennsylvania, January 21, 1886, reprinted in ibid., 229.

64   Ronald William Yanosky, "Seeing the Cat: Henry George and the Rise of the Single Tax Movement, 1879–1890" (PhD diss., University of California, Berkeley, 1993), 178–79.

65   Henry George, New York Labor Conference address, August 26, 1886, Henry George Papers, NYPL.

66   Philip Sheldon Foner, *History of the Labor Movement in the United States*, vol. 2 (New York: International Publishers, 1955), 123–24.

67   George Jr., *The Life of Henry George*, 472.

68   Foner, *History of the Labor Movement*, 33; and George Jr., *The Life of Henry George*, 480–81.

69   George Jr., *The Life of Henry George*, 481–82.

70   Leon Fink, *Workingmen's Democracy: The Knights of Labor and American Politics* (Urbana: University of Illinois Press, 1983), 25–26.

71   Henry George, New York Labor Conference address, August 26, 1886.

72   "The Strike," *The Standard*, February 5, 1887, 4.

73   "The 'Fight in the Dark,'" *The Standard*, February 12, 1887, 4.

74   "The Strike," 4.

75   Foner, *History of the Labor Movement*, 99–100.

76   Kim Voss, *The Making of American Exceptionalism: The Knights of Labor and Class Formation in the Nineteenth Century* (Ithaca, N.Y.: Cornell University Press, 1993), 2.

77   James R. Green, *Death in the Haymarket: A Story of Chicago, the First Labor Movement, and the Bombing That Divided Gilded Age America* (New York: Pantheon, 2006), 185.

78   Ibid., 225–26.

79   Powderly, *Thirty Years of Labor*, 280.

80   Ibid., 281–82.

81   Ibid., 284.

82   Ibid., 284–86.

83   Green, *Death in the Haymarket*, 319.

84   Powderly, *Thirty Years of Labor*, 276.

85   Ibid., 271.

86   George, *Progress and Poverty*, 320–21.

87   Henry George and H. M. Hyndman, July 2, 1889, St. James Hall, London, transcription at http://www.cooperativeindividualism.org/george-henry_single-tax-versus-social-democracy-1889.html.

88   Yanosky, "Seeing the Cat," 221.

89   Powderly, *Thirty Years of Labor*, 191.

90   Ibid., 197.

91   "To Workingmen," *The Standard*, New York, June 16, 1888, reprinted in George, *Our Land and Land Policy*, ed. Wenzer, 189.

92   Henry George to Terence V. Powderly, New York City, April 19, 1883, Terence V. Powderly Papers [microfilm], Stanford University Library.

93   Henry George, form letter, New York City, March 23, 1884, Terence V. Powderly papers [microfilm], Stanford University Library.

94   George, "The 'Fight in the Dark,'" 4.

95   Ibid., 2.

96   Ibid., 1.

97   Ibid.

98   Ibid.

99   Foner, *History of the Labor Movement*, 149–50.

100  Ibid., 153.

101  Weir, "A Fragile Alliance," 431–32.

102   Foner, *History of the Labor Movement*, 152–53.

103   Weir, "A Fragile Alliance," 431–32.

104   "The New York Election," *The Standard*, November 12, 1887, 1.

105   Fink, *Workingmen's Democracy*, 221.

106   Ibid., 29–30; and Foner, *History of the Labor Movement*, 78–79.

107   Foner, *History of the Labor Movement*, 157; and Norman J. Ware, *The Labor Movement in the United States, 1860–1895: A Study in Democracy* (Gloucester, Mass.: Peter Smith, 1959), 298, 373.

108   In 1894, Knights of Labor Secretary John Hayes forced Powderly to resign under accusations that he had withheld Knights' properties from the other officers. These charges reflected the estrangement that had developed between Powderly and the more radical factions within the general executive board, who saw him as too conservative and as the main obstacle to their plans. Powderly's overthrow signaled the Knights' rejection of his antimonopolism for a more radical agenda. See Powderly, *The Path I Trod*, ix, 299–301; and Ware, *The Labor Movement in the United States*, 103.

109   Terence Powderly, unpublished document written at the Department of Labor, possibly to the mayor of Birmingham, Alabama, n.d., Terence V. Powderly papers [microfilm], Stanford University Library.

110   Robert D. Johnston, *The Radical Middle Class: Populist Democracy and the Question of Capitalism in Progressive Era Portland, Oregon* (Princeton, N.J.: Princeton University Press, 2003), 161–63; David Montgomery, *Citizen Worker: The Experience of Workers in the United States with Democracy and the Free Market During the Nineteenth Century* (Cambridge: Cambridge University Press, 1993), 113; and Arthur Nichols Young, *The Single Tax Movement in the United States* (Princeton, N.J.: Princeton University Press, 1916), 287–88.

111   The term "single tax" was borrowed from eighteenth-century French political economists who advocated *l'impôt unique* on rent to relieve the burden of taxation on the "productive class," farmers, and other agricultural laborers, and to delimit the role of the state in the economy. See Fox-Genovese, *The Origins of Physiocracy*, 10.

112   *George and the Scholars: A Century of Scientific Research Reveals the Reformer Was an Original Economist and a World-Class Social Philosopher*, ed. Will Lissner and Dorothy Burnham Lissner (New York: Robert Schalkenbach Foundation, 1991), 95.

113   Henry George to Louis F. Post, New York City, April 2, 1891, Henry George Papers, NYPL.

114   George, address before the U.S. House of Representatives, March 9, 1893, Henry George Papers, NYPL.

115   Ibid.

116   Ibid.

117   George Jr., *The Life of Henry George*, 607–8.

118   George Raymond Geiger, *The Philosophy of Henry George* (New York: Macmillan, 1933), 428–36.

CHAPTER   FIVE

1    The best studies of the Battle of Mussel Slough are Richard Maxwell Brown, *No Duty to Retreat: Violence and Values in American History and Society* (New York: Oxford University Press, 1991), 95–96, 109–10; Irving McKee, "Notable Memorials to Mussel Slough," *Pacific Historical Review* 17, no. 1 (1948): 20–22; and Orsi, *Sunset Limited*, 99–102.

2    Charles Edward Russell's *Stories of the Great Railroads* included a discussion of the "Massacre at Mussel Slough," which was the first historical account of the event; see *Stories of the Great Railroads* (Chicago: Charles H. Kerr & Co., 1912), chap. 9, "Speaking of Widows and Orphans." The most famous novel inspired by the events at Mussel Slough was and remains Frank Norris's *The Octopus: A Story of California* (New York: Doubleday, Page & Co., 1901). It was preceded by several other novels, including the three discussed at length in this chapter as well as William C. Morrow's *Blood-Money* (San Francisco: F. J. Walker & Co., 1882).

3    Kusmer, *Down and Out, On the Road*, 47–48.

4    Kevin Starr, *Americans and the California Dream, 1850–1915* (New York: Oxford University Press, 1973), 110–11.

5    Ibid., 116–18.

6    With few exceptions, historians of California writing in the twentieth century continued to cite Bancroft and his interpretation of squatters. See, for example, Leonard Pitt's criticism of fellow historian Paul Wallace Gates in *The Decline of the Californios*, 89. More recently, Orsi's *Sunset Limited* has recapitulated a Bancroftian interpretation of squatterism as criminality.

7    Hubert Howe Bancroft, *California Pastoral* (San Francisco: History Company, 1888), 293.

8    Ibid., 262–63.

9    Ibid., 293.

10   Phoebe S. Kropp (Phoebe S. K. Young), *California Vieja: Culture and Memory in a Modern American Place* (Berkeley: University of California Press, 2006), 41.

11   Bancroft, *California Inter Pocula*, 397.

12   Ibid., 397–98.

13   Hubert Howe Bancroft et al., *History of California*, vol. 6, *1848–1859*, The Works of Hubert Howe Bancroft 23 (San Francisco: History Company, 1884), 334n25.

14   Ibid., 333n25.

15   Jacquelyn Ann K. Kegley, *Josiah Royce in Focus* (Bloomington: Indiana University Press, 2008), 4.

16   Josiah Royce, "Tests of Right and Wrong," in *Fugitive Essays*, introduction by Jacob Loewenberg (Cambridge, Mass.: Harvard University Press, 1920), 187–90.

17    Robert V. Hine, *Josiah Royce: From Grass Valley to Harvard* (Norman: University of Oklahoma Press, 1992), 17–21.

18    See John Clendenning, *The Life and Thought of Josiah Royce* (Madison: University of Wisconsin Press, 1985), 136; and Kegley, *Josiah Royce in Focus*, 8.

19    Hine, *Josiah Royce*, 47–70.

20    Quoted in ibid., 39.

21    Peter Fuss, *The Moral Philosophy of Josiah Royce* (Cambridge, Mass.: Harvard University Press, 1965), 24.

22    Quoted in Clendenning, *The Life and Thought of Josiah Royce*, 133.

23    Josiah Royce, *California: A Study of American Character: From the Conquest in 1846 to the Second Vigilance Committee in San Francisco*, introduction by Ronald A. Wells (Berkeley, Calif.: Heyday Books, 2002). Royce concluded: "After all, however, our lesson is an old and simple one. It is the State, the Social Order that is divine. We are all but dust, save as this social order gives us life. When we think it our instrument, our plaything, and make our private fortunes the one object, then this social order rapidly becomes vile to us; we call it sordid, degraded, corrupt, unspiritual, and ask how we may escape from it forever. But if we turn again and serve the social order, and not merely ourselves, we soon find that what we are serving is simply our own highest spiritual destiny in bodily form. It is never truly sordid or corrupt or unspiritual; it is only we that are so when we neglect our duty" (394).

24    John Locke, *Second Treatise of Government*, ed. C. B. Macpherson (Indianapolis, Ind.: Hackett, 1980), 65–66.

25    Clendenning, *The Life and Thought of Josiah Royce*, 145–46; and Josiah Royce, *The Letters of Josiah Royce*, ed. John Clendenning (Chicago: University of Chicago Press, 1970), 140, 176–77. Royce's book *California: A Study of American Character* was the California installment of Houghton Mifflin's American Commonwealth series, which the editors marketed as highly interpretive state histories written by non-historians.

26    Josiah Royce, "The Squatter Riot of '50 in Sacramento," *Overland Monthly* 6, no. 33 (1885): 226–27.

27    Royce, *California: A Study of American Character*, 385.

28    Royce, "The Squatter Riot of '50 in Sacramento," 226–27.

29    Ibid., 237. New Helvetia (New Switzerland) was the name of the Swiss-born Sutter's settlement on the Alvarado land grant.

30    Royce, *California: A Study of American Character*, 216. Further citations of this work are given in the text.

31    See also George, "What the Railroad Will Bring Us," 302–3; and Charles Howard Shinn, *Mining Camps: A Study in American Frontier Government* (New York: Scribner's, 1885), 110.

32    This sentiment echoed an older critique of the Gold Rush that had denounced the mass migration of miners as driven by greed and portended that California society would devolve into barbarity and lawlessness. See Rohrbough, *Days of Gold*, 50.

33   Historians and biographers who write about *California: A Study of American Character* tend to hold up Royce's discussion of the way in which squatters dispossessed Mexican land grantees as evidence of his racially progressive attitude. For one representative example, see Clendenning, *The Life and Thought of Josiah Royce*, 153–55. See also Starr, *Americans and the California Dream, 1850–1915*, 162–63. Certainly, one can point to a number of passages in the "Land Titles and Politics" chapter in Royce's *California: A Study of American Character* in which he attributed the dispossession of Mexican landowners to Anglo-American racism and discriminatory land policies. I argue in this book, however, that Royce did not deviate as much from the racist narrative of Manifest Destiny as has been suggested in the scholarship on him.

34   For examples, see chapter 2 of this book and Pisani, "Squatter Law in California, 1850–1858," 277–310.

35   Royce, "The Squatter Riot of '50 in Sacramento," 246.

36   Bowman, "Index of the Spanish-Mexican Private Land Grant Records and Cases of California." See also Pitt, *The Decline of the Californios*, 110, 131.

37   In the 1960s, Paul Wallace Gates was the first to rehabilitate the image of the California squatter in *Land and Law in California*. Other historians, including Donald Pisani, Mark Eifler, David Vaught, and I, have built on his work. There is also a rich scholarship on Californios and Indians and the experience of conquest. See, for example, Miroslava Chavez-Garcia, *Negotiating Conquest: Gender and Power in California, 1770s to 1880s* (Tucson: University of Arizona Press, 2004); Lisbeth Haas, *Conquests and Historical Identities in California, 1769–1936* (Berkeley: University of California Press, 1995); Hurtado, *Indian Survival*; Pitt, *The Decline of the Californios*; and Louise Pubols, *The Father of All: The de la Guerra Family, Power, and Patriarchy in Mexican California* (San Marino, Calif.: Huntington Library; Berkeley: University of California Press, 2009).

38   John E. Bodnar, *Remaking America: Public Memory, Commemoration, and Patriotism in the Twentieth Century* (Princeton, N.J.: Princeton University Press, 1991), 17, 113; and Ron Theodore Robin, *Signs of Change: Urban Iconographies in San Francisco, 1880–1915* (New York: Garland, 1990), 11.

39   As historian Richard Maxwell Brown argues, "The lesson of the deaths of the five farmers who opposed the railroad seemed to be that one of the greatest of all American corporations, the Southern Pacific Railroad . . . would not rest content with its campaign to deprive hard-working farmers and family men of their land but would demand the ultimate sacrifice and have them shot down in cold blood" (*No Duty to Retreat*, 112).

40   Ibid., 112–14; Orsi, *Sunset Limited*, 98–99; and Williams, *The Democratic Party and California Politics, 1880–1896*, 26.

41   C. C. Post, *Driven from Sea to Sea; or, Just a Campin'* (Chicago: J. E. Downey & Co., 1884; Philadelphia: Elliot and Beezley, 1890), 47. Citations are to the 1890 edition.

42   Ibid., 47–48.

43   Ibid., 32–33.

44    Ibid., 340.

45    Royce made the circumstances of the fictional squatters at Oakfield Creek essentially identical to those of the real-life squatters of Mussel Slough. In the novel, a California corporation—the Land and Improvement Company—stands in the place of the Southern Pacific, and its land rights stem not from a federal land grant but a Mexican private grant. Before the novel begins, the Land and Improvement Company recruited settlers by promising the free use of the land until the official survey and patenting of the grant. At that time, the corporation stipulated that settlers would pay a predetermined amount per acre, the same agreement made by Southern Pacific with the settlers at Mussel Slough. Like the Southern Pacific, Royce's fictional corporation plans to run a railroad through its land grant, and the proposed railroad—although never built in the novel—increases the speculative value of the land. When the grant is finally confirmed at the outset of the novel, the Land and Improvement Company demands that the settlers pay up at a higher price than originally agreed or get off the claim. As in the real-life case of Mussel Slough, the fictional Oakfield Creek settlers resist eviction with armed force and tragic consequences. Royce, *The Feud of Oakfield Creek: A Novel of California Life* (Boston: Houghton, Mifflin, 1887), 33–38. One of the characters gives a summary of the major plot points on these pages. Further citations of this work are given in the text.

46    María Amparo Ruiz de Burton, *The Squatter and the Don*, ed. Rosaura Sánchez and Beatrice Pita (Houston: Arte Público Press, 1992), 12–13. Further citations of this work are given in the text.

47    In a letter to one of her lawyers, Ruiz de Burton explained her hopes as a writer: "I would like to make the venture a little bit profitable. I do not write for glory." See María Amparo Ruiz de Burton to S. M. L. Barlow, San Francisco, California, September 9, 1872, reprinted in María Amparo Ruiz de Burton, *Conflicts of Interest: The Letters of María Amparo Ruiz de Burton*, ed. Rosaura Sánchez and Beatrice Pita (Houston: Arte Público Press, 2001), 438.

48    Bancroft, *California Pastoral*, 331; and Ruiz de Burton, *Conflicts of Interest*, 5–7.

49    Ruiz de Burton, *Conflicts of Interest*, 100–101.

50    Ibid., 97–99; and María Amparo Ruiz de Burton to Pío Pico, Staten Island, New York, January 10, 1870, FAC667 (1136), De la Guerra Family Collection, Huntington Library.

51    "Ya tambien yo se lo dije pero comon jamas hace aprecio alguno de mis cartos dudo que le importe un pito que se pierda todo Jamul" (I already told him, but as he never acknowledges my letters, I doubt he gives a damn if we lose all of Jamul). María Amparo Ruiz de Burton to M. G. Vallejo, Staten Island, New York, January 10, 1870, FAC667 (1135), De la Guerra Family Collection, Huntington Library. Author's translation.

52    Ruiz de Burton, *Conflicts of Interest*, 228–29.

53    "Es terrible estar en esta incertidumbre, en un Limbo de dudas y ansias." María Amparo Ruiz de Burton to M. G. Vallejo, Staten Island, New York,

January 31, 1870, FAC667 (1135), De la Guerra Family Collection, Huntington Library. Author's translation.

54   Ibid.; and María Amparo Ruiz de Burton to C. Scott, San Francisco, California, November 1, 1870, reprinted in Ruiz de Burton, *Conflicts of Interest*, 420.

55   María Amparo Ruiz de Burton to George Davidson, Jamul, California, March 5, 1874, reprinted in Ruiz de Burton, *Conflicts of Interest*, 449.

56   *Maria A. Burton et al. Plaintiffs and Respondents, v. W. N. Robinson, Appellant and Defendant* (San Diego, Calif.: Douglas Gunn, Book and Job Printer, 1874), 10.

57   Conditions north of the border were mirrored to the south; Ruiz de Burton's property in Baja California was also occupied by squatters, who told the Mexican government that she had abandoned it. See Ruiz de Burton, *Conflicts of Interest*, 387–88.

58   Ibid., 387.

59   Her homestead was land on which she or one of her close family members had continuously resided since the 1850s, and the property in Ensenada was adjacent to land claimed by her grandfather. See María Amparo Ruiz de Burton to George Davidson, San Diego, California, April 13, 1883, reprinted in Ruiz de Burton, *Conflicts of Interest*, 493; and María Ruiz de Burton to S. L. M. Barlow, San Diego, California, May 13, 1883, reprinted in Ruiz de Burton, *Conflicts of Interest*, 404.

60   "Yo tengo mucho interes en buen suceso del Southern Pacific RR, o mejor dicho el 'Memphis & El Paso RR'. . . . Pasa por esquinita de la casa en Jamul y si se lleva a cabo hara el rancho muy valuable [*sic*]." María Amparo Ruiz de Burton to M. G. Vallejo, Staten Island, New York, March 27, 1870, FAC667 (1135), De la Guerra Family Collection, Huntington Library. Author's translation.

61   María Amparo Ruiz de Burton to M. G. Vallejo, San Diego, California,t January 7, 1874, FAC667 (1135), De la Guerra Family Collection, Huntington Library; and María Amparo Ruiz de Burton to George Davidson, San Francisco, California, December 4, 1875, reprinted in Ruiz de Burton, *Conflicts of Interest*, 461.

62   Richard White recounts the competition between Huntington and Scott over the southern transcontinental route in chapter 3 of *Railroaded*.

63   María Amparo Ruiz de Burton to George Davidson, San Francisco, California, December 4, 1875.

## CHAPTER SIX

1   Henry Carter Adams, *Relation of the State to Industrial Action* (Baltimore, Md.: American Economic Association, 1887), 47.

2   The underlying notion was not new. John Stuart Mill, in his book *Principles of Political Economy*, had described capital-intensive gasworks and waterworks as "practical monopolies," and he fretted that without government regulation, such industries would exploit their position as sole provider to

overcharge and neglect their customers. See Mill, *Principles of Political Economy, with Some of Their Applications to Social Philosophy* (1848; London: Longmans, Green, 1909), 962–63.

3   Historians have differed on the moral and economic value of the railroad land grants. Representing one pole in the spectrum of opinion, Albro Martin argues in *Railroads Triumphant* that the grants have been unjustly maligned in the scholarship. Martin claims the railroads more than compensated for the gifts of free government land by spurring economic growth and raising land values. Moreover, railroad corporations did not profit from the grants but used revenues from land sales to cover construction and upkeep with none to spare. Far from an undeserved windfall, the land grants were in fact the gift that kept on taking from the railroads, entrapping them in a complicated relationship with the federal government, forcing them to take on costs of administering that relationship, and fomenting discord with squatters. Richard White adopts the near-opposite position from Martin on both the railroad land grants in particular and Gilded Age transcontinental railroad construction as a whole. He argues that the railroads were built ahead of demand, and that their costs far exceeded their benefits. White critiques the land grants' "free-lunch logic," the notion that the government could subsidize the railroads at no cost by recouping its losses through increased revenues from land sales along the railroad line. There were, in fact, costs: costs borne by states and localities denied taxes on railroad lands, costs borne by Indian peoples dispossessed of their territory, costs borne by an irrevocably changed environment. For a detailed and measured analysis of the "creative destruction" wrought by the transcontinental railroads, see White, *Railroaded*, chap. 11.

4   John Powell Irish, "California and the Railroad: Julian Ralph Reviewed," *Overland Monthly*, 2nd ser., 25 (1895): 678.

5   Ibid., 681.

6   For a detailed description of the major acts that extended railroad land grants, see Mercer, *Railroads and Land Grant Policy*, 3–6.

7   Ibid., 15.

8   G. Frederick Keller, "Curse of California," *The Wasp*, August 19, 1892, 520–21.

9   Orsi, *Sunset Limited*, 6–7.

10  Ibid., 10–11.

11  Deverell, *Railroad Crossing*, 28; and Mercer, *Railroads and Land Grant Policy*, 35.

12  George, *Our Land and Land Policy*, 14.

13  Orsi's *Sunset Limited* exhaustively and painstakingly debunks the notion of the Southern Pacific as land monopolist; see pp. 65–91.

14  Henry Haight to L. T. Carr, January 25, 1871, San Francisco, box 6, file 172, Henry Haight Papers, Huntington Library.

15  Quoted in Davis, *History of Political Conventions in California*, 296.

16  Henry Haight to L. T. Carr, January 25, 1871.

17    Quoted in Davis, *History of Political Conventions in California*, 296.

18    Newton Booth, *Newton Booth, of California: His Speeches and Addresses,*
      ed. Lauren E. Crane (New York: G. P. Putnam's Sons, 1894), 123–24.

19    Quoted in Davis, *History of Political Conventions in California*, 304.

20    Newton Booth, "Speech of Acceptance," reprinted in *Newton Booth, of Cali-
      fornia*, 143.

21    Ibid.

22    Quoted in Davis, *History of Political Conventions in California*, 307.

23    Sidney Fine, "Richard T. Ely, Forerunner of Progressivism, 1880–1901,"
      *The Mississippi Valley Historical Review* 37, no. 4 (1951): 604–5.

24    Gordon, "Attitudes Towards Trusts," 164.

25    Ibid., 166.

26    Thorelli, *The Federal Antitrust Policy*, 53.

27    Adams, *Relation of the State to Industrial Action*, 35.

28    Richard T. Ely, "Ethics and Economics," *Science* 7, no. 175 (1886): 530; and Ely,
      "Political Economy in America," *The North American Review* 144, no. 363
      (1887): 119.

29    Richard T. Ely, *Recent American Socialism* (Baltimore, Md.: Johns Hopkins
      University, 1885), 16.

30    Richard T. Ely, "Natural Monopolies and the Workingman: A Programme
      of Social Reform," *The North American Review* 158, no. 448 (1894): 296–97;
      and Ely, "The Telegraph Monopoly," *The North American Review* 149, no. 392
      (1889): 45–46.

31    Ely, "Ethics and Economics," 530.

32    Fine, "Richard T. Ely, Forerunner of Progressivism, 1880–1901," 609–11.

33    In *Network Nation*, Richard John argues that the theory of "natural monopo-
      lies" reflected the "anti-investor" bias of its proponents. Part of the impulse
      to define monopolies as natural was to diminish the power and privilege of
      investor-managers like Jay Gould over indispensable industries like the tele-
      graph. See John, *Network Nation*, 194–98.

34    Arthur P. Dudden, "Men against Monopoly: The Prelude to Trust-Busting,"
      *Journal of the History of Ideas* 18, no. 4 (1957): 587–93; and Herbert Hoven-
      kamp, "Regulatory Conflict in the Gilded Age: Federalism and the Railroad
      Problem," *The Yale Law Journal* 97, no. 6 (1988): 1043–44.

35    Gerald D. Nash, "The California Railroad Commission, 1876–1911," *Southern
      California Quarterly* 44, no. 4 (1962): 288.

36    Historians have debated the impetus and effects of railroad regulation. The
      scholarship has largely focused on the question of who gained the most from
      government regulation. Was it the public at large, special-interest groups (for
      example, farmers, shippers, merchants), or the railroads themselves? For an
      overview of the major positions in the historiography of railroad regulation, see
      Herbert Hovenkamp, *Enterprise and American Law, 1836–1937* (Cambridge,

Mass.: Harvard University Press, 1991), 132–37. For the purposes of this study, the question of who gained the most from state and federal regulation is subordinate to the question of how government regulation emerged from the collision between older ideals of antimonopolism and new economic theories of natural monopoly in the Gilded Age.

37   Dobie, *The Political Career of Stephen Mallory White*, 26.

38   Curtis Edwin Grassman, "Prologue to Progressivism, Senator Stephen M. White and the California Reform Impulse, 1875–1905" (PhD diss., UCLA, 1970), 14–15.

39   Untitled, undated, printed loose-leaf pamphlet from box 99, folder 4, Stephen Mallory White Papers, Stanford University Library.

40   Davis, *History of Political Conventions in California*, 332.

41   Ibid.

42   David B. Griffiths, "Anti-Monopoly Movements in California, 1873–1898," *Southern California Quarterly* 52, no. 2 (1970): 93.

43   Dobie, *The Political Career of Stephen Mallory White*, 24–26.

44   Davis, *History of Political Conventions in California*, 366–67.

45   For detailed biographies of the "antimonopoly wing" of the Democratic party, see Williams, *The Democratic Party and California Politics, 1880–1896*.

46   Davis, *History of Political Conventions in California*, 433–34.

47   Deverell, *Railroad Crossing*, 60–61.

48   Davis, *History of Political Conventions in California*, 439–41.

49   Deverell, *Railroad Crossing*, 60; and Williams, *The Democratic Party and California Politics, 1880–1896*, 26.

50   Nash, "The California Railroad Commission, 1876–1911," 294; and Williams, *The Democratic Party and California Politics, 1880–1896*, 29–30. Nash's study of the Railroad Commission of the State of California details the challenges the commissioners faced. Lack of expertise, active opposition from the Central Pacific and Southern Pacific Railroad companies, and limited decision rights—combined with impatient and critical legislators and voters—made it almost impossible for the Railroad Commission to effect substantial change.

51   Donald R. Burrill, *Servants of the Law: Judicial Politics on the California Frontier 1849–89: An Interpretive Exploration of the Field-Terry Controversy* (Lanham, Md.: University Press of America, 2010), 13; and Paul Kens, *Justice Stephen Field: Shaping Liberty from the Gold Rush to the Gilded Age* (Lawrence: University Press of Kansas, 1997), 41.

52   Burrill, *Servants of the Law*, 15–17.

53   Stephen J. Field and George C. Gorham, *Personal Reminiscences of Early Days in California: With Other Sketches* (Union, N.J.: Lawbook Exchange, 2001), 49. Field's decisions on the California Supreme Court and, later, on the U.S. Supreme Court reflected a logic based in what his biographer Paul Kens calls "the radical individualist strain of the Jacksonian free-labor tradition." See Kens, *Justice Stephen Field*, 9.

54   Field and Gorham, *Personal Reminiscences*, 125; and Kens, *Justice Stephen Field*, 77–78.

55   Field and Gorham, *Personal Reminiscences*, 123.

56   Quoted in Hovenkamp, *Enterprise and American Law, 1836–1937*, 113.

57   Kens, *Justice Stephen Field*, 165.

58   Williams, *The Democratic Party and California Politics, 1880–1896*, 33–39.

59   Stephen White to Governor [Stoneman], Los Angeles, California, June 23, 1884, box 1, Stephen Mallory White Papers, Stanford University Library.

60   Grassman, "Prologue to Progressivism," 66–67.

61   For more detail, see Williams, *The Democratic Party and California Politics, 1880–1896*, 33–40.

62   Ibid., 48.

63   Stephen Mallory White to George Stoneman, Los Angeles, California, June 23, 1884, box 1, Stephen Mallory White Papers, Stanford University Library.

64   Deverell, *Railroad Crossing*, 62.

65   Thorelli, *The Federal Antitrust Policy*, 150.

66   The dynamic nature of corporate and industrial organization at the end of the nineteenth century challenged the enforcement of the Interstate Commerce Act and the various antitrust laws. See Hovenkamp, *Enterprise and American Law, 1836–1937*, 41–167.

67   Grassman, "Prologue to Progressivism," 150–51.

68   White's biographers reach no consensus about his work with the Southern Pacific. Edith Dobie claims that the experience soured White on "railroad affairs" and deepened his commitment to regulation, whereas Kenneth Johnson offers a more cynical interpretation of White's motives: "The railroad was becoming extremely unpopular in Southern California, and White undoubtedly felt that his connection with it was damaging his political career." See Dobie, *The Political Career of Stephen Mallory White*, 100; and Johnson, *Stephen Mallory White* (Los Angeles: Dawson's Book Shop, 1980), 23.

69   Henry George had mixed feelings about the Populists. He favored paper currency but preferred silver to gold, which he believed to be the currency of monopolists. But George could not get past his feeling that the Populists replaced one form of monopoly with another. In a letter to Louis Post, then president of the Manhattan Single Tax Club and a successful New York publisher, George wrote, "Farmers combinations that would help farmers by making them participants in the plunder of the treasury . . . can no more help the masses than can those rosewater reformers who would curb political corruption by electing good men to office and solve the awful problem of poverty by doles of alms." George's goal was to restore independence and free competition among equal proprietors and not simply to transfer government privilege from corporate monopolists to farmers' and producers' cooperatives. Nonetheless, many single taxers joined the Populist Party because it approximated George's anti–land monopolist vision by demanding that the government restore alien landholdings and unreasonably large corporate land

grants to the public domain. The Populist Party also supported free silver, a currency reform that promised to reduce inflation and appealed to the small proprietors that dominated the single-tax movement. See Chester McArthur Destler, "Western Radicalism, 1865–1901: Concepts and Origins," *The Mississippi Valley Historical Review* 31, no. 3 (1944): 353–54; George Jr., *The Life of Henry George*, 581; and Postel, *The Populist Vision*, 229–31. See also Henry George to Louis F. Post, New York City, April 2, 1891, Henry George Papers, NYPL.

70    Destler, "Western Radicalism, 1865–1901: Concepts and Origins," 353–54; and Robert C. McMath Jr., *American Populism: A Social History, 1877–1898* (New York: Hill and Wang, 1993), 6–8.

71    "National People's Party Platform," in *A Populist Reader: Selections from the Works of American Populist Leaders*, ed. George Brown Tindall (New York: Harper & Row, 1966), 90–96.

72    Postel, *The Populist Vision*, 171.

73    Ibid., 288.

74    *A Populist Reader*, ed. Tindall, 90–96.

75    Edward Bellamy, *Looking Backward, 2000–1887*, ed. Cecelia Tichi (New York: Penguin Books, 1982), 7–8.

76    Griffiths, "Anti-Monopoly Movements in California," 95; and Harold F. Taggart, "Thomas Vincent Cator: Populist Leader of California," *California Historical Society Quarterly* 27, no. 4 (1948): 311–12.

77    Thomas V. Cator, *Millionaires or Morals: Which Shall Rule? The Celebrated Oration of Hon. Thos. V. Cator at Metropolitan Temple, San Francisco, July 4th, 1890* (San Francisco: W. M. Langton & Co., 1890), 5.

78    Ibid., 6.

79    Ibid., 16.

80    "An Anti-Monopolist for Congress," *Weekly Star Supplement,* October 4, 1890, Thomas Vincent Cator Papers, Stanford University Library.

81    Thomas V. Cator, acceptance speech in "Read His Record!," *Weekly Star Supplement,* October 4, 1890, Thomas Vincent Cator Papers, Stanford University Library.

82    Griffiths, "Anti-Monopoly Movements in California," 96–97; and Taggart, "Thomas Vincent Cator," 313.

83    Davis, *History of Political Conventions in California*, 590.

84    Taggart, "Thomas Vincent Cator," 313–14.

85    Thomas V. Cator, *Rescue the Republic: The Necessity and Advantages of National Ownership of Railroads and Telegraphs* (San Francisco: Citizens' Alliance, 1892), 3.

86    Ibid., 4.

87    Ibid., 4, 14.

88    Quoted in "Stephen M. White," *Los Angeles Times*, December 16, 1882, 4.

89    "The Senatorship," *The Morning Call*, January 2, 1892, Thomas Vincent Cator Papers, Stanford University Library.

90    Ibid.

91    Stephen Mallory White to Thomas Vincent Cator, San Francisco, California, January 10, 1891, box 5; and Stephen Mallory White to Thomas Vincent Cator, San Francisco, California, April 2, 1891, box 5, Stephen Mallory White Papers, Stanford University Library.

92    Taggart, "Thomas Vincent Cator," 316.

93    Ibid., 316–17.

94    Stephen Mallory White to Marion Cannon, Ventura, California, December 6, 1892, box 6, Stephen Mallory White Papers, Stanford University Library. White rewarded Cannon's assistance in the senatorial bid with patronage. He secured the Ventura postmaster position for Cannon's friend and wrote, "Be assured that as far as I can affect matters you will not be compelled to accept the mail from any postmaster who is not your personal friend." Incurring the wrath of another Ventura Populist who desired the postmaster appointment, White wrote to the angry individual: "Cannon did all in the world he could to insure my election to the senate and brought down upon himself the wrath of the populist organization. He stuck by me when a great many persons who had agreed to do the same thing, refused to acquiesce. He assisted in coalitions which, while they did not all result in the election of Democrats or of men who supported me, they nevertheless resulted in the defeat of Republicans. Had Republicans been elected instead of Populists the matter would have been ended. He asks for very little of me. He simply requests as a personal matter to be allowed to name a Democrat who shall fill this local post office." Stephen Mallory White to Marion Cannon, Ventura, California, March 10, 1893; and Stephen Mallory White to John McGonigle, Ventura, California, July 7, 1893, box 7, Stephen Mallory White Papers, Stanford University Library.

95    Dobie, *The Political Career of Stephen Mallory White*, 143–44; and Taggart, "Thomas Vincent Cator," 317.

96    Douglas Steeples and David O. Whitten, *Democracy in Desperation: The Depression of 1893* (Westport, Conn.: Greenwood Press, 1998), 16–23.

97    White, *Railroaded*, 397.

98    Steeples and Whitten, *Democracy in Desperation*, 22.

99    Ibid., 29.

100   For full descriptions of the American Railway Union strike and the Los Angeles Free Harbor controversy, see Deverell, *Railroad Crossing*.

101   Ibid., 96–97.

102   Ibid., 102.

103   Stephen Mallory White, "Speech Delivered in the Senate of the United States, Friday, May 8, and Saturday, May 9, 1896, and Tuesday, May 12, 1896," reprinted in Leroy E. Mosher, *Stephen M. White: Californian, Citizen, Lawyer, Senator,* comp. Robert Woodland Gates, 2 vols. (Los Angeles: Times-Mirror, 1903), 1:373.

104   Deverell, *Railroad Crossing*, 118–20; and Dobie, *The Political Career of Stephen Mallory White*, 181–84.

105   Stephen Mallory White, "San Pedro Jubilee Speech, April 26, 1899," reprinted in Mosher, *Stephen M. White*, 2:333.

106   Telfair Creighton to Stephen Mallory White, Los Angeles, California, April 25, 1896, Stephen Mallory White Scrapbooks, Seaver Center, Natural History Museum of Los Angeles.

107   Stephen Mallory White to Marion Cannon, Santa Paula, California, May 16, 1894, series 1, box 1, folder 9, Cannon Walker Papers, University of the Pacific.

108   Ibid.

109   Thomas Vincent Cator to E. M. Wardall, Chicago, Illinois, July 8, 1896, box 1, folder 1, Thomas Vincent Cator Papers, Stanford University Library.

110   "For Bryan and the People," *Daily Evening Expositor*, October 24, 1896, Thomas Vincent Cator Papers, Stanford University Library.

111   Stephen Mallory White to Thomas Vincent Cator, Los Angeles, California, September 28, 1896, box 12, Stephen Mallory White Papers, Stanford University Library.

112   Griffiths, "Anti-Monopoly Movements in California," 111.

113   Grassman, "Prologue to Progressivism," 346–47.

114   Ibid., 349; and Stephen Mallory White to Thomas Vincent Cator, Los Angeles, California, November 12, 1896, box 12, Stephen Mallory White Papers, Stanford University Library. Cator, ever the rolling stone, switched political allegiances again and joined the Republican Party in 1898. See Griffiths, "Anti-Monopoly Movements in California," 120.

115   Maury Klein, *Union Pacific*, 2 vols. (Garden City, N.Y.: Doubleday, 1987–89), 1:466.

116   Grassman, "Prologue to Progressivism," 269. Maury Klein details the Union Pacific's response to the debt-repayment controversy in his two-volume history of the railroad company. The Union Pacific's president, Charles Francis Adams, adopted a similar approach to Huntington's, essentially daring Congress to take the railroad off his hands. See Klein, *Union Pacific*, 1:465–66, 654.

117   Grassman, "Prologue to Progressivism," 272; and Klein, *Union Pacific*, 2:16–17.

118   "Are the Debts of the Railroad to Remain Unpaid," San Francisco *Examiner*, January 24, 1895, 3; "With One Voice," San Francisco *Examiner*, January 27, 1895, 2; and "Against Reilly's Bill," San Francisco *Examiner*, January 30, 1895, 1.

119   Marion Cannon, "The Pacific Railroad Debts," printed version of an address before Congressional Committee on Railways and Canals, 1894, series 1, box 1, folder 8, Cannon Walker Papers, University of the Pacific.

120   Porter and Johnson, *National Party Platforms*, 99.

121   Grassman, "Prologue to Progressivism," 272; and Klein, *Union Pacific*, 2:18.

122   "Let the Railroads Pay Up," *Los Angeles Times*, March 23, 1896, 6; and H. R. Meyer, "The Settlements with the Pacific Railways," *Quarterly Journal of Economics* 14, no. 4 (1899): 442–43.

123    Grassman, "Prologue to Progressivism," 274–75.

124    "Let Justice Be Done," *Los Angeles Times*, January 17, 1897, 26.

125    Cong. Rec., 55th Congress, 2d Sess., vol. 31, pt. 8, pp. 6464–65 (June 29, 1898).

126    Stephen White to E. L. Andrews, June 29, 1898; Stephen White to L. E. Mosher, June 29, 1898, box 15, Stephen Mallory White Papers, Stanford University Library; and "Foreclosure Avoided," *Los Angeles Times*, February 17, 1899, 3.

127    The Harvard economist H. R. Meyer deemed the settlement a success, as it recouped the principal and interest of the debt and as it protected the government from engaging in the thankless task of railroad operation. See Meyer, "The Settlements with the Pacific Railways," 443–44.

128    Daniel Rodgers, "In Search of Progressivism," *Reviews in American History* 10, no. 4 (1982): 113–32.

## CONCLUSION

1    Henry George, "Thy Kingdom Come," reprinted in George, *Our Land and Land Policy*, ed. Wenzer, 196–97.

2    State Land Settlement Act, S 584, chap. 755 (passed June 1, 1917), reprinted in *Information Regarding Progress under the Land Settlement Act of the State of California and about the Plans for Soldier Settlement in the Future* (Sacramento, Calif.: State Land Settlement Board, 1919), 35–39.

3    William A. Hartman, "State Policies in Regulating Land Settlement Activities," *Journal of Farm Economics* 13, no. 2 (1931): 261–62, 264.

4    Robbins, *Our Landed Heritage*, 273.

5    Pisani, *Water, Land, and Law in the West*, 181–82.

6    Ibid., 185.

7    Elwood Mead, *Helping Men Own Farms: A Practical Discussion of Government Aid in Land Settlement* (New York: Macmillan, 1920), 9–10.

8    State Land Settlement Board, *Report of the State Land Settlement Board of the State of California, September 30, 1920* (Sacramento: California State Printing Office, 1921), 45.

9    Mead, *Helping Men Own Farms*, 10.

10    Ibid., 198–99.

11    *How California Helps Men Own Farms and Rural Homes* (Sacramento: California State Printing Office, 1920), 12.

12    James R. Kluger, *Turning on Water with a Shovel: The Career of Elwood Mead* (Albuquerque: University of New Mexico Press, 1992), 22; Tyrrell, *True Gardens of the Gods*, 155; and Donald Worster, *Rivers of Empire: Water, Aridity, and the Growth of the American West* (New York: Pantheon, 1985), 157–58.

13    Kluger, *Turning on Water with a Shovel*, 30–31, 34; Pisani, *Water, Land, and Law in the West*, 185; and Worster, *Rivers of Empire*, 158–59.

14    Tyrrell, *True Gardens of the Gods*, 155; and Richard White, *"It's Your Misfortune and None of My Own": A History of the American West* (Norman: University of Oklahoma Press, 1991), 405–6.

15    Kluger, *Turning on Water with a Shovel*, 35; and Tyrrell, *True Gardens of the Gods*, 155.

16    Tyrrell, *True Gardens of the Gods*, 156–57.

17    Elwood Mead, *State Aid in Land Settlement: An Address by Elwood Mead* (Stockton, Calif.: International Irrigation Congress, 1915), Elwood Mead Papers, Water Research Center Archives, University of California, Riverside (formerly at University of California, Berkeley; hereafter cited as WRCA).

18    Elwood Mead, *The Rural Credit System Needed in Western Development* (Berkeley, Calif.?: 1916), 5, Elwood Mead Papers, WRCA.

19    Ibid.

20    Ibid., 6.

21    Elwood Mead, *Reform in Land Settlement Methods* (Kansas City, Mo.: National Conference of Social Work, 1918), 2, Elwood Mead Papers, WRCA.

22    Tyrrell, *True Gardens of the Gods*, 158–59.

23    Elwood Mead, "Solution of the Land Question," *New Republic*, April 29, 1916, 348.

24    Kluger, *Turning on Water with a Shovel*, 85.

25    U. S. Bureau of the Census, *Thirteenth Census of the United States Taken in the Year 1910*, vol. 6, *Agriculture* (Washington, D.C.: Government Printing Office, 1913), 134, available at http://www.agcensus.usda.gov/Publications/Historical_Publications/1910/Reports_by_state_Alabama_Montana/41033898v6.pdf (accessed May 22, 2013).

26    Ibid., 136.

27    Ibid., 148.

28    Pisani, *Water, Land, and Law in the West*, 184.

29    Elwood Mead, *The Tenant Farmer and Land Monopoly* (Kansas City, Mo.: National Conference of Social Work, 1918), 1, Elwood Mead Papers, WRCA.

30    Ibid., 2.

31    S 584, reprinted in *Information Regarding Progress under the Land Settlement Act*, 37.

32    Ibid., 37–38; and State Land Settlement Board, *Farm Allotments and Farm Laborers' Allotments in the Durham State Land Settlement, Located at Durham, Butte County, Calif.* (Sacramento, Calif.: State Printing Office, 1918), 3.

33    S 584, reprinted in *Information Regarding Progress under the Land Settlement Act*, 35.

34    In 1906, the San Francisco Board of Education ordered all Japanese and Korean students to join the Chinese school, satisfying the city's anti-Japanese activists, who had campaigned to segregate Japanese and white schoolchildren. In the same period, a coalition of California nativist groups, including the

American Legion and the Native Sons of the Golden West, orchestrated the drive for federal legislation curtailing Japanese immigration. They achieved their first results with President Theodore Roosevelt's concession, the 1908 Gentlemen's Agreement, wherein the American government convinced the Japanese government to limit the number of passports issued to laborers wishing to immigrate to the United States. In the early 1920s, Valentine Stuart "V. S." McClatchy, the elder of James McClatchy's two sons, led the California Joint Immigration League (originally called the Japanese Exclusion League) in pressuring Congress to pass the 1924 National Origins Act, which set quotas for immigration from each foreign country and eliminated all Japanese immigration. See Roger Daniels, *The Politics of Prejudice: The Anti-Japanese Movement in California and the Struggle for Japanese Exclusion*, 2nd ed. (Berkeley: University of California Press, 1977), 34, 41–42, 91–92.

35    Consequently, rural California experienced the greatest gains in Japanese residents, from 6,905 in 1900 to 22,744 in 1910. In the same years, the Chinese population in California decreased from 45,753 to 36,348 due to the extension of the 1882 Chinese Exclusion Act and its restrictions on new and return migration from China. Although the Chinese continued to outnumber the Japanese in the cities by a margin of four to three, the Japanese dominated in the countryside, where they outnumbered the Chinese two to one. As a proportion of the total rural population, the Japanese remained a tiny minority, at 2.5 percent of the population in 1910, but up from 0.9 percent in 1900. See Daniels, *Asian America*, 107. Data gathered from the U.S. Bureau of the Census, Population Census, California, 1910, 157, http://factfinder2.census.gov (accessed May 22, 2013).

36    Carey McWilliams, *Factories in the Field* (Boston: Little, Brown, 1939), 202–3.

37    Ibid., 203–4; and Elwood Mead, *Land Settlement and Rural Credits: Statement of the Need for an Investigation* (Berkeley, Calif.: 1916?), 2, Elwood Mead Papers, WRCA.

38    Neil Foley's study of western Texas in the late nineteenth and early twentieth centuries has similarly argued that agrarian ideals were inseparable from notions of white manhood and white womanhood for cotton farmers, tenants, and sharecroppers. See Foley, *The White Scourge: Mexicans, Blacks, and Poor Whites in Texas Cotton Culture* (Berkeley: University of California Press, 1997), 12.

39    Mead, *The Tenant Farmer and Land Monopoly*, 2–3.

40    State Land Settlement Board, *Report of the State Land Settlement Board of the State of California, September 30, 1920*, 50.

41    Mead, *Helping Men Own Farms*, 5.

42    Ibid.

43    George, *Our Land and Land Policy*, 46–47.

44    Mead, *Helping Men Own Farms*, 7.

45    State Land Settlement Board, *Report of the State Land Settlement Board of the State of California, September 30, 1920*, 51.

46    In the American system, to purchase a farm or farm laborer's allotment, the
      Land Settlement Act set the terms at 5 percent down payment on the value
      of the land and 40 percent on the total value of improvements already in
      place. Settlers repaid the state-sponsored loans in semiannual installments
      with a 5 percent interest rate. These terms are outlined in the 1917 legislation.
      The Australian system was just slightly different: settlers paid 3 percent down
      on the land and 25 percent for improvements. They then repaid the state
      loan at 4.5 percent interest. Mead outlined these terms in "Systematic Aid to
      Settlers, the First Need in Irrigation Development," an address delivered at
      the Irrigation Conference, Denver, Colorado, on April 9, 1914, Victoria, Aus-
      tralia, Elwood Mead Papers, WRCA.

47    Mead, "Solution of the Land Question," 348.

48    S 584, reprinted in *Information Regarding Progress under the Land Settlement
      Act*, 38.

49    Mead, *The Tenant Farmer and Land Monopoly*, 4.

50    State Land Settlement Board, *Farm Allotments and Farm Laborers' Allot-
      ments in the Durham State Land Settlement, Located at Durham, Butte
      County, Calif.*

51    State Land Settlement Board, *Report of the State Land Settlement Board of
      the State of California, September 30, 1920*, 53.

52    Ibid.

53    State Land Settlement Board, *Report of the State Land Settlement Board of
      the State of California, June 30, 1918* (Sacramento: California State Printing
      Office, 1918), 9.

54    State Land Settlement Board, *Report of the State Land Settlement Board of
      the State of California, September 30, 1920*, 53.

55    George, *Progress and Poverty*, 319.

56    Kluger, *Turning on Water with a Shovel*, 90.

57    State Land Settlement Board, *Farm Allotments and Farm Laborers' Allot-
      ments in the Durham State Land Settlement, Located at Durham, Butte
      County, Calif.*, 3; and McWilliams, *Factories in the Field*, 204–5.

58    "Application for Farm Allotments or Farm Laborers' Allotments," State Land
      Settlement Act, chap. 755, Statutes (1917), in State Land Settlement Board,
      *Farm Allotments and Farm Laborers' Allotments in the Durham State Land
      Settlement, Located at Durham, Butte County, California*.

59    *Information Regarding Progress under the Land Settlement Act*, 20.

60    Mead, *The Rural Credit System Needed in Western Development*, 5.

61    *Information Regarding Progress under the Land Settlement Act*, 12–13.

62    *How California Helps Men Own Farms and Rural Homes*, 10.

63    George P. West, "Riveted Down—and They Like It," *Collier's*, July 9, 1922, 26.

64    *Information Regarding Progress under the Land Settlement Act*, 13.

65    Ibid., 24.

66    Kluger, *Turning on Water with a Shovel*, 91.

67    Ibid., 92–93; and McWilliams, *Factories in the Field*, 205.

68    State Land Settlement Board, *Report of the State Land Settlement Board of the State of California, September 30, 1920*, 51.

69    State Board of Control, *California and the Oriental: Japanese, Chinese, and Hindus* (Sacramento: California State Printing Office, 1922), 123–24.

70    U.S. Bureau of the Census, Population Census, Merced County, California, 1910 and 1920, http://factfinder2.census.gov (accessed May 22, 2013).

71    State Board of Control of California, *California and the Oriental*, 124.

72    Daniels, *The Politics of Prejudice*, 88–91; and Cecilia Tsu, "Grown in the 'Garden of the World': Race, Gender, and Agriculture in California's Santa Clara Valley, 1880–1940" (PhD diss., Stanford University, 2006), 160. Rising Japanese-American birthrates and land-tenure statistics after 1913 convinced the state legislature to pass a second Alien Land Law in 1920. Tsu has shown that the increasing number of Japanese-American families with American-born children caused a resurgence in anti-Japanese sentiment and led to the more restrictive Alien Land Law of 1920. Japanese immigrants capitalized on loopholes in the original law and availed themselves of legal counsel when necessary. They had the support of organizations like the Japanese Agricultural Association, the Japanese Association of America, and the American Committee of Justice, which disseminated information and countered anti-Japanese propaganda. The 1920 law closed the loopholes of the 1913 law by prohibiting leases to Japanese immigrants, but the legislature could do nothing to prevent American-born Japanese children from becoming landowners without violating their constitutional rights as American citizens. As a result, historians have agreed that the effects of the Alien Land Laws on Japanese land tenure in California were minimal. Roger Daniels claims that the 1920 measure "was an attempt to lock the door after the horse had been stolen. Had it been enacted in 1913, when native-born Japanese were less numerous, it would have seriously inhibited Japanese acquisition of agricultural land. By 1920, its enactment was an empty gesture, an ineffective irritant" (88).

73    Daniels, *The Politics of Prejudice*, 91.

74    Kluger, *Turning on Water with a Shovel*, 91.

75    Ibid., 94–95.

76    Ibid., 99, McWilliams, *Factories in the Field*, 206–7; and Worster, *Rivers of Empire*, 185–86.

77    Kluger, *Turning on Water with a Shovel*, 96–97; and Tyrrell, *True Gardens of the Gods*, 163–64.

78    Kluger, *Turning on Water with a Shovel*, 100.

79    Ellis Hawley has shown how regulatory antimonopolism, untethered from the land question, shaped the New Deal's business policy and how late nineteenth-century ambivalence toward concentrated ownership persisted in the era of the Great Depression. See Hawley, *The New Deal and the Problem of Monopoly: A Study in Economic Ambivalence* (New York: Fordham University Press, 1995).

80    Brian Q. Cannon, *Remaking the Agrarian Dream: New Deal Rural Resettle-ment in the Mountain West* (Albuquerque: University of New Mexico Press, 1996), 1–2.

81    Ibid.; Jess Gilbert, "Low Modernism and the Agrarian New Deal: A Different Kind of State," in *Fighting for the Farm: Rural America Transformed*, ed. Jane Adams (Philadelphia: University of Pennsylvania Press, 2003), 132–33; and Donald Worster, *Dust Bowl: The Southern Plains in the 1930s* (New York: Oxford University Press, 2004).

82    Louis Uchitelle, "The Richest of the Rich, Proud of a New Gilded Age," *New York Times*, July 15, 2007; Steve Fraser, "The Gilded Age, Past and Present," *Salon*, April 28, 2008, http://www.salon.com/news/opinion/feature/2008/04/28/gilded_age (accessed January 3, 2011); and David Kennedy, "Throwing the Bums Out for 140 Years," *New York Times*, November 6, 2010.

# Bibliography

## Manuscript Sources

Bancroft Library, University of California, Berkeley
    J. N. Bowman, "Index of the Spanish-Mexican Private Land Grant Records and Cases of California"
    William Prince Papers

California Historical Society, San Francisco
    Samuel Brown Correspondence

Center for Sacramento History (formerly Sacramento Archives and Museum Collection Center)
    City Directories
    Common Council Meeting Minutes
    Eleanor McClatchy Collection
    Preemption Claims Index and Register
    Tax Assessor's Records

History San Jose, San Jose, California
    Anastasio Chabolla Last Will and Testament
    Antonio Chabolla Last Will and Testament
    Santa Clara County Recorder Papers

Huntington Library, San Marino, California
    Cave Johnson Couts Papers
    De la Guerra Family Collection
    Henry Dalton Collection
    Henry Haight Papers
    Kansas State Historical Society
    Charles and Sara Robinson Papers

Kenneth Spencer Research Library, University of Kansas at Lawrence
    Charles Robinson Collection
    Sara Tappan Doolittle Robinson Collection

New York Public Library
    Henry George Papers

San Jose Public Library
    Hanging Maps Collection
    Signposts Scrapbooks

Seaver Center, Natural History Museum of Los Angeles
    Stephen Mallory White Scrapbooks

Stanford University Library, Stanford, California
    Thomas Vincent Cator Papers
    Terence V. Powderly Papers [microfilm]
    Stephen Mallory White Papers

State Archive of California
    Governors' Papers

University of the Pacific, Stockton, California
    Cannon Walker Papers

Water Research Center Archives, University of California at Riverside (formerly at
    University of California at Berkeley)
    Elwood Mead Papers

## *Periodicals*

*Alta California*
*Daily Bee* (Sacramento)
*Daily Herald* (New York)
*Irish World* (New York)
*Journal of United Labor*
*Los Angeles Times*
*The Morning Call* (San Francisco)
*New York Times*
*New-York Tribune*
*Overland Monthly*
*Sacramento Daily Union*
San Francisco *Examiner*
*Settlers and Miners Tribune*
*The Standard* (New York)
*The Wasp*

## Pamphlets and Books

Adams, Henry Carter. *Relation of the State to Industrial Action*. Baltimore, Md.: American Economic Association, 1887.

Bancroft, Hubert Howe. *California Inter Pocula*. San Francisco: History Company, 1888.

———. *California Pastoral*. San Francisco: History Company, 1888.

Bancroft, Hubert Howe, et al. *History of California*. Vol. 6, *1848–1859*. The Works of Hubert Howe Bancroft 23. San Francisco: History Company, 1884.

Board of Supervisors. *San Francisco Municipal Reports for the Fiscal Year 1868–1869*. San Francisco: Cosmopolitan Printing, 1869.

Brown, George W. *False Claims of Kansas Historians Truthfully Corrected*. Rockford, Ill.: the author, 1902.

———. *Reminiscences of Gov. R. J. Walker: With the True Story of the Rescue of Kansas from Slavery*. Rockford, Ill.: the author, 1902.

Cator, Thomas V. *Millionaires or Morals: Which Shall Rule? The Celebrated Oration of Hon. Thos. V. Cator at Metropolitan Temple, San Francisco, July 4th, 1890*. San Francisco: W. M. Langton & Co., 1890.

———. *Rescue the Republic: The Necessity and Advantages of National Ownership of Railroads and Telegraphs*. San Francisco: Citizens' Alliance, 1892.

Congressional Record, 55th Congress, 2d Session (1898).

Davis, Winfield J. *History of Political Conventions in California, 1849–1892*. Sacramento: Publications of the California State Library, 1893.

———. *An Illustrated History of Sacramento County, California. Containing a History of Sacramento County from the Earliest Period of its Occupancy to the Present Time*. Chicago: Lewis Publishing, 1890.

Ely, Richard T. "Ethics and Economics." *Science* 7, no. 175 (1886): 529–33.

———. "Natural Monopolies and the Workingman: A Programme of Social Reform." *The North American Review* 158, no. 448 (1894): 294–303.

———. "Political Economy in America." *The North American Review* 144, no. 363 (1887): 113–19.

———. *Recent American Socialism*. Baltimore, Md.: Johns Hopkins University, 1885.

———. "The Telegraph Monopoly." *The North American Review* 149, no. 392 (1889): 44–53.

George, Henry. "The Kearney Agitation in California." *Popular Science Monthly* 17 (1880): 433–53.

———. *Why Work Is Scarce, Wages Low, and Labor Restless: A Lecture by Henry George, Delivered in the Metropolitan Temple, San Francisco, Cal. March 26, 1878*. San Francisco: The California Tax Reform League, 1885.

Hartman, William A. "State Policies in Regulating Land Settlement Activities." *Journal of Farm Economics* 13, no. 2 (1931): 259–69.

*History of Alameda County, California.* Oakland, Calif.: M. W. Wood, 1883.

*History of Sacramento County, California.* Edited by George F. Wright. Oakland, Calif.: Thompson & West, 1880.

*How California Helps Men Own Farms and Rural Homes.* Sacramento: California State Printing Office, 1920.

*Illustrated History of Sonoma County, California.* Chicago: Lewis Publishing, 1889.

*Information Regarding Progress under the Land Settlement Act of the State of California and about the Plans for Soldier Settlement in the Future.* Sacramento, Calif.: State Land Settlement Board, 1919.

*Journals of the Legislature of the State of California.* San Jose, Calif.: Eugene Casserly, State Printer, 1851.

Kinney, Abbott, and Helen Hunt Jackson. *Report on the Conditions and Needs of Mission Indians.* Washington, D.C.: Office of Indian Affairs, 1883.

*Maria A. Burton et al. Plaintiffs and Respondents, v. W. N. Robinson, Appellant and Defendant.* San Diego, Calif.: Douglas Gunn, Book and Job Printer, 1874.

McClatchy, James. Deposition in United States v. Sutter, 319. N.D. Calif. 1861.

McKune, John Hill. *Minority Report of the Hon. J. H. McKune of the Judiciary Committee, to Which Was Referred Assembly Bill to Repeal the Act for the Protection of Actual Settlers, and to Quiet Land Titles in this State, Submitted April 25th, 1857, in the Assembly of the State of California.* Sacramento, Calif.: James Anthony & Co., 1857.

Mead, Elwood. *Helping Men Own Farms: A Practical Discussion of Government Aid in Land Settlement.* New York: Macmillan, 1920.

———. "Solution of the Land Question." *New Republic* (1916).

Meyer, H. R. "The Settlements with the Pacific Railways." *Quarterly Journal of Economics* 14, no. 4 (1899): 427–44.

Morrow, William C. *Blood-Money.* San Francisco: F. J. Walker & Co., 1882.

Mosher, Leroy E. *Stephen M. White: Californian, Citizen, Lawyer, Senator.* Compiled by Robert Woodland Gates. 2 vols. Los Angeles: Times-Mirror, 1903.

Norris, Frank. *The Octopus: A Story of California.* New York: Doubleday, Page & Co., 1901.

Painter, C. C. *A Visit to the Mission Indians of Southern California, and Other Western Tribes.* Philadelphia: Press of Grant and Faires, 1886.

*Report of Special Committee on Resolutions of Mr. Barker of Nevada, Concerning Land Monopoly.* Sacramento, Calif.: T. A. Springer, State Printer, 1872.

*Report of the Debates in the Convention of California, on the Formation of the State Constitution, in September and October, 1849.* Washington, D.C.: John T. Towers, 1850.

*Report of the Joint Committees on Swamps and Overflowed Lands and Land Monopoly: Presented at the Twentieth Session of the Legislature of California.* Sacramento, Calif.: G. H. Springer, State Printer, 1874.

Report of the Special Committee Appointed to Investigate the Troubles in Kansas. 34th Congress, 1st Session, 1856.

Robinson, Charles. *The Kansas Conflict.* Lawrence, Kans.: Journal Publishing Company, 1898.

Robinson, Sara T. L. *Kansas: Its Interior and Exterior Life,* 10th ed. Lawrence, Kans.: Journal Publishing Company, 1899.

Royce, Josiah. *The Feud of Oakfield Creek: A Novel of California Life.* Boston: Houghton, Mifflin, 1887.

Russell, Charles Edward. *Stories of the Great Railroads.* Chicago: Charles H. Kerr & Co., 1912.

Shinn, Howard. *Mining Camps: A Study in American Frontier Government.* New York: Scribner's, 1885.

State Board of Control. *California and the Oriental: Japanese, Chinese, and Hindus.* Sacramento: California State Printing Office, 1922.

State Land Settlement Board. *Farm Allotments and Farm Laborers' Allotments in the Durham State Land Settlement, Located at Durham, Butte County, Calif.* Sacramento, Calif.: State Printing Office, 1918.

———. *Report of the State Land Settlement Board of the State of California, June 30, 1918.* Sacramento: California State Printing Office, 1918.

———. *Report of the State Land Settlement Board of the State of California, September 30, 1920.* Sacramento: California State Printing Office, 1921.

Upham, Samuel C. *Notes of a Voyage to California Via Cape Horn, Together with Scenes in El Dorado, in the Years of 1849–'50. With an Appendix Containing Reminiscences . . . Together with the Articles of Association and Roll of Members of "The Associated Pioneers of the Territorial Days of California."* Philadelphia: the author, 1878.

U.S. Bureau of the Census, Population Census and Vital Statistics.

West, George P. "Riveted Down—and They Like It." *Collier's* (1922).

## Published Primary Sources

Bancroft, Hubert Howe. *California Pioneer Register and Index.* Baltimore, Md.: Regional Publishing Company, 1964.

Bellamy, Edward. *Looking Backward, 2000–1887.* Edited by Cecilia Tichi. New York: Penguin Books, 1982.

Booth, Newton. *Newton Booth, of California: His Speeches and Addresses.* Edited by Lauren E. Crane. New York: G. P. Putnam's Sons, 1894.

Brannan, Samuel. *Scoundrel's Tale: The Samuel Brannan Papers.* Edited by Will Bagley. Logan: Utah State University Press, 1999.

*"Chink!" A Documentary History of Anti-Chinese Prejudice in America.* Edited by Cheng-Tsu Wu. New York: World Pub., 1972.

Delano, Alonzo. *Alonzo Delano's California Correspondence: Being Letters Hitherto Uncollected from the Ottawa (Illinois)* Free Trader *and the New Orleans* True Delta, *1849–1952*. Edited by Irving McKee. Sacramento, Calif.: Sacramento Book Collectors Club, 1952.

Doten, Alfred. *The Journals of Alfred Doten, 1849–1903*. Edited by Walter Van Tilburg Clark. Reno: University of Nevada Press, 1973.

Field, Stephen J., and George C. Gorham. *Personal Reminiscences of Early Days in California: With Other Sketches*. Union, N.J.: Lawbook Exchange, 2001.

George, Henry. *Our Land and Land Policy: Speeches, Lectures, and Miscellaneous Writings*. Edited by Kenneth C. Wenzer. East Lansing: Michigan State University Press, 1999.

———. *Progress and Poverty: An Inquiry into the Cause of Industrial Depressions and of Increase of Want with Increase of Wealth*. New York: Robert Schalkenbach Foundation, 1936.

*George and the Scholars: A Century of Scientific Research Reveals the Reformer Was an Original Economist and a World-Class Social Reformer*. Edited by Will Lissner and Dorothy Burnham Lissner. New York: Schalkenbach Foundation, 1991.

Jefferson, Thomas. *Notes on the State of Virginia*. Edited by Frank Shuffleton. New York: Penguin, 1999.

Lincoln, Abraham, and Stephen A. Douglas et al. *In the Name of the People: Speeches and Writings of Lincoln and Douglas in the Ohio Campaign of 1859*. Edited by Harry V. Jaffa and Robert W. Johannsen. Columbus: Ohio State University Press, 1959.

Locke, John. *Second Treatise of Government*. Edited by C. B. Macpherson. Indianapolis, Ind.: Hackett, 1980.

Lord, Israel Shipman Pelton. *At the Extremity of Civilization: A Meticulously Descriptive Diary of an Illinois Physician's Journey in 1849 Along the Oregon Trail to the Goldmines and Cholera of California, Thence in Two Years to Return by Boat Via Panama*. Edited by Necia Dixon Liles. Jefferson, N.C.: McFarland & Co., 1995.

Mill, John Stuart. *Principles of Political Economy, with Some of Their Applications to Social Philosophy*. London: Longmans, Green, 1909.

Plumbe, John. *A Faithful Translation of the Papers Respecting the Grant Made by Governor Alvarado to John A. Sutter*. Translated by William E. P. Hartnell. With an introduction by Neal Harlow. Sacramento, Calif.: Sacramento Book Collectors Club, 1942.

*A Populist Reader: Selections from the Works of American Populist Leaders*. Edited by George Brown Tindall. New York: Harper & Row, 1966.

Post, C. C. *Driven from Sea to Sea; or, Just a Campin'.* Chicago: J. E. Downey & Co., 1884; Philadelphia: Elliot and Beezley, 1890.

Powderly, Terence Vincent. *The Path I Trod: The Autobiography of Terence V. Powderly.* Edited by Harry J. Carman, Henry David, and Paul N. Guthrie. New York: Columbia University Press, 1940.

———. *Thirty Years of Labor, 1859–1889.* New York: A. M. Kelley, 1967.

Royce, Josiah. *California: A Study of American Character: From the Conquest in 1846 to the Second Vigilance Committee in San Francisco.* Berkeley, Calif.: Heyday Books, 2002.

———. *Fugitive Essays.* Introduction by Jacob Loewenberg. Cambridge, Mass.: Harvard University Press, 1920.

———. *The Letters of Josiah Royce.* Edited by John Clendenning. Chicago: University of Chicago Press, 1970.

Ruiz de Burton, María Amparo. *Conflicts of Interest: The Letters of María Amparo Ruiz de Burton.* Edited by Rosaura Sánchez and Beatrice Pita. Houston: Arte Público Press, 2001.

———. *The Squatter and the Don.* Edited by Rosaura Sánchez and Beatrice Pita. Houston: Arte Público Press, 1992.

Sacramento City Settlers' Association. *Notice to Immigrants!!* Sacramento, 1850; reprint, New York: Argus Books, 1977.

Soulé, Frank, John H. Gihon, and James Nisbet. *The Annals of San Francisco.* Berkeley, Calif.: Berkeley Hills Books, 1999.

## Primary Source Databases

Ancestry.com (http://www.ancestry.com)

California Governors' Gallery (http://governors.library.ca.gov)

Cooperative Individualism (http://www.cooperativeindividualism.org)

Library of Congress (http://www.loc.gov)

U.S. Bureau of the Census (http://factfinder2.census.gov)

## Unpublished Secondary Sources

Grassman, Curtis Edwin. "Prologue to Progressivism, Senator Stephen M. White and the California Reform Impulse, 1875–1905." PhD diss., UCLA, 1970.

Haines, Michael R., and Robert A. Margo. "Railroads and Local Economic Development: The United States in the 1850s." Working paper 12381, National Bureau of Economic Research, July 2006.

Tsu, Cecilia. "Grown in the 'Garden of the World': Race, Gender, and Agriculture in California's Santa Clara Valley, 1880–1940." PhD diss., Stanford University, 2006.

Yanosky, Ronald William. "Seeing the Cat: Henry George and the Rise of the Single Tax Movement, 1879–1890." PhD diss, University of California, Berkeley, 1993.

## Published Secondary Sources

Aarim-Heriot, Najia. *Chinese Immigrants, African Americans, and Racial Anxiety in the United States, 1848–82*. Urbana: University of Illinois Press, 2003.

Adams, Jane, ed. *Fighting for the Farm: Rural America Transformed*. Philadelphia: University of Pennsylvania Press, 2003.

Aron, Stephen. *American Confluence: The Missouri Frontier from Borderland to Border State*. Bloomington: Indiana University Press, 2006.

Barker, Charles A. *Henry George*. New York: Oxford University Press, 1955.

Benson, Lee. *Merchants, Farmers, & Railroads: Railroad Regulation and New York Politics, 1850–1887*. Cambridge, Mass.: Harvard University Press, 1955.

Blackmar, Frank W. *The Life of Charles Robinson: The First State Governor of Kansas*. Topeka, Kans.: Crane & Company, 1902.

Bodnar, John E. *Remaking America: Public Memory, Commemoration, and Patriotism in the Twentieth Century*. Princeton, N.J.: Princeton University Press, 1991.

Bronstein, Jamie L. *Land Reform and Working-Class Experience in Britain and the United States, 1800–1862*. Stanford, Calif.: Stanford University Press, 1999.

Brown, Richard Maxwell. *No Duty to Retreat: Violence and Values in American History and Society*. New York: Oxford University Press, 1991.

Brown, Thomas N. *Irish-American Nationalism, 1870–1890*. Philadelphia: Lippincott, 1966.

Burrill, Donald R. *Servants of the Law: Judicial Politics on the California Frontier 1849–89: An Interpretive Exploration of the Field-Terry Controversy*. Lanham, Md.: University Press of America, 2010.

Cannon, Brian Q. *Remaking the Agrarian Dream: New Deal Rural Resettlement in the Mountain West*. Albuquerque: University of New Mexico Press, 1996.

Carstensen, Vernon Rosco, ed. *The Public Lands: Studies in the History of the Public Domain*. Madison: University of Wisconsin Press, 1963.

Cashman, Sean Dennis. *America in the Gilded Age: From the Death of Lincoln to the Rise of Theodore Roosevelt*. 3rd ed. New York: New York University Press, 1993.

Chan, Sucheng. *This Bittersweet Soil: The Chinese in California Agriculture, 1860–1910*. Berkeley: University of California Press, 1986.

Chase, Malcolm. *"The People's Farm": English Radical Agrarianism, 1775–1840*. Oxford and New York: Clarendon Press and Oxford University Press, 1988.

Chavez-Garcia, Miroslava. *Negotiating Conquest: Gender and Power in California, 1770s to 1880s*. Tucson: University of Arizona Press, 2004.

Clay, Karen B. "Property Rights and Institutions: Congress and the California Land Act of 1851." *Journal of Economic History* 59, no. 1 (1999): 122–42.

Clendenen, Clarence C. "Dan Showalter—California Secessionist." *California Historical Society Quarterly* 40 (1961): 309–25.

Clendenning, John. *The Life and Thought of Josiah Royce.* Madison: University of Wisconsin Press, 1985.

Cohen, Nancy. *The Reconstruction of American Liberalism, 1865–1914.* Chapel Hill: University of North Carolina Press, 2002.

Cook, Sherburne. *The Population of the California Indians, 1769–1970.* Berkeley: University of California Press, 1976.

Cronon, William. *Nature's Metropolis: Chicago and the Great West.* New York: W. W. Norton, 1991.

Currarino, Rosanne. *The Labor Question in America: Economic Democracy in the Gilded Age.* Urbana: University of Illinois Press, 2011.

Danhof, Clarence. "Farm-Making Costs and the 'Safety-Valve': 1850–1860." *Journal of Political Economy* 49 (1941): 317–59.

Daniels, Roger. *Asian America: Chinese and Japanese in the United States since 1850.* Seattle: University of Washington Press, 1988.

———. *The Politics of Prejudice: The Anti-Japanese Movement in California and the Struggle for Japanese Exclusion.* 2nd ed. Berkeley: University of California Press, 1977.

Destler, Chester McArthur. "Western Radicalism, 1865–1901: Concepts and Origins." *The Mississippi Valley Historical Review* 31, no. 3 (1944): 335–68.

Deverell, William. *Railroad Crossing: Californians and the Railroad, 1850–1910.* Berkeley: University of California Press, 1994.

———. "To Loosen the Safety Valve: Eastern Workers and Western Lands." *Western Historical Quarterly* 19, no. 3 (1988): 269–85.

Dobie, Edith. *The Political Career of Stephen Mallory White: A Study of Party Activities under the Convention System.* Stanford, Calif.: Stanford University Press, 1927; reprint, New York: AMS Press, 1971.

Dudden, Arthur P. "Men against Monopoly: The Prelude to Trust-Busting." *Journal of the History of Ideas* 18, no. 4 (1957): 587–93.

Earle, Jonathan Halperin. *Jacksonian Antislavery and the Politics of Free Soil, 1824–1854.* Chapel Hill: University of North Carolina Press, 2004.

Eifler, Mark A. *Gold Rush Capitalists: Greed and Growth in Sacramento.* Albuquerque: University of New Mexico Press, 2002.

Eisinger, Chester E. "The Freehold Concept in Eighteenth-Century American Letters." *William and Mary Quarterly* 4 (1947): 42–59.

Ellison, William Henry. *A Self-Governing Dominion: California, 1849–1860.* Chronicles of California. Berkeley: University of California Press, 1950.

Etcheson, Nicole. *Bleeding Kansas: Contested Liberty in the Civil War Era.* Lawrence: University Press of Kansas, 2004.

Fink, Leon. *Workingmen's Democracy: The Knights of Labor and American Politics.* Urbana: University of Illinois Press, 1983.

Foley, Neil. *The White Scourge: Mexicans, Blacks, and Poor Whites in Texas Cotton Culture*. Berkeley: University of California Press, 1997.

Foner, Eric. *Free Soil, Free Labor, Free Men: The Ideology of the Republican Party before the Civil War*. Oxford: Oxford University Press, 1995.

Foner, Philip Sheldon. *History of the Labor Movement in the United States*. Vol. 2. New York: International Publishers, 1955.

Fox-Genovese, Elizabeth. *The Origins of Physiocracy: Economic Revolution and Social Order in Eighteenth-Century France*. Ithaca, N.Y.: Cornell University Press, 1976.

Fine, Sidney. "Richard T. Ely, Forerunner of Progressivism, 1880–1901." *The Mississippi Valley Historical Review* 37, no. 4 (1951): 599–624.

Fuss, Peter. *The Moral Philosophy of Josiah Royce*. Cambridge, Mass.: Harvard University Press, 1965.

Gates, Paul Wallace. *Fifty Million Acres: Conflicts over Kansas Land Policy, 1854–1890*. Ithaca, N.Y.: Cornell University Press, 1954.

———. *Land and Law in California: Essays on Land Policies*. Henry A. Wallace Series on Agricultural History and Rural Studies. Ames: Iowa State University Press, 1991.

———. "An Overview of American Land Policy." *Agricultural History* 50, no. 1 (1976): 213–29.

Geiger, George Raymond. *The Philosophy of Henry George*. New York: Macmillan, 1933.

George, Henry, Jr. *The Life of Henry George*. Garden City, N.Y.: Doubleday, 1911.

Gilbert, Benjamin Franklin. "California and the Civil War: A Biographical Essay." *California Historical Society Quarterly* 40 (1961): 289–307.

———. "The Confederate Minority in California." *California Historical Society Quarterly* 20 (1941): 154–70.

Gordon, Sanford D. "Attitudes Towards Trusts Prior to the Sherman Act." *Southern Economic Association* 30, no. 2 (1963): 156–67.

Green, James R. *Death in the Haymarket: A Story of Chicago, the First Labor Movement, and the Bombing that Divided Gilded Age America*. New York: Pantheon, 2006.

Griffiths, David B. "Anti-Monopoly Movements in California, 1873–1898." *Southern California Quarterly* 52, no. 2 (1970): 93–121.

Grob, Gerald N. *Workers and Utopia: A Study of Ideological Conflict in the American Labor Movement, 1865–1900*. Evanston, Ill.: Northwestern University Press, 1961.

Gyory, Andrew. *Closing the Gate: Race, Politics, and the Chinese Exclusion Act*. Chapel Hill: University of North Carolina Press, 1998.

Haas, Lisbeth. *Conquests and Historical Identities in California, 1769–1936*. Berkeley: University of California Press, 1995.

Hawley, Ellis. *The New Deal and the Problem of Monopoly: A Study in Economic Ambivalence.* New York: Fordham University Press, 1995.

Hibbard, Benjamin Horace. *A History of the Public Land Policies.* New York: P. Smith, 1939.

Hine, Robert V. *Josiah Royce: From Grass Valley to Harvard.* Norman: University of Oklahoma Press, 1992.

Hovenkamp, Herbert. *Enterprise and American Law, 1836–1937.* Cambridge, Mass.: Harvard University Press, 1991.

———. "Regulatory Conflict in the Gilded Age: Federalism and the Railroad Problem," *The Yale Law Journal* 97, no. 6 (1988): 1017–72.

Hurtado, Albert L. *Indian Survival on the California Frontier.* New Haven, Conn.: Yale University Press, 1988.

———. *John Sutter: A Life on the North American Frontier.* Norman: University of Oklahoma Press, 2006.

Huston, Reeve. *Land and Freedom: Rural Society, Popular Protest, and Party Politics in Antebellum New York.* New York: Oxford University Press, 2000.

Jacobson, Matthew Frye. *Whiteness of a Different Color: European Immigrants and the Alchemy of Race.* Cambridge, Mass.: Harvard University Press, 1998.

John, Richard R. *Network Nation: Inventing American Telecommunications.* Cambridge, Mass.: Harvard University Press, 2010.

Johnson, Susan Lee. *Roaring Camp: The Social World of the California Gold Rush.* New York: W. W. Norton, 2000.

Johnston, Robert D. *The Radical Middle Class: Populist Democracy and the Question of Capitalism in Progressive Era Portland, Oregon.* Princeton, N.J.: Princeton University Press, 2003.

Kegley, Jacquelyn Ann K. *Josiah Royce in Focus.* Bloomington: Indiana University Press, 2008.

Kens, Paul. *Justice Stephen Field: Shaping Liberty from the Gold Rush to the Gilded Age.* Lawrence: University Press of Kansas, 1997.

King, Russell. *Land Reform: A World Survey.* Boulder, Colo.: Westview Press, 1977.

Klein, Maury. *Union Pacific.* 2 vols. Garden City, N.Y.: Doubleday, 1987–89.

Kluger, James R. *Turning on Water with a Shovel: The Career of Elwood Mead.* Albuquerque: University of New Mexico Press, 1992.

Kropp, Phoebe S. (Phoebe S. K. Young). *California Vieja: Culture and Memory in a Modern American Place.* Berkeley: University of California Press, 2006.

Kusmer, Kenneth L. *Down and Out, On the Road: The Homeless in American History.* Oxford: Oxford University Press, 2002.

Lause, Mark A. *Young America: Land, Labor, and the Republican Community.* Urbana: University of Illinois Press, 2005.

Malin, James Claude. *John Brown and the Legend of Fifty-Six*. Memoirs of the American Philosophical Society 17. Philadelphia: American Philosophical Society, 1942.

Martin, Albro. *Railroads Triumphant: The Growth, Rejection, and Rebirth of a Vital American Force*. New York: Oxford University Press, 1992.

McKee, Irving. "Notable Memorials to Mussel Slough." *Pacific Historical Review* 17, no. 1 (1948): 19–27.

McMath, Robert C., Jr. *American Populism: A Social History, 1877–1898*. New York: Hill and Wang, 1993.

McWilliams, Carey. *Factories in the Field*. Boston: Little, Brown, 1939.

Melendy, H. Brett, and Benjamin F. Gilbert. *The Governors of California: Peter H. Burnett to Edmund G. Brown*. Georgetown, Calif.: Talisman Press, 1965.

Mercer, Lloyd J. *Railroads and Land Grant Policy: A Study in Government Intervention*. New York: Academic Press, 1982.

Miner, H. Craig. *Seeding Civil War: Kansas in the National News, 1854–1858*. Lawrence: University Press of Kansas, 2008.

Montgomery, David. *Citizen Worker: The Experience of Workers in the United States with Democracy and the Free Market During the Nineteenth Century*. Cambridge: Cambridge University Press, 1993.

Montoya, Maria E. *Translating Property: The Maxwell Land Grant and the Conflict over Land in the American West, 1840–1900*. Berkeley: University of California Press, 2002.

Mullis, Tony R. *Peacekeeping on the Plains: Army Operations in Bleeding Kansas*. Columbia: University of Missouri Press, 2004.

Nash, Gerald D. "The California Railroad Commission, 1876–1911." *Southern California Quarterly* 44, no. 4 (1962): 287–305.

———. *State Government and Economic Development: A History of Administrative Politics in California, 1849–1933*. Berkeley: Institute of Governmental Studies, University of California, 1964.

Oertel, Kristen Tegtmeier. *Bleeding Borders: Race, Gender, and Violence in Pre–Civil War Kansas*. Baton Rouge: Louisiana State University Press, 2009.

Orsi, Richard J. *Sunset Limited: The Southern Pacific Railroad and the Development of the American West, 1850–1930*. Berkeley: University of California Press, 2005.

Overton, Richard Cleghorn. *Burlington West: A Colonization History of the Burlington Railroad*. Cambridge, Mass.: Harvard University Press, 1941.

Phillips, Catherine Coffin. *Cornelius Cole, California Pioneer and United States Senator: A Study in Personality and Achievements Bearing upon the Growth of a Commonwealth*. San Francisco: J. H. Nash, 1929.

Phillips, George Harwood. *Indians and Indian Agents: The Origins of the Reservation System in California, 1849–1852*. Norman: University of Oklahoma Press, 1997.

————. *Vineyards and Vaqueros: Indian Labor and the Economic Expansion of Los Angeles, 1771–1877.* Norman, Okla.: Arthur H. Clark, 2010.

Pisani, Donald J. "Squatter Law in California, 1850–1858." *Western Historical Quarterly* 25, no. 3 (1994): 277–310.

————. *Water, Land, and Law in the West: The Limits of Public Policy, 1850–1920.* Development of Western Resources. Lawrence: University Press of Kansas, 1996.

Pitt, Leonard. *The Decline of the Californios: A Social History of the Spanish-Speaking Californians, 1846–1890.* Berkeley: University of California Press, 1966.

Porter, Kirk Harold, and Donald Bruce Johnson. *National Party Platforms, 1840–1968.* Urbana: University of Illinois Press, 1970.

Postel, Charles. *Populist Vision.* Oxford and New York: Oxford University Press, 2007.

Pubols, Louise. *The Father of All: The de la Guerra Family, Power, and Patriarchy in Mexican California.* San Marino, Calif.: Huntington Library; Berkeley: University of California Press, 2009.

Rawls, James J., Richard J. Orsi, and Marlene Smith-Baranzini, eds. *A Golden State: Mining and Economic Development in Gold Rush California.* Berkeley: University of California Press, 1999.

Rezneck, Samuel. "Distress, Relief, and Discontent in the United States during the Depression of 1873–78." *Journal of Political Economy* 8, no. 6 (1950): 494–512.

Richmond, Robert W. *Kansas: A Land of Contrasts.* Saint Charles, Mo.: Forum Press, 1974.

Ritter, Gretchen. *Goldbugs and Greenbacks: The Antimonopoly Tradition and the Politics of Finance in America.* Cambridge: Cambridge University Press, 1997.

Robbins, Roy M. *Our Landed Heritage: The Public Domain, 1776–1970.* 2nd ed. Lincoln: University of Nebraska Press, 1976.

Robin, Ron Theodore. *Signs of Change: Urban Iconographies in San Francisco, 1880–1915.* New York: Garland, 1990.

Robinson, W. W. *Land in California: The Story of Mission Lands, Ranchos, Squatters, Mining Claims, Railroad Grants, Land Scrip, Homesteads.* Berkeley: University of California Press, 1948.

Rodgers, Daniel T. "In Search of Progressivism." *Reviews in American History* 10, no. 4 (1982): 113–32.

Rohrbough, Malcolm J. *Days of Gold: The California Gold Rush and the American Nation.* Berkeley: University of California Press, 1997.

Sawyer, Eugene T. *History of Santa Clara County, California.* Los Angeles: Historic Record Company, 1922.

Saxton, Alexander. *The Indispensable Enemy: Labor and the Anti-Chinese Movement in California.* Berkeley: University of California Press, 1995.

————. *The Rise and Fall of the White Republic: Class Politics and Mass Culture in Nineteenth-Century America.* London and New York: Verso, 1990.

Shah, Nayan. *Contagious Divides: Epidemics and Race in San Francisco's Chinatown.* American Crossroads 7. Berkeley: University of California Press, 2001.

Shelton, Tamara Venit. "A More Loyal, Union Loving People Can Nowhere Be Found: Squatters' Rights, Secession Anxiety, and the 1861 'Settlers' War' in San Jose." *Western Historical Quarterly* 41, no. 4 (2010): 473–94.

Silliman, Stephen W. *Lost Laborers in Colonial California: Native Americans and the Archaeology of Rancho Petaluma.* Tucson: University of Arizona Press, 2004.

Smith, Henry Nash. *Virgin Land: The American West as Symbol and Myth.* Cambridge, Mass.: Harvard University Press, 1950.

Smith, Stacey L. "Remaking Slavery in a Free State: Masters and Slaves in Gold Rush California." *Pacific Historical Review* 80, no. 1 (2011): 28–63.

Stanley, Gerald. "Racism and the Early Republican Party: The 1856 Presidential Election in California." *Pacific Historical Review* 43, no. 2 (1974): 171–87.

———. "Senator William Gwin: Moderate or Racist?" *California Historical Quarterly* 50, no. 3 (1971): 243–55.

Starr, Kevin. *Americans and the California Dream, 1850–1915.* New York: Oxford University Press, 1973.

Steeples, Douglas, and David O. Whitten. *Democracy in Desperation: The Depression of 1893.* Westport, Conn.: Greenwood Press, 1998.

Swierenga, Robert P. *Pioneers and Profits: Land Speculation on the Iowa Frontier.* Ames: Iowa State University Press, 1968.

Taggart, Harold F. "Thomas Vincent Cator: Populist Leader of California." *California Historical Society Quarterly* 27, no. 4 (1948): 311–18.

Thomas, John L. *Alternative America: Henry George, Edward Bellamy, Henry Demarest Lloyd, and the Adversary Tradition.* Cambridge, Mass.: Belknap Press, 1983.

Thorelli, Hans Birger. *The Federal Antitrust Policy: Origination of an American Tradition.* Baltimore, Md.: Johns Hopkins University Press, 1954.

Tyrrell, Ian. *True Gardens of the Gods: Californian–Australian Environmental Reform, 1860–1930.* Berkeley: University of California Press, 1999.

Unrau, William E. *Indians of Kansas: The Euro-American Invasion and Conquest of Indian Kansas.* Topeka: Kansas State Historical Society, 1991.

Vaught, David. *After the Gold Rush: Tarnished Dreams in the Sacramento Valley.* Baltimore, Md.: Johns Hopkins University Press, 2007.

Voss, Kim. *The Making of American Exceptionalism: The Knights of Labor and Class Formation in the Nineteenth Century.* Ithaca, N.Y.: Cornell University Press, 1993.

Ware, Norman J. *The Labor Movement in the United States, 1860–1895: A Study in Democracy.* Gloucester, Mass.: Peter Smith, 1959.

Watson, Harry L. *Liberty and Power: The Politics of Jacksonian America.* New York: Hill and Wang, 1990.

Weir, Robert E. "A Fragile Alliance: Henry George and the Knights of Labor." *American Journal of Economics and Sociology* 56, no. 4 (1997): 421–39.

White, Richard. *"It's Your Misfortune and None of My Own": A History of the American West.* Norman: University of Oklahoma Press, 1991.

———. *Railroaded: The Transcontinentals and the Making of Modern America.* New York: W. W. Norton, 2011.

Wilentz, Sean. *Chants Democratic: New York City and the Rise of the American Working Class, 1788–1850.* New York: Oxford University Press, 1984.

Williams, R. Hal. *The Democratic Party and California Politics, 1880–1896.* Stanford, Calif.: Stanford University Press, 1973.

Wilson, Don W. *Governor Charles Robinson of Kansas.* Lawrence: University Press of Kansas, 1975.

Wolff, David A. *Industrializing the Rockies: Growth, Competition, and Turmoil in the Coalfields of Colorado and Wyoming, 1868–1914.* Boulder: University of Colorado Press, 2003.

Worster, Donald. *Dust Bowl: The Southern Plains in the 1930s.* New York: Oxford University Press, 2004.

———. *Rivers of Empire: Water, Aridity, and the Growth of the American West.* New York: Pantheon, 1985.

Young, Arthur Nichols. *The Single Tax Movement in the United States.* Princeton, N.J.: Princeton University Press, 1916.

# INDEX

Page numbers in boldface type refer to illustrated material.